THE "CONCEITED NEWES"
OF SIR THOMAS OVERBURY
AND HIS FRIENDS

A man's best fortune or his worst's a wife.
Yet I, that know nor mariage peace nor strife,
Live by a good, by a bad one lost my life.

A wife like her I writ, man scarse can wed:
Of a false friend like mine, man scarse hath read.

for Ric=Baldwin.

Frontispiece, 1616 Printing

The "Conceited Newes" Of Sir Thomas Overbury And His Friends

A FACSIMILE REPRODUCTION
OF THE NINTH IMPRESSION OF 1616 OF
Sir Thomas Ouerbury His Wife

WITH A COMMENTARY AND TEXTUAL NOTES
ON THE "NEWES"

BY

James E. Savage
University of Mississippi

GAINESVILLE, FLORIDA

SCHOLARS' FACSIMILES & REPRINTS

1968

SCHOLARS' FACSIMILES & REPRINTS

1605 N.W. 14TH AVENUE

GAINESVILLE, FLORIDA, 32601, U.S.A.

HARRY R. WARFEL, GENERAL EDITOR

L. C. CATALOG CARD NUMBER: 68-29084

Manufactured in the U.S.A.

PREFACE

The facsimile reprint which is here offered is a composite, including items from several of the different impressions. Primarily, there is a reproduction of the Ninth Impression (1616) of *Sir Thomas Ouerbury HIS WIFE* as it appears in The Folger Shakespeare Library. Bound with that copy is an excerpt, containing "Paradoxes," "Receipts," and "Songs," taken from the Gray's Inn *Masque of Mountebankes* (presented in February, 1618) and appearing first in the Eleventh Impression (1622). Following the text of the Ninth Impression is a facsimile of part of the introductory matter as it appeared in the Second Impression (1614). Finally, two individual characters are reproduced from the Sixth Impression (1615), one of which was omitted from the Ninth, while the other was shortened. These items are all taken, with the permission of the Directors, from the copies in The Folger Shakespeare Library.

Though the introductory material is directed principally toward the "Conceited Newes," since one of the suggestions made is that the "Newes" strongly influenced the "Characters", it is thought advisable to provide the reader with the entire content of the curious miscellany to which Overbury's name is attached. The Ninth Impression is chosen for reprint, for it was only in that edition that the accepted canon of "Newes" and "Characters" was reached.

v

Invaluable help in the preparation of this work has been provided me by my research assistant, Miss Virginia Morgan. My daughter Margaret did much useful research for me in the Library of the University of Illinois. My colleagues, Professor Charles D. Cannon and Mrs. Martha L. Adams, offered many helpful suggestions. I am grateful to the staffs of The British Museum, The Bodleian Library, The Henry E. Huntington Library, and The Folger Shakespeare Library. All have responded most courteously to requests for material or information.

TABLE OF CONTENTS

CHARACTERS

INTRODUCTION

CIRCUMSTANCES RELATED TO THE PUBLICATION OF "A WIFE," THE "CHARACTERS," AND THE "NEWES"

The station in English literature which Sir Thomas Overbury occupies is almost unique, for much of the writing associated with his name is not in reality his, and the shocking circumstances accompanying his death have made his name more familiar to readers than is perhaps warranted by the importance of his work. Selections from the "Characters" appear frequently in anthologies of English writing; and in any book dealing with the *genre*, the sequence of eighty-two sketches associated with Overbury's name occupies a position second in importance only to that of the *Characters* of Theophrastus.

Accompanying the "Characters" in all seventeenth-century editions of his work are not only his poem "A Wife," but also a kindred group of sketches called "Newes." This "Newes" has not been reprinted since 1856, and has never been closely examined. I propose to reproduce the items in their context in the Overbury volume, and, in the introductory essay, to look into the circumstances of their writing and to suggest some of their influence on the "Characters."

Sir Thomas Overbury had written "A Wife" early

xiii

enough in his career for an impression to appear in 1611.[1]
If we are to believe Ben Jonson, as quoted by Drummond in this passage, Sir Thomas' intentions with regard
to the poem were not so virtuous as the subject matter
of the poem itself:

> The Countess of Rutland was nothing jnferior to her
> Father S. P. Sidney jn Poesie. Sir Th: Overburie was
> in love with her, and caused Ben to read his wyffe to
> her, which he with ane excellent grace did & praised
> the Author. that the Morne Therafter he discorded
> with Overburie, who would have him to jntend a sute
> yt was unlawfull. the lines my Lady Keepd jn remem-
> brance he comes to near, who comes to be denied.[2]

The amazing popularity which "A Wife" was to enjoy
over the next quarter of a century is hardly to be accounted for by its intrinsic excellence, or by any spright-
liness in its subject matter. It begins on this rugged
philosophical note:

> Each Woman is a *briefe* of Woman-kind,
> And doth in little euen as much containe;
> As, in one Day & Night, all life we find,
> Of Either, More, is but the same againe,
>   *God* fram'd Her so, that to Her *husband*, She,
>   As *Eue*, should all the *world of Women* be.[3]

---

[1]On the flyleaf of the Fifteenth Impression is a note in MS., "1st
in 1611. Edn. of Overbury's Wife." For this information, and for
much other assistance, I am indebted to *A Bibliography of English
Character-Books, 1608-1700*, by Gwendolen Murphy (Supplement
to the Bibliographical Society's Transactions, No. 4; Printed at the
Oxford University Press for the Bibliographical Society, 1925), p.
24.

[2]*Ben Jonson*, ed. C. H. Herford and Percy and Evelyn M. Simpson (Oxford: Clarendon Press, 1925-1952), I, 138.

[3]The complete text of "A Wife" appears on pp. 45-61 of the
facsimile, although excerpts from the "Newes" in the introduction
are, where possible, taken from the Second Impression.

After thirty-five stanzas not greatly different from the initial one, we find this one, which contains the line admired by the Countess of Rutland, who was "nothing jnferior to her Father S. P. Sidney jn Poesie":

> Womens *Behauior* is a surer barre
> Then is their *No* : *That* fairely doth *deny*
> Without *denying, thereby* kept they are
> Safe eu'n from *Hope* ; in part to blame is shee,
>   Which hath *without consent* bin only tride ;
>   He comes too *neere,* that comes *to be denide.*

At some time subsequent to the year 1611, however, the "Wife" was apparently put to a different use from the one which Jonson suggests. Sir Thomas was secretary to Robert Carr, the fast-rising favorite, and—if Queen Anne may be believed—was Carr's "governor."[4] Carr probably had Overbury's support—perhaps with "A Wife"—in his pursuit—or *vice versa*—of the Countess of Essex as mistress. By the middle of the year 1612, however, it became apparent that Carr, now Sir Robert and Viscount Rochester, sought to change the status of the Countess (the former Frances Howard, daughter to Thomas Howard, Earl of Suffolk) from that of mistress

---

[4]For the general and the specific information about the life and death of Overbury and about the parts that Somerset and Lady Essex played in his murder, I have relied on no one source. However, I am indebted particularly to the following works for much of the biographical material: *The Letters of John Chamberlain,* ed. Norman Egbert McClure (2 vols.; Philadelphia: The American Philosophical Society, 1939); Philip Gibbs, *King's Favorite: The Love Story of Robert Carr and Lady Essex* (2nd ed.; Philadelphia: George W. Jacobs & Co., 1908); Miriam Allen deFord, *The Overbury Affair: The Murder Trial That Rocked the Court of King James I* (Philadelphia: Chilton Company, 1960); Beatrice White, *Cast of Ravens: The Strange Case of Sir Thomas Overbury* (New York: George Braziller, 1965).

to that of wife. This latter intention on the part of his
master Overbury bitterly opposed. The wifely virtues
in "A Wife" were now brought to bear to demonstrate
the unsuitability, as wife, of the fair Frances. Possibly
also some of the "Characters" were used in Overbury's
efforts to prevent the marriage. The first of them, "A
good Woman," is in material analogous to "A Wife." But
the second, "A very very Woman," and the third, "Her
next part," are almost certainly bitter attacks on the
Countess herself, *e.g.*:

> She is *Mariageable* and *Fourteene* at once: and after
> shee doth not liue but tarry. Shee reads ouer her face
> euery morning, and somtime blots out pale, and writes
> red. Shee thinks shee is faire, though many times her
> opinion goes alone, and shee loues her glasse and the
> knight of the *Sunne* for lying. Shee is hid away all but
> her face, and that's hang'd about with toyes and deuices,
> like the signe of a Tauerne to draw *Strangers*. If shee
> shew more, shee preuents desire, and by too free-giuing,
> leaues no *Gift*. Shee may escape from the Seruingman,
> but not from the chamber-maide. Shee commits with
> her eares for certaine, after that shee may goe for a
> Maide, but shee hath been lyen with in her vnderstand-
> ing.
> ("A very very Woman")

In August of 1612 there was talk of divorce between
the Earl of Essex and his wife. A Royal Commission
having been appointed and having been reinforced by
complaisant bishops, the divorce became a fact on 25
September 1613, *"propter latens et incurabile impedi-
mentum."*

In the meantime, however, Sir Thomas, presumably
so that his bitter opposition might not endanger these

A WIFE

Novv
The Widdow
O F
SIR THOMAS OVERBVRYE.

Being
A moſt exquiſite and ſingular Poem
of the choice of a Wife.

WHEREVNTO ARE ADDED
many witty Characters, and conceited
Newes, written by himſelfe and other
learned Gentlemen his
friends.

Dignum laude virum muſa vetat mors,
Cælo muſa beat. Hor: car: lib. 3.

LONDON
Printed for *Lawrence Liſle,* and are to bee ſold at his
ſhop in *Paules Church-yard,* at the ſigne of
the *Tigers head.* 1614.

Title page of the Second Impression of *A Wife,*
reproduced by permission of the Director
of The Folger Shakespeare Library.

proceedings, was confined in the Tower, incommunicado. By 15 September 1613 he was dead and had been buried in the Tower, like Polonius, "in hugger mugger."

The triumphant marriage rites of Carr and Frances were held on Sunday, 26 December 1613, as it were over the body of Overbury, with pomp which included a masque by Thomas Campion and another by Ben Jonson.

These goings-on did not escape the attention of the publisher Lawrence Lisle, who entered "A Wife" in the *Stationers' Register* on 13 December 1613. The market must have been brisk, for during the year 1614 Lisle issued the second, third, fourth and fifth impressions of the poem, with title-pages varying only slightly from that of the Second Impression, as here reproduced.

"A Wife" itself would hardly be of sufficient length to carry a quarto, so Lisle reinforced it with whatever came to hand: a mass of commendatory verse of indifferent quality; the first twenty-one of the Overbury characters; and a segment called "conceited *Newes*," presumably by Overbury and his friends.

In 1615, further stirring events were to contribute to the popularity, and add to the reinforcement, of Lisle's little book, which was to become an octavo in the Sixth Impression. Rumors that Overbury had been poisoned by Carr, now Earl of Somerset, and his wife, reached the ears of James, who by now had a second favorite, George Villiers, later to be the notorious Duke of Buckingham. James ordered a trial. Several of the lesser actors in the poisoning were convicted and executed. Robert Carr, Earl of Somerset, the waning favorite, was, with his wife, found guilty, sentenced to death, and in the meantime confined in the Tower.

Nine new characters, in addition to the initial twenty-one, had appeared in the Fourth Impression. In the Sixth, however, forty-two more characters were added, three of which are claimed by "I. Cocke" (John Cooke?), and thirty-two of which are, on the basis of verbal parallels, attributed to John Webster.[5]

Lisle produced his Sixth Impression in 1615, a more ambitious project than had been the four editions preceding it. He may have employed John Webster as an editor, for the Latin motto on the title-page changes to "Mar.—*non norunt haec monumenta mori,*" which is also on the title-pages of Webster's *White Devil* and his *Monumental Column.*[6] There are also added one item of "Newes" and Lady Southwell's "Edicts." But the earth-shaking events attending the great trial are not noticed.

That notice remained for the Seventh Impression, 1616. The contents of this octavo remain essentially the same as those of the Sixth, with the exception of the commendatory verses that had been in all earlier ones. One of those poems is dropped—"A Morning-Sacrifice," by "*I. S. Lincolniensis,* Gentleman" (cf. p. 311 of the facsimile)—and the rest give way to "NEW ELEGIES / vpon his (now knowne) / *vntimely death.*" Of these there are eighteen, many taking cognizance of the trial and its shocking findings. Though Webster's motto is gone, and

---

[5]Cf. H. Dugdale Sykes, *Notes & Queries,* 11th ser., Vol. VIII (September 20, 27, October 4, 11, 1913) and Vol. XI (April 24, May 1, 8, 15, 1915) and Baron A. F. Bourgeois, *Notes & Queries,* 11th ser., Vol. X (July 4, 1914). The same group of thirty-two ("A Worthy Commander in the Warres" through "A Rimer," which appear on pp. 149-215 of the facsimile) is attributed to Webster by F. L. Lucas (ed.), *The Complete Works of John Webster* (London: Chatto & Windus, 1927), IV, 7.

[6]This motto appeared only in the Sixth Impression. See Lucas, IV, 10.

perhaps his editorship, these new elegies are the work of some of the more noted writers of the time. They included verses that may be by John Ford, John Fletcher, John Marston, William Brown, and others of less note. Also added were two additional items of "Newes."

With this impression, however, *The Wife* had taken its final form, except for the addition of eleven more characters, some excerpts from a court masque, and an irrelevant poem addressed to the Countess of Rutland. But it had not lost its popularity. In 1616 also appeared the Eighth and Ninth Impressions. In the Folger copy of the Ninth Impression appear, of course, the additional characters and, fortuitously, an added gathering, from the Twelfth Impression, which includes the "Paradoxes," "Receipts," and "Songs" excerpted from the *Masque of Mountebankes.*[7] For these reasons the Folger copy of the Ninth Impression is used as the basis of the facsimile, though the Second and Sixth Impressions would give a more correct text of the "Newes."

After 1616, there were to be ten more impressions, the last in 1664. There were to be two "Miscellaneous Works" of Overbury, one in 1756 and one in 1856. The latter edition, by Edward F. Rimbault, was the last ap-

---

[7]For the information that these pages, though bound with the Folger copy of the Ninth Impression, actually belong to the Twelfth Impression, I am indebted to Mr. Giles E. Dawson of the Folger Library Staff. There are two twelfth impressions, one printed in Dublin in 1626 and one in London in 1627. Pages V2-V8ᵛ belong to the latter. Miss Murphy assigns them to the Eleventh Impression, and in the Folger Library copy of the Eleventh Impression they appear on pages V2-V8ᵛ (see pp. 293-307 of the facsimile). Three items added in the Eleventh Impression— "*Ad Comitissam Rutlandiae*" (sig. C4-C5), "The true Character of a Dunce" (sig. G3-G5), and "An Essay of Valour" (sig. Q6-R) — are not included in the facsimile.

pearance of the "Newes."[8] "A Wife" and the characters
appeared again in the edition of W. J. Paylor in 1936,
and the characters in an anthology by Richard Aldington
in 1924.[9]

Non norunt haec monumenta mori—the motto which
may have been given to the Sixth Impression by John
Webster—gives a nice instance of irony. Though "A
Wife" and the characters may be found fairly easily, the
"Newes" must be sought in Rimbault's rare and inac-
curate imprint of 1856, or in a rare-book room.

In the edition by Rimbault examined for this essay,
on the title-page in a faded, shaky Victorian script, is the
notation: "The best thing in the book is the 'Newes.'"
A new discussion of the "Newes" is offered, in the hope
of lending some help to John Webster's (?) motto and to
the judgment of the unknown critic. Lawrence Lisle, in
his "The Printer to the Reader," in the Second Impression (1614), thus accounts for the "Characters" and the
"Newes":

> The surplusage, that now exceeds the last edition
> [the lost edition of 1611], was (that I may bee
> honestly impartiall) in some things only to be chal-
> lenged by the first author, but others now added,
> (little inferior to the residue) being in nature an-
> swerable, and first transcrib'd by Gentlemen of the
> same qualitie, I haue vpon good inducements, made
> publike with warrantie of their and my owne credit.

---

[8]Edward F. Rimbault (ed.), *The Miscellaneous Works in Prose
and Verse of Sir Thomas Overbury, Knt.* (London: J. R. Smith,
1856).

[9]W. J. Paylor (ed.), *The Overburian Characters* (The Percy
Reprints, XIII; Oxford: Basil Blackwell, 1936); and Richard Al-
dington (comp. and trans.), *A Book of "Characters"* (New York:
E. P. Dutton & Co., 1924).

In the second impression of "A Wife," the "Newes" occupies eighteen pages of the quarto, F4 through H4ᵛ. It has its own title-page: "NEWES, / FROM ANY WHENCE: / OR / Old Truthes vnder a supposall of / *Noueltie.* / Occasioned by diuers Essayes and priuate / *passages of wit between sundry Gentlemen* / vpon that subiect." The items of news, with the initials of their authors, are these:

Newes from Court.	*T.O.*
Answer to the Court newes.	*A.S.*
Country Newes.	Sʳ.T.R.
Newes from the very Country.	*I.D.*
Answer to the very Country	
Newes.	*A.S.*
Newes to the Vniuersitie.	
Newes from Sea.	*W.S.*
Forrein Newes of the yeere 1604.	
From France.	
From Spaine.	
From Rome.	
From Venice.	
From Germanie.	
From the Low Countries.	
Newes from my Lodging.	*B.R.*
Newes of my morning worke.	Mʳⁱˢ.B.
Newes from the lower end of the	
Table	*J.C.*
Newes from the Bed.	*R.S.*

The Sixth Impression adds one new item:

Newes from the Church	*Io. Ruddiard.*

The only other additions to the news appear first in the Seventh Impression:

> *Newes from Shipbord.* H.R.
> *Newes from the Chimney corner.*

The sequence of the news paragraphs is changed in the Ninth Impression, in which "Newes from the Church," with the author's signature omitted, is inserted before "Newes from the Bed" and the other two new items are printed last.

Along with these three new paragraphs, the Sixth Impression presented for the first time "Certaine *Edicts* from a Parlia- / *ment in Eutopia;* / Written by the LADY SOVTHWELL." It is likely that the "Parliament" which produced the "Edicts" was no more than the courtier group which produced the "Newes," and I suggest that both the "Newes" and the "Edicts" are part of an elaborate courtly game which occurred in the early years of the reign of James I.

The commentary which follows will be much more comprehensible if the "Newes" and the "Edicts" are read at this point. They appear on pages 218 to 265 of the facsimile.

THE CIRCUMSTANCES OF THE "GAME"

The rules of this game of "Newes" seem to have been very strict, both as to the manner of composition and the social status of the writers. The closest analogies in better-known literature are perhaps to be found in the plays of Ben Jonson: the "dorring" game in *Cynthia's Revels;* the "vapours" of *Bartholomew Fair;* and the "Jeering" of *The Staple of News.* It is my purpose to suggest the probable circumstances of the contest, to identify several of the participants, and to show that these items of "Newes" were probably a stage in the development of the Overburian character out of the abstract characters of Joseph Hall.

The reader will already have observed that there are items of three different sorts in the passages.[10] The "Forrein Newes of the yeere 1604"[11] is a unit in itself, entirely different in conception from such items as "Newes from Court." He will also have noticed that "Newes to the Vniuersitie" is written not in the manner of the items of "Newes from," but in that of the "Characters." Our first concern will be with circumstances and participants in the category of "Newes from."

Commentary on these items of "Newes" should perhaps begin with the "pit" where the game was played, which was, very probably, the "Chamber" of Cecily Bulstrode—the "M^{ris}. B." of "Newes of my morning worke." Cecily Bulstrode was a lady-in-waiting to the Queen, and had had the temerity to "censure" Ben Jonson. That censure elicited from Jonson one of the bitterest of his poems, "An Epigram on The Court Pucell." That epigram, I believe, throws a great deal of light on the circumstances under which the "Newes" was written, and suggests at least some of the rules of the game. I quote relevant lines:

---

[10]The "Newes" items appear on pp. 223-265 of the facsimile.

[11]In later editions, the "Forrein Newes" is dated, first, 1614, then 1616, and, in the Eleventh Impression, 1622.

Do's the Court-Pucell then so censure me,
  And thinkes I dare not her? let the world see.
What though her Chamber be the very pit
  Where fight the prime Cocks of the Game, for wit?
And that as any are strooke, her breath creates
  New in their stead, out of the Candidates?
What though with Tribade lust she force a Muse,
  And in an Epicoene fury can write newes
Equall with that, which for the best newes goes,
  As aerie light, and as like wit as those?
What though she talke, and cannot once with them,
  Make State, Religion, Bawdrie, all a theame?
And as lip-thirstie, in each words expence,
  Doth labour with the Phrase more then the sense?
.   .   .   .

Shall I advise thee, *Pucell*? steale away
  From Court, while yet thy fame hath some small day;
The wits will leave you, if they once perceive
  You cling to Lords, and Lords, if them you leave
For Sermoneeres: of which now one, now other,
  They say you weekly invite with fits o'th' Mother,
And practise for a Miracle, take heed
  This Age would lend no faith to *Dorrels* Deed;
Or if it would, the Court is the worst place,
  Both for the Mothers, and the Babes of grace,
For there the wicked in the Chaire of scorne,
  Will cal't a Bastard, when a Prophet's borne.[12]

These bitter lines, as has been said, give the location
for the game—at Court, in the chamber of the "Pucell";
the purpose of the game—the production of "newes"; the
participants—"wits," "Lords," and "Sermoneeres," and
perhaps, in the word "Cocks," a pun on the name of one
of the participants; the subjects—"State, Religion, Baw-

---

[12]Herford and Simpson, VIII, 222-223, lines 1-14 and 35-46.

drie." The items of news should be "aerie light," and
"like wit," but should clearly not "labour with the Phrase
more then the sense."

THE PARTICIPANTS

For the evidence linking "M^{rls}. B." with "the Court
Pucell"[13] we need only to go to the *Conversations with
Drummond* and let Jonson make the connection:

> Verses on the Pucelle of the Court Mistriss Boul-
> stred, whose Epitaph Done made.
>
> .   .   .   .
>
> that piece of the Pucelle of the Court, was stollen
> out of his pocket by a Gentleman who drank him
> drousie & given Mistress Boulstraid, which brought
> him great displeasur.[14]

Since the death of Cecily Bulstrode came in 1609, it is
probable that 1609 is the terminal date for the composition of the "Newes" and of course marks the termination
of the game. Her death was the occasion of one of
Donne's finest elegies, and its circumstances are given in
a letter to Sir Henry Goodyer. Since Donne, as will be
shown later, is one of the more skillful players of the

---

[13]Perhaps Jonson had Cecily in mind when, in *The Silent Woman*, he gave these lines to Truewit, who is warning Morose against
marriage:
> . . . shee may censure *poets*, and authors, and stiles,
> and compare 'hem, DANIEL with SPENSER, IONSON
> with the tother youth, and so foorth; or, be thought
> cunning in controuersies, or the very knots of diuin-
> itie; and haue, often in her mouth, the state of the
> question:, and then skip to the *Mathematiques*, and
> demonstration and answere, in religion to one; in state,
> to another, in baud'ry to a third. (Herford and Simp-
> son, V, 182, lines 116-123.)

[14]Herford and Simpson, 1, 135 and 150.

game, it is appropriate here to quote relevant passages
from both the poem and the letter:

> Her Soule is gone to usher up her corse,
> Which shall be'almost another soule, for there
> Bodies are purer, then best Soules are here.
> Because in her, her virtues did outgoe
> Her yeares, would'st thou, O emulous death, do so?
> And kill her young to thy losse? must the cost
> Of beauty, 'and wit, apt to doe harme, be lost?
> What though thou found'st her proofe 'gainst sins
>   of youth?[15]

. . . but (by my troth) I fear earnestly that Mistresse *Bolstrod* will not escape that sicknesse in
which she labours at this time. I sent this morning
to aske of her passage of this night; and the return
is, that she is as I left her yesternight, and then by
the strength of her understanding, and voyce, (pro-
portionally to her fashion, which was ever remisse)
by the eavenesse and life of her pulse, and by her
temper, I could allow her long life, and impute all
her sicknesse to her minde. But the History of her
sicknesse, makes me justly fear, that she will scarce
last so long, as that you when you receive this letter,
may do her any good office, in praying for her; for
she hath not for many days received so much as a
preserved Barber[r]y, but it returnes, and all accompanied with a Fever, the mother, and an extream
ill spleen.[16]

Cecily may also be the subject of this epigram (Num-

---

[15]Sir H. J. C. Grierson (ed.), *The Poems of John Donne* (London: Oxford University Press, 1939), *"Elegie on Mris* Boulstred,"
p. 258, lines 46-53.
[16]Charles Edmund Merrill (ed.), *Letters to Severall Persons of
Honour, by John Donne* (New York: Sturgis and Walton Company,
1910), p. 187.

ber 42) in John Cooke's *Epigrames Served Out in 52
Several Dishes* (1604) :

> SI*slie* reports Angels appeare to her,
> And comforts her in all extremity,
> Nay and besides they do presse neare to her,
> Promising aide in great'st calamity,
> But this you must suppose they come in night,
> For *Sislies* Angels neuer came in sight.[17]

The accusation—religion as pretense for illicit visiting—
is so close to that in Jonson's poem that one is led to believe Cooke spoke of the same Cecily-Sislie.

Before we leave the unfortunate Cecily we should
perhaps do her, and Ben Jonson, the justice of quoting
his own "Epitaph," a graceful recantation of his earlier
attack:

> Stay, view this stone: And, if thou beest not such,
> Read here a little, that thou mayst know much.
> It couers, first, a Virgin; and then, one
> That durst be that in Court: a vertu' alone
> To fill an Epitaph. But she had more.
> She might haue claym'd t'have made the Graces foure;
> Taught Pallas language; Cynthia modesty;
> As fit to haue encreas'd the harmony
> Of Spheares, as light of starres; She was earthes Eye:
> The sole Religious house, and Votary,
> Wᵗh Rites not bound, but conscience. Wouldst thou All?
> She was *'Sell Boulstred*. In wᶜh name, I call
> Vp so much truth, as could I it pursue
> Might make the Fable of *Good Women* true.[18]

Having tentatively established on the authority of

---

[17]Sig. Dᵛ. I am indebted to the Curators of the Bodleian Library
for permission to quote from Cooke's *Epigrams*.
[18]Herford and Simpson, VIII, 371-372.

Ben Jonson the locale of our game of "Newes" and the identity of one of the players, and having also given a terminal date to the "Newes," we need to identify as many as possible of the other players. "Newes from the very Country" is followed by the initials "*I.D.*," and as one would expect from the unusual skill with which its conceits are handled, it is indeed the work of John Donne. His son, John Donne the younger, includes it in the edition of his father's poems of 1650 and in subsequent editions.[19]

It was during the years just prior to 1609 that Donne, with his family settled at Mitcham, had himself taken lodgings in the Strand and was seeking employment at Court. In a letter of June 13, 1607, he requests Sir Henry Goodyer, Gentleman of the Privy Chambers and Donne's weekly correspondent, to help him to (the reversion of?) the office of Mr. Fowler, the Queen's Secretary.[20] Several other of Donne's letters of this period, about 1605 to 1609, indicate Donne's presence at Court, and those to Carr would have gone through the hands of Overbury,[21] who is one of the participants in our game of "Newes."

The first item, "Newes from Court," is followed by "*T.O.*" in the second and third impressions, "S^r.*T.O.*" in the fourth, and, by the time the ninth is reached (in 1616), "Sir, *T.Ouer.*" Overbury and Carr had been friends since the former's visit to Scotland in 1601 and had been associates at Court before Carr came to the attention of James in 1607. Thereafter, Overbury's influ-

---

[19]The only modern reprint of "Newes from the very Country" is in *John Donne, Dean of St. Paul's: Complete Poetry and Selected Prose*, ed. John Hayward (Bloomsbury: The Nonesuch Press, 1929).

[20]Merrill, pp. 70-71.

[21]Cf. Merrill, Letters CII, CXII, CXIII.

ence over the rising favorite was so great that the Queen
could refer to him as Carr's "governor." His knighthood came in 1608, and by 1611 he had written his poem
"A Wife," according to Ben Jonson as a part of his im-
proper suit to the Countess of Rutland, and possibly such
of the "Characters" as "A very very Woman" and "Her
next part." At any rate, he probably used both the
"Wife" and the characters as part of his constant effort
to discourage Carr in his pursuit of the wife of the Earl
of Essex. Since the first printed version of the "Newes"
does not have the "Sir" before his initials, we may perhaps make the assumption that the "Newes from Court"
was written before June 19, 1608, the date on which
Overbury was knighted.

One of the most skillful players is the author of
"Newes from the lower end of the Table," "J.C." He is
in all probability the "I. Cocke" who claims three of the
"Characters" and also the John Cooke who is listed in
the *STC* as author of *Greenes Tu quoque; or, the Cittie
Gallant* and of *Epigrames Served Out in 52 Several
Dishes.* Bits of his writing turn up in other places also.
He has a commendatory poem, of indifferent worth, in
the 1607 Quarto of *Volpone.* There are several pages of
his writing in the introductory material to the second
impression of John Stephens' *Essayes* (1615). It is there
that he claims three of the Overbury characters, "A Tinker," "An Apparatour," and "An Almanacke-maker."[22]

---

[22]Cooke inserts the following footnote after line 74 of his poem,
"To the nameless Author": "*I am heere enforced to claime 3
Characters following the *Wife:* viz: the *Tinker,* the *Apparatour,*
and *Almanack-maker,* that I may signify the ridiculous and bold
dealing of an vnknown botcher . . . ." (John Stephens, *Essayes
and Characters, Ironicall, and Instructive, The second impression,*
1615, sig. A8).

What he says there is of little consequence to us, but we should note the company he keeps. John Stephens is of Lincoln's Inn, as is another contributor to the front matter, George Greene, "Gentleman." Cooke is listed as "Gent." on the title-page of his *Epigrames*. All these circumstances suggest the possibility of his presence in the Court circle of Overbury, Donne, and the lady-in-waiting, Cecily Bulstrode.

The content of the *Epigrames* is not inconsistent in writing techniques and subject matter with the work of our "J.C." Consider Number 29:

> *IAnus* the ritch fat vsurer desird,
> To be a knight and yet was loath to giue,
> The compleate summe which of him was requird,
> And once a year a feast while he did liue.
> Ambition yet gaue couetousnes a blow,
> That stroke two hundred pounds out of his purse,
> But of his knighthood such great charge doth grow
> That he repents of what he did disburse,
> And wisely now his knighthood doth compare,
> To pickle herring or tough martlemas beife,
> (Which being eaten not for common faire)
> Though it be ready bought yet playes the theefe,
> meaning as those salt meates do steale down drinke
> So doth his knight-hood steale away his chinke.[23]

He ends his little book of epigrams with this verse, conceived in the imagery of food, and punning on his own name:

> REader I know not how I haue pleas'd thy mind,
> With these rude Epigrams harsh vnrefind,

---

[23]*Epigrames*, sig. C1ᵛ.

But if they be not drest vnto thy taste,
Then blame the Cooke for making too much hast,
Ile ne're make promise to remaine thy debter,
But if thou likst them not, would thou hadst better.[24]

In "Newes from the lower end of the Table," "J.C." shows almost uncanny skill for uniting the imagery of a meal at the table with religious and ethical observations, using conceits liberally in the process: "That grace before meat is our election before we were; grace after, our saluation when we are gone"; "A rich foole among the wise is a gilt empty bowle among the thurstie."

Greenes Tu quoque; or the Cittie Gallant, written in 1611, deals in general with persons and incidents that would certainly belong to the lower end of the Court table—a rich merchant who has just bought his knighthood, his daughters, and young men of the lower gentry or upper citizen class. Much of the flavor of "Newes from the lower end of the Table" appears in such a passage as this:

STAINES. That I should live to be a servingman! a fellow which scalds his mouth with another man's porridge; brings up meat for other men's bellies, and carries away the bones for his own; changes his clean trencher for a foul one, and is glad of it. And yet did I never live so merry a life when I was my master's master as now I do, being man to my man. And I will stand to't, for all my former speeches, a serving-man lives a better life than his master; and thus I prove it: The saying is, the nearer the bone the sweeter the flesh; then must the serving-man needs eat the sweeter flesh, for he always picks the bones. And again, the proverb says, the deeper the sweeter. There has the serving-man the advantage again, for he drinks still in the bot-

---

[24]*Ibid.,* sig. D7ᵛ.

tom of the pot. He fills his belly, and never asks what's
to pay . . . .[25]

This John Cocke, or Cooke, gives also an excellent
demonstration of the kinship between the "Newes" and
the "Characters." One of the "Characters" for which he
claims authorship is Number 33, "A Tinker."[26] Aside
from the noun clauses beginning with "That," it shows
all the techniques of the "Newes": a conceited beginning
and a liberal sprinkling of conceits throughout; the use of
a specific body of images, those of the tinker's tools and
occupational techniques; a collective, epigrammatic ending. The text of "A Tinker" appears on pages 123 to
125 of the facsimile.

The next of the players to be easily identifiable is
"S^r.T.R.," author of "Country Newes," who is in all probability Sir Thomas Roe.[27] He was friend and correspondent to Donne, and Donne's letters to Roe, or men-
tions of him in Donne's letters to Goodyer and others, indicate the presence of Sir Thomas at Court during the
years 1605-1609.[28] Ben Jonson has two epigrams addressed to Roe (Nos. XCVIII and XCIX), one of which
touches on the Knight's literary endeavors:

> THat thou hast kept thy loue, encreast thy will,
> Better'd thy trust to letters; that thy skill;
> Hast taught thy selfe worthy thy pen to tread,
> And that to write things worthy to be read:
> How much of great example wert thou, ROE,
> If time to facts, as vnto men would owe?

[25]W. Carew Hazlitt (ed.), *A Select Collection of Old English
Plays* (London: Reeves and Turner, 1875), XI, 207.
[26]I use the number assigned in Miss Murphy's *Bibliography*.
[27]Rimbault (p. 309) identifies the "Sir T.R." of the Ninth Impression as Sir Thomas Roe.
[28]Cf. Merrill, Letters XIV, LXV, LXX.

> But much it now auailes, what's done, of whom:
> The selfe-same deeds, as diuersly they come,
> From place, or fortune, are made high, or low,
> And euen the praisers iudgement suffers so.
> Well, though thy name lesse then our great ones bee,
> Thy fact is more: let truth encourage thee.[29]

John Chamberlain notes, on December 30, 1609, that "Sir Walter Raleigh hath a ship come from Guiana richly laden they say with gold ore, and Sir Thomas Rowe with a ship and pinnesse is going that way to seeke his fortune."[30] Since his knighthood had come in 1604, we again have suggestions for terminal dates for the composition of the "Newes."

The writer of "Newes from Sea," "*W.S.*," is a serious-minded man, both cynical and devout. He gives only lip-service to the subject of bawdry, and he uses religion only for his epigrammatic ending. But the perils of the sea are to him nothing so dangerous as the "crosse gale" of Court. He is almost certainly an experienced traveller, both at sea and at Court. I take "*W.S.*"[31] to be William Strachey, one of those shipwrecked in 1609 in the Bermudas with Sir George Somers and Sir Thomas Gates. His *A True Repertory of the Wracke and Redemption of Sir Thomas Gates, Knight* is a source of Shakespeare's *Tempest,* though Shakespeare must have seen it in manuscript, for it was not published until 1625.[32]

Strachey went to Constantinople in 1606 as secretary to the Ambassador, Sir Thomas Glover. He returned

---

[29]Herford and Simpson, VIII, 63, Epigram No. XCIX.
[30]McClure, I, 292.
[31]In the Fifteenth Impression a note in MS. offers "(Wye Saltonstall?)" for "*W.S.*" Rimbault (p. 310) repeats the query.
[32]E. K. Chambers, *William Shakespeare: A Study of Facts and Problems* (Oxford: The Clarendon Press, 1930), I, 492,

almost immediately to England, however, and we do not hear of him again until he sailed for Virginia, on June 2, 1609, as a grantee of the Second Virginia Charter with an investment of £25. In the meantime, perhaps he was, like Donne, seeking preferment at Court: "I haue liued to see the Sunne a bankerout, being ready to starue for cold in his perpetuall presence." A good sample of Strachey's prose style, with a flavor remarkably like that of "Newes from Sea," is the following, from a letter addressed to "his Maiesties Councell for the Colonie":

> Nor let it afflict the patience of such full and well instructed iudgments, vnto whom many of these constitutions and Lawes Diuine or Marshall may seeme auncient and common, since these grounds are the same constant, Asterismes, and starres, which must guide all that trauell in these perplexed wayes, and paths of publique affairs; & whosoeuer shall wander from them, shall but decline a hazardous and by-course to bring their purposes to good effect.[33]

A similar tone pervades his *A True Repertory:* "It being now the fourth morning, it wanted little, to have shut vp hatches, and commending our sinfull soules to God, the Shippe to the mercy of the Sea."[34]

His verse has the same somber quality, if one may judge by the dedicatory sonnet which appears in the Quarto of Ben Jonson's *Sejanus:*

---

[33]"For the Colony in Virginea Britannia," p. (6), in *Tracts and Other Papers*, coll. Peter Force (New York: Peter Smith, 1947), Vol. III, no. 2.

[34]Quoted from *The Tempest, A New Variorum Edition of Shakespeare*, ed. Horace Howard Furness (9th ed.; Philadelphia: J. B. Lippincott Company, c. 1892), p. 314.

> And as the Lightning comes behind the Thunder
> From the torne Cloud, yet first inuades our Sense,
> So euery violent Fortune, that to wonder
> Hoists men aloft, is a cleere euidence
> Of a vaunt-curring blow the *Fates* haue giuen
> To his forst state: swift Lightning blindes his
>   eyes,
> While Thunder from comparison-hating Heauen
> Dischargeth on his height, and there it lyes:[35]

Such verse hardly deserves Thomas Campion's praise, *"Summus Pieridum unicus que Cultor,"*[36] but all the passages quoted display qualities very evident in "Newes from Sea." It may be worth noting that of the commendatory poems which begin the Ninth Impression (1616) one has the initials "W.S." and another is signed *"W: Stra:."*[37] The first of them (see pp. 9-11 of the facsimile), expressing profound shock at the revelations about the nature of Overbury's death, has much the same imagery and tone of the lines quoted above.

If we are safe in assuming that "W.S." is William Strachey, then again we have a terminal date for composition of the "Newes," 1609, and an early limit of about 1606.

The writer of "Newes from my Lodging" is identified by Rimbault as Sir Benjamin Rudyerd, with this addi-

---

[35]Herford and Simpson, XI, 316, *"Vpon* SEIANVS," lines 5-12.

[36]"Highest and only cultivator of the Muses," in *"Ad Gulielmum Stracheum,"* quoted from Percival Vivian (ed.), *Poetical Works of Thomas Campion* (London: George Routledge & Sons, Ltd., [n. d.]). p. xlviii.

[37]S. G. Culliford, in his *William Strachey, 1572-1621* (Charlottesville: The University of Virginia Press, 1965), assigns the *"W: Stra:"* sonnet with confidence to Strachey and suggests that the *"W.S."* poem is also his. Culliford does not, however, make any reference to "Newes from Sea."

tional comment: "He was of the Middle Temple, and probably well acquainted with Overbury. His poems, in conjunction with those of the Earl of Pembroke, were printed in 1660."[38] John Aubrey records that he was a close friend to Sir Walter Raleigh to the extent of having fought a duel with Raleigh and of having participated in the famous dinner at which Raleigh's son sent a box on the ear around the table to his father.[39]

Ben Jonson has three epigrams to Rudyerd (CXXI, CXXII, CXXIII), and the *"B.R."* who says in "Newes from my Lodging" that "the best prospect is to looke inward" is certainly not essentially different from the Rudyerd to whom Jonson addresses these lines:

> If I would vertue set, as shee was yong,
>   And heare her speake with one, and her first tongue;
> If holiest friend-ship, naked to the touch,
>   I would restore, and keepe it euer such;
> I need no other arts, but studie thee:
>   Who prou'st, all these were, and again may bee.
>
> .   .   .   .   .
>
> Writing thy selfe, or iudging others writ,
>   I know not which th'hast most, candor, or wit:
> But both th'hast so, as who affects the state
>   Of the best writer, and iudge, should emulate.[40]

In connection with Sir Benjamin, it should be noted

---

[38]Rimbault, p. 310.

[39]Anthony Powell (ed.), *Brief Lives and Other Selected Writings by John Aubrey* (London: The Cresset Press, 1949), pp. 202-203, 326.

[40]Herford and Simpson, VIII, 78, Epigrams CXXII, lines 5-10, and CXXIII.

that the new item in the Sixth Impression, "Newes from the Church," is there attributed to *"Io. Ruddiard,"* whose signature does not appear in the Ninth Impression. Of him, Rimbault has this note: "Perhaps John Rudyerd, the elder brother of Sir Benjamin Rudyerd, the lawyer and poet? He matriculated at Oxford in 1587."[41]

Only one of the players of the game has two items of news: the *"A.S."* who responds to the "Newes from Court" and to the "Newes from the very Country," *i. e.,* to Sir Thomas Overbury and to John Donne. For the identity of *"A.S."* only speculative suggestions can be proposed. It has been suggested by students and colleagues that the writer of the two paragraphs may be a woman, and I suggest a young lady who might have been a participant in courtly goings-on during the years 1605-1609. She is Lady Anne Clifford, who early in 1609 became Lady Sackville and three days thereafter Countess of Dorset.

Lady Anne's diary is well-known.[42] Its early pages are the writings of a girl of thirteen at Court about the time of the accession of James I. That they are remarkably well-written is probably due to the tutorship of Samuel Daniel during the preceding year or two. Unfortunately, there is a hiatus in the diary between the years 1603 and 1616. But we know that she was at Court during the years 1605-1609, for she was one of the Nymphs in Ben Jonson's *Masque of Beautie* on Twelfth Night, 1608, and about a year later was one of the Queens (Valasea?) in the Jonson masque of that name.[43]

---

[41]Rimbault, p. 311.
[42]V. Sackville-West (ed.), *The Diary of the Lady Anne Clifford* (New York: George H. Doran Company, [n. d.]).
[43]Herford and Simpson, VII, 191 and 317.

One note which associates her with the group of courtiers who produced the "Newes" is an aside by John Chamberlain: "Sir Robert Carre, (who is likewise in speach to marry the Lady Anne Clifford)."[44] Chamberlain's news is in a letter dated January 10, 1609, and Anne became Lady Sackville on February 25th. The accuracy of Chamberlain's news is to be questioned, for on March 3, 1609, he wryly reports Anne's marriage: "The earle of Dorset died on Monday night leaving a heavie widow God wot, and his sonne seeing him past hope, the Satterday before maried the Lady Anne Clifford."[45] But one may safely infer that Chamberlain, in coupling Anne's name with Carr's, was faithfully reporting gossip he had heard.

Players in the game for whom no identities have been proposed are the authors of "Newes from the Bed," "*R.S.*," and "Newes from Shipboard," "*H.R.*"[46] The only *R. S.* who seems in any way associated with the other participants in the courtly game is one Sir Ralph Shelton, and he only vicariously, through his inclusion in Ben Jonson's circle of acquaintance. He was knighted by James at Whitehall in December of 1607.[47] Ben Jonson's Epigram CXIX is complimentary but has no reference to literary abilities, and it suggests that Shelton "flies the court."[48] It is perhaps a dubious honor that he is one of those who make the epic, but noisome voyage on the Thames described in Jonson's final epigram, No. CXXXIII.[49]

---

[44]McClure, I, 280.
[45]*Ibid.*, I, 287.
[46]I have no suggestions for the identity of "*H.R.*"
[47]John Nichols, *The Progresses, Processions, and Magnificent Festivities of King James the First* (London: J. B. Nichols, 1828), II, 160.
[48]Herford and Simpson, VIII, 76, "To Sir Ralph Shelton."
[49]*Ibid.*, VIII, 84-89, "On the Famous Voyage."

The "Edicts" of Lady Southwell, "from a Parliament in Eutopia,"[50] have much of the cynicism shown by the writers of the "Newes" about the conduct of courtiers—whether men or women—and they concern themselves almost exclusively with the third subject proposed by Ben Jonson, bawdry.[51] Lady Frances Southwell has good credentials for presence among the courtly group which produced the "Newes." Her father was Charles Howard, Earl of Nottingham, the Lord Admiral, who had been in command of the English fleet in 1588. Her mother was the daughter of Henry Cary, Lord Hunsdon, first cousin of Elizabeth and her Lord Chamberlain, and she was principal Lady-in-Waiting to the Queen. She was the widow of Sir Robert Southwell (d. 1598), who had commanded the *Elizabeth Jonas* at the time of the Armada. She was herself, about 1609, lady-in-waiting to Queen Anne.[52]

Perhaps the tone of bitterness and disillusionment of the "Edicts" can be explained by a few choice bits of contemporary gossip. Lady Southwell had been maid of honor to Queen Elizabeth, and the Earl of Essex was supposed to have been her lover. In 1605 her daughter Elizabeth followed Sir Robert Dudley to Italy, disguised as a

---

[50]Cf. pp. 219-222 of the facsimile.
[51]One item of Lady Southwell's "Edicts" provides an interesting literary footnote. The courtier who, lacking wit, relies on bawdry is excused only if he wears "white for *William*, and greene for *Sommer*" (see p. 220 of the facsimile). This obvious pun on the name and calling of Will Sommer, Henry VIII's fool, can be found in Richard Brathwaite's *The Good Wife*, not published until 1618. Leslie Hotson, in *Shakespeare's Motley* (New York: Oxford University Press, 1952), pp. 40 and 78, cites the lines from Brathwaite without reference to the "Edicts."
[52]*DNB*

page,[53] after he had repudiated his own wife. John
Chamberlain reports: "We heare out of Italie that the
Pope hath expressely commaunded Sir Robert Dudley to
forsake his mistris, who they say hath ben with child and
miscaried five times within the yeare."[54]
This Sir Robert Dudley was himself the illegitimate
son of Elizabeth's first great favorite, Robert Dudley,
Earl of Leicester.[55] He tried, and failed, to establish
legitimacy and, as a consequence of the elopement, had
all his property confiscated.

There remains to be proposed only the authorship of
the "Forrein Newes of the yeere 1604."[56] A suggestion
as to the identity of its author could not well be handled
until after other players in the game had been introduced,
and it should be preceded by some analysis of the nature
of the "Forrein Newes."

There are six of these little items, all depending on
the initial gambit "IT is deliuered from." The sources
from which delivery is taken are France, Spain, Rome,
Venice, Germany, and the Low Countries. There is nothing in any of them to indicate the place to which delivery
has been made, but the process would of course have been
letters, diplomatic and otherwise.

These items, I believe, constitute a penetrating, informed, and cryptic commentary on diplomatic, ecclesias-
tic, and social conditions prevailing on the Continent in
the first decade of the seventeenth century. The commentary is in some cases, notably the items from France

[53]Logan Pearsall Smith, *The Life and Letters of Sir Henry
Wotton* (2 vol.; Oxford: The Clarendon Press, 1907), I, 69-70; see
also I, 373, letter of 15 December 1606 to Salisbury and footnote.
[54]McClure, I, 257.
[55]*DNB.*
[56]See footnote 11 above.

and Spain, in "metaphors"; in the cases of Venice and
Rome, however, it is factual and can be documented. I
believe also that the terminal date for them should be, not
1604, but 1610. Substantiation of these contentions will
come as part of the process of identifying the writer. The
author of these items shows marked facility in the use of
words; he accepts the format of the other items of
"Newes"—at least to the extent of the "That" clauses;
he has extensive knowledge of affairs on the Continent.
The subject of James I who most nearly fulfills these
qualifications is Sir Henry Wotton, contributor to the
"Characters," good friend to John Donne, to Sir Thomas
Roe, to Lady Southwell, and to Sir Thomas Overbury, and
His Majesty's "leiger" in Venice from 1604 to 1610. I
shall attempt to establish that, in the word of Lawrence
Lisle, he may "challenge" this "Forrein Newes," by re-
counting something of his career, by showing his familiarity with other items of the "Newes," and by showing
to what extent the news delivered from certain of the
places can be documented by reference to his letters.

Born in 1568, Henry Wotton came of a family in Kent
characterized by his biographer, Logan Pearsall Smith,
as being "distinguished by a peculiar honesty, and old-
fashioned piety, and simplicity of nature," a family which
"habitually declined, rather than sought, court honours
and preferment."[57]   After being put to school at Win-
chester, he went to New College, Oxford, and then to Hart
College, where his lifelong friendship with Donne was
formed, and thence to Queens. While in college he wrote
a play and three discourses in Latin on the construction

---

[57]Smith, I, 1. I am indebted to Smith's study for many biographical details of Sir Henry's career.

of the eye. His primary interest, however, was in civil law, as preparation for a career of public service.

After leaving Oxford, he began the grand tour in 1589. This journey ended in August, 1594. He had spent more than a year in Germany, had become highly proficient in the language, and had sought out the most distinguished professors of civil law. Passing as a German and a Roman Catholic, he went to Rome. During a stay in Italy of three years, he visited numerous cities, seeking out writers, scholars, statesmen. In 1593 he went to Geneva, where he lived in the house of Isaac Casaubon, who also was to become his lifelong friend. In August of 1594 he began his journey to England. After leisurely travel through the Low Countries, he arrived in England before the year was out.

Once back in England, he was preferred by his older half-brother, Lord Wotton, to the service of the Earl of Essex, and he soon became one of the secretaries. He also entered the Middle Temple. He accompanied Essex on the Cadiz expedition of 1596 and on that to the Azores in 1597. His friend John Donne was a member of the retinue of Essex on the Cadiz expedition. Wotton continued in the service of Essex through the unfortunate Irish campaign. While there, he was associated in the negotiations for the treaty with Tyrone. After his return to England, he found it expedient, before the Essex uprising and subsequent trial, to make another voyage to Italy.

This trip was the means of bringing Henry Wotton to the notice of James in 1601. Wotton went, as envoy of the Grand Duke of Tuscany, to Scotland, to warn James of a proposed plot to poison him. He also carried antidotes, which were fortunately not needed. Fortunately, too, his identity as the Italian Ottavio Baldi was not penetrated, though of course he identified himself to James. He remained in Scotland for some months, making a most favorable impression on the King. As a consequence of these actions, in 1604, when the Scottish King was now James I of England, Wotton was knighted and appointed ambassador to Venice.

The qualities, circumstances, and friendships recounted above constitute fairly valid ground for assigning to Sir Henry the authorship of the "From France" and its companion pieces. The fact that he wrote "The Character of a Happy Life" (*c.* 1614), one of the most famous of the characters, adds weight to the argument. Considerably more weight, however, is added by the fact that Sir Henry was very familiar with at least three of the items of "Conceited Newes": Overbury's "Newes from Court," Donne's "Newes from the very Country," and Rudyerd's "Newes from my Lodging."

In his *Life and Letters of Sir Henry Wotton,* Smith lists in Appendix IV a group of items which he calls "Table Talk."[58] They occur in the *Burley M.S.,*[59] apparently a commonplace book which "belonged to him [Wotton], or to some one connected with him."[60] Of these items of "Table Talk," there are one hundred and forty-five. The group, on the basis of contemporary references (*e. g.,* the assassination of Henry IV), must be assigned to the year 1610, or earlier. Smith assumes that most of the items may be attributed to Wotton himself. Of these one hundred forty-five items, the first thirty-four

---

[58]*Ibid.,* II, 489-500.
[59]*Burley MS.,* p. 255, pp. 82-86 (Smith, II, 489).
[60]Smith, II, 490.

are aphoristic and sententious, and several are elaborate conceits. It remained for Mrs. Evelyn M. Simpson in "John Donne and Sir Thomas Overbury's 'Characters,' "[61] to point out that the first thirty-four of these bits of so-called table talk are taken, almost verbatim, from the three items of "Newes" mentioned above, those of Overbury, Donne, and Rudyerd. Some samples are these:

10. Next to no wife and children, your own wife and children are best pastime; another's wife and your children worse; your wife and another's children worst. [*I.D.* (John Donne)]

16. Wit and a woman are two frail things, and both the frailer by concurring. [*T.O.* (Sir Thomas Overbury)]

19. The best bed-fellow for all times in the year is a bed without a fellow. [B.R. (Sir Benjamin Rudyerd)]

As has been said above, these thirty-four extracts could not have gotten into the Wotton commonplace book later than 1610. The earliest extant impression of *A Wife* is the second, one of the four issued in 1614.[62] Wotton, therefore, could only have seen the thirty-four items of Overbury, Donne, and Rudyerd in manuscript. Since the terminal date for most of the items is 1609,[63] in all probability he saw them at Venice. It is suggested that they were sent to him along with letters, probably by Donne, with whom he was in frequent correspondence. There was traffic in such items in the other direction, for

---

[61]*Modern Language Review*, XVIII (October, 1923), 410-415.
[62]There had been an issue of *A Wife* in 1611 (cf. footnote 1 above), but it is not known whether it contained the "Newes."
[63]Cf. pp. xxii, xxx, xxxiv, xxxvi above.

Wotton frequently sent to England "epigrams, pasquils, and such sport of the time,"[64] for the amusement of the King and the Earl of Salisbury.

Wotton had the wide experience and the literary ability to write the pungent little items from Rome and elsewhere, and he had knowledge of some of the more ambitious items of "Newes from." The final step in building a case for his authorship of the "Forrein Newes" is the setting of them against his letters. No strong verbal parallels will be discovered, but many of the cryptic utterances, *e.g.*, "vice is a state-commoditie" ("From Rome"), can be copiously documented by reference to Wotton's letters, official and personal. Before detailed documentation is attempted, however, it may be well to look at some of the less specific items, with some speculation about what meaning may lie under their surfaces— meanings that Wotton as ambassador at Venice, in frequent correspondence with ambassadors at other capitals, might have felt or uttered. Reading of his letters offers abundant evidence that he had an informed view of events in Europe.

In a letter to Sir Edmund Bacon, of 7 May 1613, Wotton, speaking of the imprisonment of Sir Thomas Overbury, offers the following curious observation:

> The nature of his alteration was (as you rightly judge it) in the first access somewhat apoplectical, but yet mingled in my opinion with divers properties of a lethargy; whereof we shall discourse more particularly when we meet; which I now long for, besides other respects, that we may lay aside these metaphors.[65]

---

[64]Letter, 14 July 1606, to the Earl of Salisbury (Smith, I, 356).
[65]Smith, II, 22.

It is my suggestion that certain items of the "Forrein Newes"—"From France," "From Spaine," and "From the Low Countries"—contain some of the Wotton "metaphors." I suggest that underneath the various images in "From France" lies the conversion to Catholicism of Henry IV, with its consequences for Henry himself and for France and the Continent. This great sovereign, as Henry of Navarre, had been a champion of Protestantism. With the death of Henry III in 1589 he became heir to the throne of France. As a step toward gaining his throne, and upon the advice of his great friend and minister, the Duc de Sully, he was converted to Catholicism on July 25, 1593. With his entry into Paris on March 22, 1594, he became in reality Henry IV, King of France. Thereafter, through such devices as his "great design" for uniting Protestant, or disaffected, states, for the purpose of driving the Spaniards out of Italy, even while seeming to take the part of the Papacy (as in the quarrel of the mid-1590's between Venice and the Pope), he to some extent negated his own official Catholicism. By the Edict of Nantes in 1598 he enormously furthered the Protestant cause. His embracement of Catholicism was regarded by Wotton as not only the indirect cause of his death, but also the cause of its own terrible punishment:

> I must crave pardon for the private comfort and benefit of mine own conscience, to note these two visible circumstances of God's heavy judgement in the fall of that King: first, that he wanted in his extremity the Sacraments of that Church which had abused him, having with the blow (as we hear) been strangely deprived of all speech, though not of life for some hours after it. Secondly, that he was taken away by that doctrine to which he had passed:

for that which he did abandon is no killer of princes, nor no rewarder of homicides with Paradise.[66]

Now for the metaphors in the news "From France." The "wines" of the first sentence may refer to the conversion of Henry to Catholicism. The "torrent"[67] of the second sentence may refer to his support of the Protestant cause while giving lip-service to Catholicism. The third sentence—"a penetrating iudgment may enter into a mans minde"—may wonder that a man so "setled" in judgment as Henry could embrace Catholicism. It is not unlikely also that the phrase "a Princes pleasurable vices" takes note of the flagrant extramarital conduct, not only of Henry, but also of his Queen.

This same speech through metaphors, I believe, can be found in the news "From Spaine," especially when it is considered in conjunction with "From the Low Countries." For approximately forty years before 1610, the United Provinces in the Low Countries—a republic—had been resisting valiantly, and on the whole successfully, the efforts of the King of Spain to impose his claim of sovereignty. From the persecutions of the Duc de Alva to the skillful military operations of Spinola, they had repelled all Spanish aggression. During those forty years, the Dutchmen had created the world's greatest seapower; they had driven the Spaniards almost completely out of trade to the East Indies; and had been most successful in disrupting the return of her treasure ships from the In-

---

[66]Letter, 28 May 1610, to the Earl of Salisbury (Smith, I, 490-491).

[67]In a letter to the Earl of Salisbury, 21 July 1607, Wotton refers to the rebellion among the Grisons as a "trimestral torrent" (Smith, I, 393).

dies to the West. Says the writer of "From Spaine":
"That the shortest cutt to the riches of the Indies is by
their contempt."

It may be argued, of course, that the "shortest cutt
to the riches of the Indies" is only a generalized, Stoic
statement about the unimportance of wealth. The consideration of this and other such mystifying statements
prompted a rereading of the sixth volume of John L.
Motley's *History of the United Netherlands*,[68] and one
feels that these little pieces about Spain and the Low
Countries say in brief much of what Motley says at
length—that they are much more likely to be metaphors
than mere moralizing.

Speculation about the fifth item in "From Spaine"—
"That it is a grosse flattering of tired crueltie to honest
it with the title of clemencie"—is perhaps a little safer
than that of the preceding paragraphs. On the 9th of
April, 1609, there was signed a treaty of truce, of twelve
years' duration, between United Netherlands on the one
hand and the "Archdukes" Albert and Clara, rulers of
the Spanish Netherlands, with the full concurrence of
Philip III of Spain. This treaty was a triumph for the
Netherlands: it recognized their absolute independence
as a state; it established their freedom on the high seas;
it eliminated the danger of Spanish aggression; and it did
not require that the Netherlands foster Roman Catholics.

The "crueltie" of Spain—and of the Roman Catholics
—through Inquisitions, through the burning of heretics,
through massacres such as that on St. Bartholomew's Day
—is well known indeed. That that "crueltie" was "tired"

---

[68]Vol. XI, *The Complete Works of John L. Motley* (New York:
The Kelmscott Society, c. 1900).

needs to be elaborated a bit. This truce was necessary to Spain for many reasons. Spinola's campaign in the summer of 1606 had been an expensive failure; two great Spanish fleets had been destroyed by the Dutch, one at Malacca and one at Gibraltar; with the expulsion in 1607 of the half-million Moors, much of Spain's productive capacity had been lost; the Duke of Lerma governed Philip III absolutely, and his rapacity—plus that of the Church and nobility—had utterly drained Spain's resources. Spain must be relieved of the burden of chastising the heretics in the North. "Tired crueltie." There were, no doubt, those who felt indeed that this truce was "clemencie" on the part of Spain—and the Archdukes—but not, I believe, the writer of "From Spaine"—whether he was Wotton or another.

"From the Low Countries"—if read after the more vigorous "From Spaine"—appears to contain a quiet assessment, and approval, of the fortitude and foresight which kept the intrepid Duchmen free of the yoke of Spain: "grounds of a mans libertie"; "in the likelyhood of good, prouide for ill"; "the euill fortune of the wars as well as the good is variable."

If the "metaphors" of the three items discussed above could be Wotton's, the more specific charges of "From Rome" are much more likely to be his, for they can be copiously documented from his dispatches to Salisbury and King James, or his letters to his friends during his first appointment as "leiger" in Venice.

The first two sentences of "From Rome" concern themselves with the fact that "vice is a state-commoditie." In the "Table Talk," not all of which, of course, is Wotton's, there are several items which point out this state (Papal) policy:

40. The murderer must be wrought to the fact either by great promises of estate, or pardons and indulgences.

43. Sixtus IV built the *bordello* in Rome which yieldeth £4,000 *per annum.* A whore there cannot turn to an honest life without paying so much to have her name razed out of the book as it cost to enroll.

108. Since the example of Alexander VI, and then Bianca Capella, the use of poisoning is lost in Italy —not to give place to a better custom, but to a more convenient vice, the stiletto.

The next item in the news from Rome is "That Iewes and Curtezans there, are as beasts that men feed to feed on." This observation is, of course, related to the preceding one—"vice is a state-commoditie"—but it is interesting to note that on at least two occasions Wotton in his letters makes the juxtaposition of Jews and courtesans. In a letter to Lord Zouche of 8 May 1592 we have this:

2. In the second, all dishonest *donne* are banished out of the corps of the city to the Piazza Padella or *hortaccio;* by which remove, the governor of the town hath openly confessed himself to have gained 15,000 crowns with artificial handling of the matter; and the Pope being desirous to know the number of these women, the *censo* was found 40,000 and certain hundreds, as the Baron of Didrichstein reported from the Pope's mouth. 3. The third edict was wholly against the jews, imposing upon them of three things, necessarily one; either to keep against the *banditi* 400 horse in Campania, or to maintain the bread at one *baiocho* the pound, or *imbagagliare.*[69]

_____
[69]Smith, I, 275.

The danger to an Englishman abiding at Rome, which is the third topic of the news from Rome, is not to Wotton primarily physical, but spiritual. He himself, on his first visit to Rome on his grand tour, travelled incognito, as a very convivial German Roman Catholic, with a large feather in his hat to suggest frivolity.[70] Upon his return as ambassador, one of his most persistent concerns was with young Englishmen, perhaps travelling with chaplain-tutors, who may succumb, in Rome, to the blandishments of the Jesuits. A general statement of the processes of converting travellers occurs in Wotton's letter of 18 August 1605 to Salisbury:

> under Clement VIII (*mutatis artibus*), began not only permission and connivency, but invitation and allurement of all nations and religions promiscuously. Through which freedom and conversation they began by little and little to take hold of such as came thither, entering into them (where they saw them weakest), not as they were wont, with certain arguments of the school, which they found to be but an overlading of your capacities, and the longer way, but working now upon every discontentment in the party (which by conversation they discovered), and upon every outward scandal at home, deriding, commiserating, and running through all affections; catching first the fancy, and by that the judgement and conscience, with certain popular observations (as I may term them) upon this or that accident.[71]

The first of Wotton's young Englishmen to whom Rome was dangerous was Lord Roos, whose tutor was

---

[70]Note that in "From Germanie," that nation is afflicted throughout by "the infectious vice of drunken goodfellowship."
[71]Smith, I, 332.

John Molle. To Lord Roos, Wotton wrote on 17 May 1608:

> I must not forget to tell your Lordship that I have hereof advertised my Lord of Salisbury more particularly, both because it was a thing (as I took it) of public consequence, and for that it seemed unto me in your Lordship a point both of politic and Christian wisdom to provide for yourself, before your going, a safe-conduct that might secure as well your conscience as your person.[72]

The young lord did go to Rome, and apparently escaped unscathed. Wotton writes on 5 December 1608 to Salisbury that he finds in Roos' "speeches a most vehement detestation of that foolish religion."[73] But the unfortunate Molle did not thrive so well, for he fell into the hands of the Inquisition. In the same letter Wotton informs Salisbury that he is sending Molle a "portion of money" for his "present necessities," and also "to be disposed in the helping of him out." The bribery was unsuccessful, for in 1618 the unfortunate Molle was still a prisoner.[74]

At the risk of too much quotation, it seems well to let Wotton sum up this matter of danger in—or from— Rome. This passage also is a part of a dispatch to Salisbury, written on 18 June 1609:

> My Lord Wentworthe on the 18th of May, coming towards Venice (as then immediately from Florence), accompanied with his brother-in-law Mr. Henry Crafts, one Edward Lichefeld, their gover-

---

[72]*Ibid.*, I, 429.
[73]*Ibid.*, I, 442.
[74]Chamberlain's letter to Sir Dudley Carleton (McClure, II, 128).

nor, and some two or three other English, through
Bologna, as they were there together at supper the
very night of their arrival, came up two Dominican
Friars, with the sergeants of the town, and carried
thence the foresaid Lichefeld, with all his papers,
into the prison of the Inquisition, where he yet remaineth. Thus standeth this accident in the bare
circumstances thereof, not different, save only in
place, from that of Mr. Mole at Rome. And doubt-
lessly (as we collect now upon the whole matter) if
Sir Jhon Harrington had either gone the Roman
journey, or taken the ordinary way in his remove
hitherwards out of Tuscany, the like would have be-
fallen his director also, a gentleman of singular suf-
ficiency; for it appeareth a new piece of counsel (in-
fused into the Pope by his artisans the Jesuits) to
separate by some device their guides from our
young noblemen (about whom they are busiest),
and afterwards to use themselves (for aught I can
yet hear) with much kindness and security, but yet
with restraint (when they come to Rome) or depart-
ing thence without leave; which form was held both
with the Lords Rosse and St. Jhons, and with this
Lord Wentworthe and his brother-in-law at their
being there.[75]

One more note on the news from Rome seems worth
while, concerning the observation "That greatnesse comes
not downe by the way it went vp." True, it is not part of
the official dispatch of an ambassador, and it comes long
after the date I have set for the "Newes." Moved by the
imprisonment of Overbury, Wotton comments in metaphor on the vicissitudes of "greatnesse":

---

[75]Smith, I, 456-457.

So as I can yet but cast towards you a longing, and
in truth an envious look, for this place of such ser-
vility in the getting, and such uncertainty in the
holding of fortunes, where methinks we are all over-
clouded with that sleep of Jacob, when he saw some
ascending, and some descending, but that those
were angels, and these are men; for in both, what
is it but a dream?[76]

It may seem strange that, if the six items are indeed
Wotton's, there are not more statements in "From Venice" that may be closely documented. If it is remembered, however, that the good Wotton was not only the
representative of His Majesty James I, but was also the
militant champion of Protestantism against the Papacy
and the power of Spain and her allies, and if it is further
remembered that during much of his residency in Venice
the city was engaged in a test of power with the Papacy,
it will not seem unreasonable that the thrust of the references will be inevitably on the iniquities of Rome.

In "From Venice" there is a reference to "Curtezans"
consistent with the attitude toward their function in
"From Rome." The "many dangerous spirits" who "lye
buried in their wants" are very prominent in Wotton's
letters to Salisbury. In the interest of England, and
Protestantism, the use of intelligencers was very necessary; equally necessary was the interception of dispatches
and letters. Says Wotton, "knaves [are] dearer than
honest men."[77] There are several requests in the letters
for an increase in allowances, for the specific purpose
of hiring these "knaves": they are almost as necessary as

---

[76]*Ibid.*, II, 21.
[77]*Ibid.*, I, 367.

honest men; [78] and "though there be great store of knaves, yet honest men are cheaper."[79]

In view of these various bits of evidence of his possession of the requisite knowledge and experience, his familiarity with other items of the "Newes," and his own literary abilities, Sir Henry Wotton should be listed with John Donne and the other writers of the "Newes"—but *in absentia.*

THE RULES

Games must have rules, and we have seen Ben Jonson, uninvited, setting himself up as both referee and custodian of the rules. But an intensive examination of the individual items of the "Newes" suggests a few observations that should be made, in addition to those of Jonson in his "Court Pucell."

The items of "Newes from" are seventeen in all and are exactly similar in rhetorical structure. Three have a declarative beginning: "It is thought heere," or "It is said among the folkes heere." In the remaining eleven, the "It is said heere" is implied. Following that beginning, the items all consist of a series of noun clauses, each beginning with "That." This structure is neglected in only four of the items—but consistently in only one, "Newes from the lower end of the Table."

Within this rigidly prescribed structure, the newsmonger must work with imagery appropriate to the place from which he is writing. Perhaps the most effective handling of this "rule" is in John Donne's "Newes from the very Country": "vnderwoods" and "great falls";

---

[78]*Ibid.*
[79]*Ibid.*, I, 359.

Apricocks"; "Pike in a pond"; "horse-taile"; references to hawking, hunting, and mill-wheels. Almost equally skillful and pervasive are the sea images in "Newes from Sea" by "W.S.": in the first few lines he works with "prospect," "putting to Sea," "forewinds," "calmes," and "crossegales." Other items that make extensive and skillful use of the appropriate place images are "Newes from the lower end of the Table" and "Newes from the Bed." As might be expected from Jonson's epigram, the "Newes of my morning worke" of Cecily Bulstrode fails almost completely to achieve the effects that the game demands.

The title-pages of impressions two, four, and five insist that the quartos contain "conceited *Newes, written by himselfe and other* learned Gentlemen his friends." The title-page of the Third Impression makes no mention of the "Newes"; those of impressions seven through ten mention it, but not as "conceited Newes." But no matter what is on the title-page, the items are "conceited" to the best of the ability of the writer, and there is represented a wide range indeed of ability.

The conceit, as it appears in these little passages written to a strict formula, seems to consist of two stages: there is first the strained, far-fetched metaphor, always the better as the distance between the things juxtaposed is the greater; secondly, there is the extension of that basic metaphor to unlikely, almost fantastic implications. Samples of the first degree of likeness are these: "That love is the taile worme" (S^r.T.R.) ; "That money is nothing but a thing which Art hath turned vp trumpe" (*T.O.*) ; "That titles of honour are rattles to still ambition" (*A.S.*, "Answer to the Court newes") ; "That guilt is the flea of the conscience" (*B.R.*).

More interesting and more abundant are those of the second sort: "That sentences in Authors like haires in an horse-taile concurre in one roote of beauty and strength, but being pluckt out one by one, serue onely for springes and snares" (*I.D.*) ; "That Iesuits are like Apricocks, heretofore here and there one succour'd in a great mans house and cost deare, now you may haue them for nothing in euery cottage" (*I.D.*) ; "That the soule in some is like an egge, hatched by a young pullet, who often rigging from her nest, makes hot and cold beget rottennesse, which her wanton youth will not beleeue, till the faire shell being broken the stinke appeareth to profit others, but cannot her" (*A.S.*, "Answer to the very Country Newes") ; "That this life is a throng in a narrow passage, hee that is first out finds ease, hee in the middle worst, hemb'd in with troubles, the hindmost that driues both out afore him, though not suffering wrong, hath his part in doing it" (Sʳ.T.R.).

The examples just given are the more fantastic, surprising, shocking of the conceits. But the vast majority of the "That" clauses are conceived in the same manner, lacking only the degree of apartness of the things examined, or the ramifications of treatment. Samples of this lesser sort of conceit are these: "That custom is the soule of circumstances" (*T.O.*) ; "That a Papist is a new word for a traytor" (Sʳ.T.R.) ; "That small faults habituated are as dangerous as little leakes vnfound, and that to punish and not preuent, is to labour in the pumpe, and leaue the leake open" (*W.S.*) ; "*That grace before meat is our election before we were; grace after, our saluation when we are gone*" (J.C.) ; "That euery ones memorie is diuided into two parts: the part loosing all is the sea, the keeping part is land" (Mʳⁱˢ.B.).

The next of the rules of the game which needs comment is the ending of the items of news. It must, in one way, or another, provide what one might call a full stop to the sententious observations which have been unified primarily by their source: court, country, sea, bed, table. In its neatest manifestations, it collects preceding material, associates it with news, or with death, the whole being given an epigrammatic flavor: "That custome hath so far preuailed, that truth is now the greatest newes" (*T.O.*); "That all this is no newes to a better wit" (S[r].T.R.); "That I care not what become of this fraile Barcke of my flesh, so I saue the passenger. And heere I cast anchor" (*W.S.*); "That if the bed should speake all it knowes, it would put many to the blush. That it is fit the bed should know more than paper" (*R.S.*); "That good deeds, in this life, are coales raked vp in embers, to make a fire next day" ("the Chimney corner").

The final word about the rules of the game has to do with content. Ben Jonson indicated "State, Religion, Bawdrie," as the principal themes. He also gives the classes of participants as "Lords," "wits," "Sermoneeres." Insofar as they participate in the game of "newes," however, all these are courtiers. And insofar as "State" is a theme of the various writers, it never rises to questions of statecraft, but ironically is almost always concerned with veniality and hollowness of the courtiers and the emptiness of titles of honor, not excluding that of King. The "*A.S.*" who says "King is fames *butt*, and feares *quiuer*," and Cecily Bulstrode, who says, "the deuill is the perfectest Courtier," may almost speak for all the players.

"Religion"—if one extends the word to include ethics —receives more attention from the newsmongers than does "State." But it is not a religion that is mystical, or even zealous. On most occasions, some phase of religious belief is merely the starting point for a conceit, or a paradox, as in the following samples: "That God made one world of *Substances;* man hath made another of Arte and Opinion" (*T.O.*) ; "That man, woman, and the deuill, are the three degrees of comparison" (*A.S.*, "Answer to the Court news") ; "That *Atheists* in affliction, like blind beggers, are forced to aske though they know not of whom" (*I.D.*) ; *"The Soule that halts between two opinions, falls between two stooles"* (J.C.).

In one matter related to religion, however, many of the writers of the "Newes" are vehement—in their denunciation of things Papist, especially the Jesuits. In fact, the attacks at this point are so bitter that one is forced to assume that the paragraphs were written after the Gunpowder Plot in 1605. Perhaps the most virulent of the references to the Papacy is in "Newes from my Lodging," by "B.R." (Sir Benjamin Rudyerd) : "That a hang'd chamber in priuate is nothing so convenient as a hang'd Traitor in publique. That the religion of *Papistry,* is like a curtaine made to keep out the light."

One of the group, however, seems out of place— "Newes from the Church." Its author (identified in the Sixth Impression as *"Io. Ruddiard"*), though working almost altogether through conceits, speaks with some conviction both in matters of dogma and of church discipline. He stoutly defends the Anglican position against both Puritan and Papist: "That the soule may be too ranke too, if wee looke not to it: and so a *Puritane* often times meets a *Papist* in superstition another way."

Jonson's third element of the "Newes," "Bawdrie," is present as the subject of philosophical disquisition or as the object of satirical attack. But it is notably absent in any erotic sense. Not many of the writers, insofar as one can tell, would disagree with the position taken in "Newes from my Lodging": "That the best bedfellow for all time in the yeere is a good bed without a fellow." The foregoing analysis has had to do with those of the items with the heading "Newes from"—seventeen in all. In the midst of that group, which purports to be written literally "from" the place whose imagery is used, there is the group of six items under the heading of "Forrein Newes of the yeere 1604," which has earlier in this paper been assigned to Sir Henry Wotton, and for which a date nearer 1610 than 1604 has been proposed. These also are "from," but the introductory declaration is different, "IT is deliuered from *France*," with the same words presumably understood to precede the news from the other five places.

They use, as did the group already described, the noun clause beginning with "That." But there the resemblance ends, for they work essentially with abstractions rather than images of the physical and take for a unifying theme a quality supposed to be in a state, rather than the physical properties of a place.

In the "Forrein Newes" the use of the conceit is not a part of the game; I find only four in the six passages, two delivered from France, and one each from Rome and Venice. Nor is there any effort to employ imagery appropriate to a France or a Rome. The unifying element in the better ones is some habit or practice popularly supposed to belong to that country or city. It may be a supposed fault, as "vice is a state-commoditie" in Rome; or "the infectious vice of drunken goodfellowship" in Germany; or cruelty in Spain. It may be a praiseworthy quality—as frugality in Venice, love of liberty in the Low Countries. Nor does the conclusion of these items really conclude, in the sense of collecting material in epigrammatic termination. The last of its "That" clauses is merely one thing more.

The third type of paragraph in the "Newes" is a single item, "Newes to the Vniuersitie." In this one the writer undertakes to work with ideas associated with place, but in general he uses abstractions rather than such physical things as those in the passages by *"I.D.,"* *"W.S.,"* or *"J.C."* He talks of "wisdome," of *"Logick,"* of *"Astronomie,"* of "perfection in this world." He touches on no state, he shuns bawdry, but he gives us about even measure of religion, ethics, and pedagogy. He does not use the format of the "That" clauses, and he is apparently not striving for conceits.

He does, however, have one little touch which may have been transmitted to the Overbury characters. His beginning is a mild conceit, "A Meere Scholler, is but a liue booke." The early characters, through number twenty-one, which are probably Overbury's, on seventeen occasions use a modification of this beginning, *e. g.*: *"A Fine Gentlemen./ IS the Cynamon tree,* whose barke is more worth then his body." (See page 89 of the facsimile.) Of the remaining sixty-one, forty-one incorporate the title into an initial conceit or metaphor.

INFLUENCE OF THE "NEWES" ON THE CHARACTERS OF THE OVERBURY GROUP

There are, however, many more affinities between the "Newes" and the "Characters" than the structure of the opening sentence. It is the purpose of this chapter to examine, in some detail, the full relationship between the items of "Newes" of Sir Thomas and his conceited friends and their more famous relative, the character.[80]

> To square out a Character by our English leuell, it is a picture (reall or personall) quaintlie drawne in various collours, all of them heightned by one shadowing.
> It is a quicke and soft touch of many strings, all shutting vp in one musicall close: It is wits descant on any plaine song.

The passage quoted above is from the Ninth Impression of *A Wife* (1616), which included a group of new characters. It is the last item in the octavo, and it is part of a passage having the heading, "What a Character is" (p. 290 of the facsimile). It can hardly be the work of Overbury, and it is not claimed for Webster by those who assign to him the major body of the character group. Even though "What a Character is" follows a group of sketches probably written by Thomas Dekker[81]—"A Prison," "A Prisoner," "A Creditour," "A Sarieant," "This Yeoman," and "A Iaylour"—it seems unlikely that writing so delicate and perceptive could be his.

Be that as it may, the character here described is not that which we see in earlier writers in the *genre*, whether Theophrastus, Ben Jonson, or Joseph Hall. The char-

---

[80]The general techniques and attitudes of the Overburian character which I have pointed out are noted by Benjamin Boyce in his *The Theophrastan Character in England* (Cambridge: Harvard University Press, 1947). He does not, however, associate these characteristics with the "Newes."

[81]See W. J. Paylor, "Thomas Dekker and the 'Overburian' Characters," *Modern Language Review*, XXXI, (April, 1936), 155-160.

acter supposed by our anonymous writer appears to me
to be one that has been subtly influenced by the "rules"
which governed the creation of the items of news.
The character of Theophrastus certainly has not the
"soft touch of many strings, all shutting vp in one musicall close." Witness his "The Arrogant Man" as typical
of his entire list:

> Arrogance is contempt for everything but one-
> self. The Arrogant Man is this sort of person. He
> tells someone who is in a hurry that he will see him
> when he takes his own after-dinner walk. He only
> remembers the benefits he has conferred. He will
> decide a case in which he is arbitrator as he walks
> through the streets. When elected to a public office
> he takes an oath that he has not sufficient leisure.
> He has never been known to make the first visit to
> anyone. He tells his workmen and tradesmen to be
> at his house at dawn. He speaks to nobody in the
> streets but walks along with his head bent forward
> or his chin in the air, according to his whim. When
> he has guests he does not come down to table but
> sends an inferior to look after them. He always
> sends someone in advance to announce his visit.
> When he is being massaged or taking his bath or
> eating he will not allow any visitors. When he set-
> tles a business matter he tells his slave to set the
> counters, reckon up and enter the total. If he
> writes a letter he does not say: "I should be much
> obliged. . ." but "This is what I want . . ." or "I
> have sent to you for . . ." or "Attend to these orders
> strictly . . ." or "Without delay."[82]

Here is no more than a casual sampling of the affairs
of the day, with the only unifying element lying in the

---

[82]Aldington, pp. 46-47.

quality of arrogance. The sketch has no "close" of any sort.

Ben Jonson makes conscious use of the character, but as an instrument of dramatic structure rather than as a self-sufficient prose entity. Examples that come immediately to mind are the characterizations of Zeal-of-the-Land Busy and Quarlous, or any one of a half-dozen descriptions of Fitzdottrell in *The Devil Is an Ass.* Nor do his more formalized characters at the beginning of *Every Man Out of His Humour* undertake more than to highlight characteristic actions that will be amplified as the play's action proceeds. His portrait of Fastidious Briske is an excellent example:

> *A neat, spruce, affecting Courtier, one that weares clothes well, and in fashion; practiseth by his glasse how to salute; speakes good remnants (notwithstanding the Base-violl and Tobacco:) sweares tersely, and with variety; cares not what Ladies fauour he belyes, or great Mans familiarity: a good property to perfume the boot of a coach. Hee will borrow another mans horse to praise, and backs him as his owne. Or, for a neede, on foot can post himselfe into credit with his marchant, only with the gingle of his spurre, and the jerke of his wand.*[83]

Much closer to the pattern set by his predecessors is Jonson's character of Amorphus, the Traveller. It may well be an ancestor of the character as it appears in Hall's work of 1608, but it lacks all the technique which became familiar in the Overbury collection.

---

[83]Herford and Simpson, III, 424.

He that is with him, is AMORPHVS, a trauailer,
one so made out of the mixture and shreds of
formes, that himselfe is truly deform'd. He walks
most commonly with a cloue, or pick-tooth in his
mouth, hee is the very mint of complement, all his
behauiours are printed, his face is another volume
of *essayes;* and his beard an *Aristarchus.* He
speakes all creame, skimd, and more affected than a
dozen of waiting women. He is his owne promoter
in euery place. The wife of the ordinarie giues him
his diet, to maintaine her table in discourse, which
(indeed) is a meere tyrannie ouer her other guests,
for hee will usurpe all the talke: ten constables are
not so tedious. He is no great shifter, once a yeere
his apparell is readie to reuolt. He doth vse much
to arbitrate quarrels, and fights himselfe, exceeding
well (out at a window.) He will lye cheaper than
any begger and lowder than most clockes.[84]

The Joseph Hall *Characters* of 1608 are examples of a
genre, each self-contained, each unified by the characteristics belonging to the man of its title—"The Flatterer,"
"The Malcontent." But they, like those of Theophrastus
and Jonson, lack the "soft touch of many strings," the
"musicall close." Hall's dignified prose marches, analytically, in terms of his subject's eyes, or his mind, or his
passions; in terms of what he does as a householder, as a
guest; in terms of what he does in church, in the courts
of law, in the commonwealth. His prose, his analyses,
vary little, whether the character be of a virtue or a vice.
He does not, more than perhaps half-a-dozen times, de-
scend to the use of the conceit, and when he does, as at
the end of "The Flatterer," he is not successful: "In
short, he is the moth of liberal men's coats; the ear-wig

---
[84]*Ibid.,* IV, 72-73.

of the mighty; the bane of courts; a friend and a slave to
the trencher; and good for nothing but to be a factor for
the Devil."[85]
It is clear, therefore, that the characters preceding
those of the Overbury collection lacked most of the qualities which make the "Newes" somewhat unique: carefully wrought beginnings and endings, uniform images,
self-conscious use of the conceit, and, in general, an approach scornful or ironic.

It cannot, of course, be established beyond doubt that
the "Newes" influenced the characters, but the kinship is
such that the relationships should be examined. I have
shown that the "Newes" paragraphs were in all probability written between the years 1605 (*i.e.*, after the Gunpowder Plot of November 5) and 1610, for Cecily Bulstrode had died in 1609.

The "Characters" fall into several groups, each isolated in the earlier editions from its predecessors by some
provision in the printer's shop. They are the work of
several men—Sir Thomas Overbury, John Cooke, Sir
Henry Wotton, and very probably John Webster and
Thomas Dekker. There are seven segments which may
be isolated; yet, as I shall show, there is in each segment
the easily recognized mark of the "Newes." There are, of
course, many of the characters to which the techniques
of the "Newes" are not applicable, or in which their effects are not sought. But examples I shall present will
show that the flavor of the "Newes" persi'sted, not only
throughout the Overbury canon, but into slightly later
work of John Stephens, Nicholas Breton, and John Earle.

The initial segment of the "Characters," the twenty-
one which appeared in the Second Impression of *A Wife*

---

[85]Aldington, p. 81.

("A good Woman" through "An Ostler"), is usually assigned to Sir Thomas Overbury.[86] These first twenty-one may have been written as early as the "Newes," but it appears more likely that they were the product of a somewhat later set of circumstances, the contemplation of a marriage between Overbury's master, Sir Robert Carr, and the Countess of Essex. Those goings-on very likely inspired "A Wife," first published in 1611, and with it such of the "Characters" as "A good Woman," "A very very Woman," and "Her next part."

If these twenty-one characters are indeed later than the "Newes," they are almost certainly indebted to it in many ways. The nature of the indebtedness can be shown by a glance at two of the shorter ones, "A golden Asse" and "An Host" (pp. 72 and 96 of the facsimile).

These short characters put to work all the "rules" suggested for the "Newes" except the employment of the subject matter—"State, Religion, Bawdrie." Their technical beginnings are outside themselves, as was frequently the case with the items of news; they begin with conceits and use others in the text; they confine themselves exclusively to imagery appropriate to the subject; and end with an epigrammatic flavor and with the collection in a phrase of preceding ideas.

To the initial group are added nine new characters in the Fourth Impression of *A Wife* (also published in 1614 by Lawrence Lisle). This group ends with the much an-

---

[86]Aldington (p. 13) suggests that "Hardly more than a quarter of Overbury's Characters can have been written by Overbury himself; the second edition of *A Wife, now a Widow*, in which the Characters first appeared, contains only twenty-one, and some of these must have been by other 'learned gentlemen.'" Paylor (p. xvii) thinks Overbury probably wrote the first eleven ("A good Woman" through "A Wise man," pp. 63-82 of the facsimile).

thologized poem, "The Character of a happy life," by Sir Henry Wotton. Typical of the group, and of the techniques of the "Newes," is "A Saylor," to be found on page 102 of the facsimile.

In the Sixth Impression (1615), entitled *NEW AND CHOISE CHARACTERS, of seuerall Authors: Together with that exquisite and vnmatcht Poeme, THE WIFE,* three new groups of characters are introduced, each segregated from the other groups. The first is a group of four (nos. 32 through 35), "A Meere Scholler," "A Tinker," "An Apparatour," and "An Almanacke-maker." The items of "Newes" appear between this little group and the thirty-one characters which had appeared in the Fourth Impression. Three of the characters in the first group are by John Cooke.[87] Cooke's "An Apparatour" displays the same ingenuity which he displayed in his "Newes from the lower end of the Table" and conforms remarkably to the description of a character given earlier: "a picture (reall or personall) quaintlie drawne in various collours, all of them heightened by one shadowing."[88] The techniques of the "Newes" are perhaps most apparent in "An Apparatour" (pp. 126-127 of the facsimile).

John Cooke's three characters and their companion— "A Meere Scholler," assigned to "D. B." in the Sixth Impression only—are followed by Lady Southwell's "Edicts." Next after the "Edicts" comes a group of six characters: "An Hypocrite," "A Maquerela, in plain English, a Bawd," "A Chamber-Mayde," "A Precisian," "A Fantasticke Innes of Court man," and "A meere Fellow of an House." These six are followed by a section title:

---

[87] See footnote 22 above.
[88] See p. lxxii above.

NEW CHARACTERS / (drawne to the life) of seuerall
/ *Persons, in Seuerall* / *qualities.*"[89]   For this group of
characters, no specific author has been proposed.
The first of this group (Nos. 36-41), "An Hypocrite,"
is very *unlike* the majority of the characters, not only in
the fact that it is perhaps four times as long as the aver-
age, but also in the fact that it works with an analytically
conceived outline. It is also very similar in subject matter to another of the group, "A Precisian." But any one
of the other five might be used as an example of characteristics heretofore noted. Suggested for examination
is "A Maquerela," beginning on page 138 of the facsimile.
All the now familiar characteristics are present: the in-
corporation of the title into the first sentence, in itself
a mild conceit; the imagery of place or occupation, this
time in combination; frequent conceits; the closing which
both collects and strives for the epigrammatical; and the
mocking tone.

Immediately after the section title quoted above, there
follows a large group of characters (Nos. 42-73), those
generally assigned to John Webster.[90]   A few of the
sketches in this group, by reason of their commendatory
subject matter, such as "A Worthy Commander in the
Warres," "A vertuous Widdow," and "A fayre and happy
Milke-mayd," avoid the scoffing tone so generally preva-
lent.   Otherwise, they conform, in general, to the techniques first noted in the "Newes." Occasionally the scoffing gives way to a more serious tone of direct condem-
nation.   On such occasions the conceits may give way to
mere exposition, or even to paradox.   But the model is

---

[89]In succeeding impressions the characters are printed contin-
uously, omitting this and the earlier section titles.
[90]See footnote 5 above.

not forgotten. "A Pirate," which begins on page 154 of
the facsimile, is an excellent example of Webster's technique.

The final group of Overburian characters does not appear until Lisle has issued his Ninth Impression. Of
these there are eight—"*A couetous man*" through "*A
Iaylour*," with the final item being "*What a Character is*,"
part of which has been quoted above. These characters,
except for "*A couetous man*" and "*What a Character is*,"
are attributed by W. J. Paylor to Thomas Dekker.[91] Certainly the experiences of debtors' prison and the knowledge of the seamier side of London life which Dekker did
indeed experience are the essential material of the six
items assigned to him. The writer's predilections with
sociological material, however, do not preclude his con-
formity to the established pattern, except perhaps in the
using of the epigrammatic closing. "*A Sarieant*" will
demonstrate Dekker's (?) application of the techniques.
It appears on pages 282 to 285 of the facsimile.

INFLUENCE OF THE "NEWES" ON THE CHARACTERS OF JOHN STEPHENS, NICHOLAS BRETON, AND JOHN EARLE

The more pervasive techniques of the "Newes," the
excessive use of conceits and the persistence in the
imagery of a particular place or occupation, must have
been highly infectious. They appear, sometimes carried
almost to extremes, in the character writings of John
Stephens and, to a lesser extent, in *The Good and the
Bad* of Nicholas Breton and in the *Micro-cosmographie*
of John Earle.

---

[91]See p. lxxii above and footnote 81.

John Stephens was associated with the courtier group which produced the items of "Newes." He is very probably the "*I.S. Lincolniensis, Gentleman*" who has an elegy, "A Morning Sacrifice," in the front matter of the Second Impression of *A Wife* (p. 311 of the facsimile). That he was acquainted with John Cooke is evident, for Cooke has a signed effusion in the Second Impression of Stephens' *Essayes* entitled "To the nameles Author of a late Character entitled, An *Excellent Actor*, following the *Wife*."[92] A commendatory poem is addressed to Stephens by Ben Jonson as "his much and worthily esteemed friend."[93] Stephens' characters appeared under two titles, *Satyrical Essayes Characters and Others* and *Essayes and Characters, Ironicall and Instructive*, both printed in 1615.

That there was some imputation of borrowing attached to Stephens' characters is strongly suggested in this, written by "GEO: GREENE *of Lincolns Inne Gentleman*":

*An Epigram to my freind the Author, of
his namelesse Detractor before mentioned.*

Fastus disdaines thy worke, because not thine,
But meerly drawne forth by anothers line:
Thou imitat'st he saith: well thou mightst one:
For thou canst imitated be by none:
Though I dare take thy word, yea 'tis well known
Ther's nothing heer but thou maist call thine own.
For (like a common theefe) the sneaking elfe
Hath slandered thee, that he might saue himselfe.

.   .   .   .   .

[92]Stephens, *Essayes and Characters*, sig. A6-B1ᵛ.
[93]Herford and Simpson, VII, 383.

*Aliud ad eundem de detractore suo
anonymo praedicto.*

Forbeare my freind to write against that man
A sharpe iambick, who hath wrong'd thy *name:*
Thou canst not right thyselfe; for he hath none:
Nor can haue, if he be the peoples Sonne.[94]

"A Falkoner" represents perhaps not the normal
Stephens character; it, however, is certainly indicative
of the extremes to which the conventions of the "Newes,"
and of some of the Overbury characters, could be carried:

A FALKONER

*IS the egge of a tame Pullet, hatcht vp among the
Hawkes and Spaniels.* Hee hath in his minority
conuersed with Kestrils, and yong Hobbies; but
growing vp he begins to handle the lure, & look a
Fawlco in the face. All his learning makes him but
a new Linguist; for to haue studied and practised
the termes of Hawkes Dictionary, is enough to excuse his wit, manners, and humanity. He hath too
many Trades to thriue; and yet if hee had fewer,
hee would thriue lesse: Hee need not bee enuied
therefore, for a *Monopolie,* though he be Barber-
surgeon, Physitian, and Apothecary, before he com-
mences *Hawk-leech:* for though he exercise all
these, and the Art of Bow-strings together, his
patients be compelled to pay him no further, then
they bee able. Hawkes be his obiect, that is, his
knowledge, admiration, labour, and all: they be indeed his idoll, or mistresse, be they Male or Female:
to them he consecrates his amorous Ditties, which

---

[94]Stephens, *Essayes and Characters,* sig B1ᵛ-2.

be no sooner framed then hallowed: Nor should he
doubt to ouercome the fairest, seeing he reclaimes
such Haggards; and courts euery one with a peculiar Dialect. . . . There is no hope of his rising,
though he doth excell; for he rather seekes to make
others ambitious of rising, then himselfe: and
therefore though he frames wings with *Daedalus*,
he therby makes his Hawke onely ambitious: Yet
if any shall (by coniecture) take a flight from
Paules Steeple; hee will (I suppose) as soone as any.
I had rather (in the meane time) take his word
then his oath; for when he speakes without an oath,
he is not troubled with the passion of his Curres,
or Haggards; and therefore cannot so well excuse
it, if he breakes his promise. As for Religion, she
is a bird of too high a wing; his *Hawkes* cannot
reach it, and therefore not Hee: And if hee flies to
heauen, it is a better flight, then any hee hath
commended: There, I meddle not with him;
thither he must carry himselfe: for I can neither
condemm, nor saue him.[95]

   Nicholas Breton has two little groups of character
writings: *Characters upon Essays Moral and Divine*,
1615, and *The Good and the Bad* of the following year.[96]
The earlier group does not lend itself to the more spec-
tacular of the traits which first manifested themselves in
the "Newes"—the pursuit of the conceit at all costs, and
the sustained imagery of a particular place or occupation.
The primary reason is, of course, that the items in the
Moral and Divine deal only with abstractions, as "Wis-

---

[95]*Satyrical Essayes Characters and Others*, 1615, pp. 257-261
(sig. S1-3).
   [96]Aldington reprints both of these little volumes in *A Book of
"Characters."*

dom," "Peace," "Time." A secondary reason is Breton's peculiar addiction to statement in fours—*e. g.,* knowledge is "begotten by grace, bred by virtue, brought up by learning and maintained by love."[97] In *The Good and the Bad,* however, he abandons abstractions for types: "A Fool," "A Beggar," "A Coward." Perhaps "A Drunkard" will serve to illustrate that vestiges of the influence of the "Newes" still remain:

A DRUNKARD

A Drunkard is a noun-adjective; for he cannot stand alone by himself; yet in his greatest weakness a great tryer of strength, whether health or sickness will have the upper hand in a surfeit. He is a spectacle of deformity and a shame of humanity, a view of sin, and a grief of nature. He is the annoyance of modesty and the trouble of civility, the spoil of wealth and the spite of reason. He is only the brewer's agent and the ale-house's benefactor, the beggar's companion and the constable's trouble. He is his wife's woe, his children's sorrow, his neighbours scoff and his own shame. In sum, he is a tub of swill, a spirit of sleep, a picture of a beast and a monster of a man.[98]

A far-fetched conceit begins the sketch, making the title part of itself; images of the habitat creep in, as in all Breton's other characters. There is a careful pretense of collection of substance at the close, though usually his "In sum" offers nothing more than a rather ineffective metaphor.

---

[97]Aldington, p. 171.
[98]*Ibid.,* p. 183.

It is of course not the purpose of this essay to pursue the fate of the "Character" through the seventeenth century. Geffray Mynshul (1618), John Earle (1628), Richard Brathwaite (1631), Wye Saltonstall (1631), all produced compilations of characters, but the flavor characteristic to the Overbury, Stephens, and even the Breton sketches is largely gone. What remains of it is perhaps most noticeable in the *Micro-cosmographie* of John Earle, but it will be seen that in, for instance, his "A handsome Hostesse" the original figurative, epigrammatic force is gone:

A HANDSOME HOSTESS

Is the fairer commendation of an inn, above the fair sign, or fair lodgings. She is the loadstone that attracts men of iron, gallants, and roarers, where they cleave sometimes long, and are not easily got off. Her lips are your welcome, and your entertainment her company, which is put into the reckoning too, and is the dearest parcel in it. No citizen's wife is demurer than she at the first greeting, nor draws in her mouth with a chaster simper; but you may be more familiar without distaste, and she does not startle at bawdry. She is the confusion of a pottle of sack more than would have been spent elsewhere, and her little jugs are accepted to have her kiss excuse them. She may be an honest woman, but is not believed so in her parish, and no man is a greater infidel in it than her husband.[99]

Yet *Micro-cosmographie* appeared while the Overbury "Wife," "Newes," and "Characters" were in their thir-

---

[99]*Ibid.*, p. 235.

teenth impression (with four more to follow). In fact, it remained in vogue long after the Overbury group, reaching its twentieth reprinting in 1904.

No formal conclusion, or summary, is appropriate to such an essay as this, for so much of what is suggested has necessarily been tentative. But the items of "Newes" in themselves are little gems in the use of language, carefully controlled in metaphor and order, which deserve more widespread attention than they have received.

Suggestions to the effect that they were a sort of courtly game, indulged in by "wits," "Lords," and "Sermoneeres"; that they were abruptly terminated by 1610; that the participants were in all cases the ones here suggested cannot of course be substantiated. There seems, however, clear enough evidence that the production of the items of "Newes" was in some manner a cooperative affair. Some constitute replies to others. They employ, in general, a common format, common material, and a uniform tone of mockery toward matters of court and a uniform religious predisposition. John Donne and John Rudyerd were almost certainly participants. It is highly probable that Sir Thomas Overbury, Sir Benjamin Rudyerd, Sir Thomas Roe, and the unfortunate Cecily Bulstrode shared in the fun. Only slightly less dependable are the identifications of "W.S." as William Strachey and "J. C." as John Cooke. Nor is it likely that any one other than Sir Henry Wotton could have written the "Forrein Newes."

That these same people, collectively as well as individually, had a strong shaping influence on the "Characters" of the early seventeenth century seems a safe conclusion. Three of them, Overbury, Cooke, and Wotton, did write characters, and one leaves consideration of the

problem with the feeling that others of them may have
fugitive pieces buried among the eighty-two items of the
Overbury collection.   And it is difficult to believe that
Ben Jonson, who had poetic correspondence with so many
of the participants, who appears to have had knowledge
of news as a conscious form of literary endeavor, and
who himself used the character so skillfully as a cutting
tool, does not make a place for himself in the Overbury
sequence.

At any rate, since throughout the essay we have relied
heavily on the evidence of Ben Jonson in various excerpts,
not only from the plays, but also from *Epigrams, The
Forest,* and *The Underwood,* in identifying both circumstance and participants, it seems not inappropriate to let
him have the last word, a word which neatly makes the
interesting association of character and epigram.   The
passage presented is from *The Magnetic Lady,* probably
written in 1632, after Overbury's work had reached its
fifteenth impression, and Earle's *Micro-cosmographie* had
passed through its sixth.   In the second scene of Act I
this exchange occurs, a sort of final word, if not on the
"Newes," at least on the character:

Iro. . . . What call you him? *Palate Please?* or *Parson Palate?*
Com.   All's one, but shorter! I can gi' you his Character.
Hee, is the Prelate of the Parish, here;
And governes all the Dames; appoints the cheere;
Writes downe the bils of fare; pricks all the Guests;
Makes all the matches and the marriage feasts
Within the ward; drawes all the parish wils;
Designes the Legacies; and strokes the Gills
Of the chiefe Mourners; And (who ever lacks
Of all the kindred) hee hath first his blacks.
Thus holds hee weddings up, and burials,

As his maine tithing; with the Gossip stals,
Their pewes; He's top still, at the publique messe;
Comforts the widow, and the fatherlesse,
In funerall Sack! Sits 'bove the Alderman!
For of the Ward-mote *Quest*, he better can
The mysterie, then the Levitick Law:
That peece of Clark-ship doth his Vestry awe.
Hee is as he conceives himselfe, a fine
Well-furnish'd, and apparaled Divine.
Iro. Who made this EPIGRAMME, you? *Com.* No, a great
  Clarke
As any'is of his bulke, (*Ben: Ionson*) made it.

TEXTUAL NOTE

The text of the "Newes" which has been reproduced is that of the Ninth Impression (1616), as it appears in the copy in The Folger Shakespeare Library. Though this text has corruptions not present in the Second Impression (1614), it has been thought advisable to present the entire text of *A Wife*, for frequent reference has been made to items of the work not in the "Newes," and not in the Second Impression. The textual comments which follow, however, will show some of the relationships among the various impressions, and, in turn, their relationship to the only modern edition of the "Newes," that of Edward F. Rimbault in 1856.

Three copies of the Second Impression have been examined: those in the Bodleian and Folger libraries and that in the British Museum. The variants are few and unimportant, and all appear to have been occasioned merely by deterioration of type. They are presented in the following table:

Sig.	Line	Bodleian	British Museum	Folger
G1	4	end[blot]an	end of man.	end of man.
G2ᵛ	2	Court: That	Court. That	Court. That
	23	sanple craft.	simple craft.	simple craft
G4ᵛ	19	waited·on	waited-on	waited·on
H4	1	*passion is dry drunke. T is easier to*	*passion* [blot] *drunke.* [blot] [blot]*ier to*	*passion is dry drunke. T is easier to*

lxxx

With these three copies of the Second Impression has been collated the Third Impression (again in microfilm) owned by The Henry E. Huntington Library. There are of course many variants, as would be inevitable with a new setting of type. They consist largely of such differences as the interchange of *-es* and *-esse* or *-ie* and *-y*, or the addition or removal of a medial or a final *-e*, of a dash, of a capital letter, or of italic letters. The few substantive variants are noted below, with the Third Impression variants enclosed in brackets:

> F4ᵛ, lines 26-27: nor the world hath not to fill his measure. [F4, line 26: Nor in the world hath not to his measure.]
> G, line 23: That to hold in knights-seruice is a slipperie tenure. [F4ᵛ, lines 21-22: . . . Knights seruice is a slippery seruice.]
> G3ᵛ, lines 1-2: Forrein Newes of the yeere 1604. [. . . yeare 1614.]
> H3-4: (text of *"Newes from the lower end of the Table."* is italicized.) [H3-3ᵛ: (no italics other than the title.)]
> H4, line 14: J.C. [H3ᵛ, line 25: *I.C.*]
> H4, lines 21-22: That the naked truth is *Eue*, and *Eue* lay without sheetes. [H4, lines 1-2: . . . is *Adam*, and *Eue* lay. . . .]

Collation of the remaining fifteen sixteenth-century impressions appears unnecessary, as well as examination of the so-called "Tenth Edition" of 1756. Of Edward F. Rimbault's edition of *The Miscellaneous Works In Prose and Verse of Sir Thomas Overbury, Knt.*, published in 1856, Miss Murphy says: "This is a reprint of the 9th ed. It omits the 'Character of a happy life.' It has various other omissions and inaccuracies."

A few corrections, and a great many corruptions, entered the text of the "Newes" between the Second Impression and the Ninth. Rimbault in general followed the Ninth Impression faithfully. He made a few corrections which suggest possible reference to earlier texts, and he, or his printer, inevitably introduced a few new corruptions. The table given below will show only substantive variations among the Second Impression, the Ninth, and the Rimbault text. In certain cases, a [c] will indicate an appropriate correction, while a [d] will indicate debasement of the text.

TEXTUAL VARIANTS

2nd Impression	(Page)	(Line)	9th Impression	Rimbault Edition
yet hopes	Nᵛ	16	yet it hopes [d]	yet it hopes
T.O.	N2	14	Sir, T.Ouer.	Sir T. Over.
to studie men is	N2ᵛ	8	to studie, men are [d]	to studie, men are
A.S.	N3	2	[deleted] [d]	[deleted]
last relique	N3	11	best relique [d]	best relique
slipperie tenure	N3	18	silipperie seruice [d]	slipperie service
three	N3ᵛ	15	3.	three
felling	N4ᵛ	10	felling	selling [d]
That Iesuits	N4ᵛ	11-12	The Iesuits [d]	The jesuits
Matachiue	N6	13	Matachine	Matachine
Action	N7	3	Action	Actions [d]

Siglum	Line			
N7	9-10	the glory of youth, is strength of the gray head, wisdome;	the glory of youth, is strength; of the gray head, wisdome; [c]	the glory of youth, is strength; of the grey head wisdome;
N8	16	aduersaries	enemies [d]	enemies
P˅	2	1604	1616	1616
P˅	6	wines	wiues [d]	wines [c]
P2	10	imitation, then	imitation. then [d]	imitation, then
P2˅	13	seeled	sillie [d]	sillie
P4	5	offendors benums . . . and that	Offenders so benums . . . as that [d]	offenders so benums . . . as that
P6	2	That to bee good is the way to bee	That to be good, the way is to be [d]	That to bee good; the way is to bee
P6	6	That most feare	That the most feare [d]	That the most feare

blowes till it	P6ᵛ	17	blowes it till it [d]	blowes it till it
constancie in women	P6ᵛ	19	constancy of women,	constancy of women,
weomens fortunes	P7	4-5	womens fortunes	womans fortunes [d]
being an acquaintance	P7	9	beeing in acquaintance [d]	being in acquaintance
[text of "Newes from the lower end of the Table" is in italics]	P7-8ᵛ		[text not italicized]	[text not italicized]
grace after, our saluation	P7ᵛ	5	grace after meat our saluation [d]	grace after meat our salvation
bowle among the	P8	17	bowle amongst the [d]	bowle amongst the
goes away and payes not for	P8ᵛ	10-11	goes away and owes for [d]	goes away and owes for
he is dead.	P8ᵛ	20	he be dead. [d]	he be dead.

J.C.	(Page)	(Line)	I. C.	I. C.
truth is *Eue*, and Eue lay	P8ᵛ	24	trueth is, *Adam* and *Eue* lay	truth is, *Adam* and *Eve* lay
soule euer wakes	Q3ᵛ	19-20	Soule euer wakes	soule ever awakes [d]
to be wak't.	Q4	12	to be awak't. [d]	to be awak't.
the vngodly Courtier	Q4ᵛ	2	the vngodlier Courtier [d]	the ungodlier courtier
That great sleepers	Q4ᵛ	4-5	That sleepers [d]	That sleepers
	Q4ᵛ	6		

6th Impression	(Page)	(Line)	*9th Impression*	*Rimbault Edition*
take heed.	Qᵛ	24-25	take heede.	take head. [d]
	Q5ᵛ	9-10	fire, it owne neede, but to reflect	the fire; he receives it not for his owne need, but to reflect [c]
	Q5ᵛ	21	to sit vp	to set up [d]
	Q6	6	tongues,	tongs [c]

TEXT

Reproduced on the following pages are these items:

1. The Ninth Impression of *Sir Thomas Ouerbury HIS WIFE*.
2. Pages V2-V8ᵛ of the Twelfth Impression, which are bound with item 1.
3. Pages A2-A3ᵛ of the Second Impression, which contain introductory matter dropped from the Ninth Impression.
4. Pages M5ᵛ-M6 of the Sixth Impression, which contain the complete text of the character, "An excellent Actor," and pages M8ʳ⁻ᵛ, also of the Sixth Impression, which contain "A Purueiour of Tobacco," a character not included in the Ninth Impression.

All of these items are reproduced with the permission of The Folger Shakespeare Library.

Sir *Thomas Ouerbury*

HIS

WIFE.

WITH

ADDITION OF

many new ELEGIES vpon his
vntimely and much lamented death.

AS ALSO

New Newes, and *diuers more* Characters,
(neuer before annexed) written by himselfe and other learned Gentlemen.

The ninth impression augmented.

LONDON,

Printed by *Edward Griffin* for *Laurence L'isle*, and
are to be sold at his shop at the Tigers head in
Paules Churchyard. 1 6 1 6.

To the Reader.

THE generall accep-
tance of this match-
leſſe *Poem* the *Wife*,
(written by SIR
Thomas Ouerbury)
is ſufficiently ap-
proued by many, the worth where-
of if any other, out of malice, ſhall
neglect to commend , hee may well
(if it proceed, from nice Criticiſme)
be exluded as a Churliſh Retainer
to the MVSES: if from direct plaine
dealing, he ſhall be degraded for in-

¶3   ſuffi-

fufficiencie. For had fuch a *Poem*
beene extant among the ancient Romanes, although they wanted our
eafie conferuations of wit by printing, they would haue cōmitted it to
braffe left iniurious time might de-
priue it of due eternitie ; If to cōuerfe
with a Creature fo amiable as is here
defcribed, be thought difficult, let
the contemplation thereof be held
admirable. To which are added
(this ninth impreffion) many new
Elegies of his vntimely death, and
diuerfe more *Characters* and *Newes*
written by himfelfe and others his
friends. Howfoeuer, they are now
expofed, not onely to the Iudicious,
but to all that cary the leaft fcruple
of mother wit about them.

Licet toto nunc Helicone frui—— Mar.

Lau: L'ifle.

Elegies of seuerall Authors,
on the vntimely death of SIR
Thomas Ouerbury poysoned in the Tower.

Vpon the vntimely Death of
Sir *Thomas Ouerbury*.

T'would ease our sorrows, t'would release our teares,
  Could we but heare those high celestiall Spheares,
Once tune their Motions to a dolefull straine
In sympathie of what we Mortalls plaine.
Or see their faire Intelligences change
Or face or habit, when blacke Deeds, so strange,
As might force pitty from the Heart of Hell
Are hatch't by Monsters, which among vs dwell.
The Stars me thinks, like men inclin'de to sleep,
Should through their chrystall casements scarcely peep,
Or at least view vs but with halfe an eye,
For feare their chaster Influence might descry
Some murdering hand, caded in guililesse bloud,
Blending vile iuices to destroy the good.
The Sunne should wed his Beames to endles Night,
And in dull darkenesse canopie his Light,
When from the ranke stewes of adulterous Brests,
Where euery base vnhallowed Proiect rests,

g 4   Is

Is belcht, as in defiance of his shine,
A streame, might make euen Death it selfe to pine.
But these things happen still ; but ne're more cleare,
Nor with more lustre did these lampes appeare:
Mercury *capers with a winged heele,*
As if he did no touch of sorrow feele,
And yet he sees a true Mercurian kill'd,
Whose birth his Mansion with much honour fil'd.
But let me not mistake those Powers aboue,
Nor taxe iniuriously those Courts of Ioue *;*
Surely, they ioy to see these Acts reueald,
Which in blinde silence haue been long conceald;
And Virtue now triumphant ; whil'st we mourne
To thinke that ere she was foule Vices scorne :
Or that poore Ouer-buries *bloud was made*
A sacrifice to Malice and darke shade.
Welton *thy Hand that* Couvre-feu Bell *did sway,*
Which did his life to endles sleepe conuay.
But rest thou where thou art ; Ile seeke no glory
By the relation of so sad a story.
If any more were priuie to the Deed,
And for the Crime must be adiudg'd to bleed,
To Heauen I pray, with heau'd vp Hands and eyes,
That as their Bodies fall, their Soules may rise.
And as those equally turne to one Dust,
So these alike may shine among the Iust.
And there make vp one glorious constellation,
Who suffred here in such a differing fashion.

D. T.

To the Memory of that generally bewailed Gentleman, Sr. *Thomas Ouerburie.*

BVt that w'are bound in Chriſtian pietie
To wiſh Gods will be done ; and Deſtinie
(In all that haps to Men, or Good, or Ill)
Suffer'd, or ſent, by that implored Will; (Breath,
Me thinks, t'obſerue how Vertue drawes faint
Subieƈt to ſlanders, Hate, and violent Dearh,
Wiſe men kept low, others aduanc'd to State,
Right checkt by wrong; and Ill men fortunate;
Theſe mou'd Effeƈts, from an vnmoued Cauſe,
Might ſhake the firmeſt faith;Heauens fixed Lawes
Might caſuall ſeeme, and each irregular Sence
Spurne at iuſt Order, blame Gods Prouidence.

But what is man, t'expoſtulate th'Intents
Of his high Will, or iudge of ſtrange Euents ?
The riſing Sunne to mortall ſight reueales
This earthly Globe ; but yet the ſtarres conceales;
So may the Sence diſcouer Naturall Things ;
Diuine, aboue the reach of Humane wings.

Then not the Fate, but Fates bad Inſtrument
Doe I accuſe, in each ſad Accident :
Good men muſt fall, rapes, inceſts,murders come;
But woe and curſes follow them by whom :
God Authors all mens Aƈtions, not their ſin,
For that proceeds from diu'liſh luſt within.

Thou

Thou then that fufferd'ft by thofe formes fo vile,
From whom thofe wicked Inftruments did file
Thy droffie part, to make thy Fame fhine cleare,
And Shrine thy foule in Heauens all glorious
Who being good,naught les to thee befel,(fphere;
Though it appear'd difguif'd in fhape of Hell;
Vanifh thy Blood and Nerues ; True life alone
In Vertue liues, and true Religion,
In both which thou art deathles : O behold,
(If thou canft looke fo low as Earths bafe mould)
How dreadfull Iuftice (late with lingring Foote)
Now comes like Whirle-winde ? how it fhakes the
Of loftie Cedars ; makes the ftately Brow (Root
Bend to the Foot ? how all men fee that now
The Breath of infamie doth moue their Sailes ;
Whiles thy deare name by loues more harty gales
Shall ftill keep Winge, vntill thy Fames extent
Fill eu'ry part of this vaft Continent.
Then you the Syre of this thus murder'd Sonne;
Repine not at his Fate ; fince he hath wonne
More Honor in his Sufferance ; and his Death
Succeeded by his Vertues endles Breath.
For him, and to his Life and Deaths example,
Loue might erect a Statue ; Zeale, a Temple :
On his true worth the Mufes might be flayne
To die his Honors Web in pureft Graine.

C. B.

Vpon the vntimely Death of
the Author of this ingenious *Poem*
Sir Tho: Overbvry
Knight poyſoned in
the Towre.

SO many *Moones* ſo many times gone round,
And roſe from *hell*, and *darknes* vnder ground,
And *yet till now*, *this darkned deed of Hell*
Not brought to Light ? ô tardie *Heauen* ! yet tell
If *Murther* layes him downe to ſleepe with *Luſt*
Or no ? reueale, as *thou* art *Truth*, and *Iuſt*,
The *Secrets* of this vniuſt Secure *Act*,
And what *our Feares* make vs ſuſpect, *compact*
With greater deedes of miſchiefe, for alone
We thinke not *This*, and do ſuſpect yet *One*,
To *which* compar'd, *This*, but a *falling Starre*,
That a bright *Firmament of Fire* : Thy *Care*
We ſee takes *meaner things* : It times the *World*
The *Signes* at rãdom thorough the *Zodiack* hurld,
The *Stars* wild wandrings, & the glib quick *hinges*
Which turne both *Poles* ; and all the *violent changes*
It ouer-lookes, which trouble th'endleſſe courſe
Of the high Firmament : *by thy bleſt Force*
Do hoary winter Froſts make forreſts bare
And ſtraight to Groues again their ſhades repaire,

By

By *Thee* doth *Autumns, Lyons-flaming Maine*
Ripen the fruits: and the full yeere suftaine
Her burdned powres : *ô being ftill the fame,*
Ruling fo much, and vnder *whom* the frame
Of this vaft world weighd, all his *Orbes* doft guide,
Why are thy Cares of Men no more applyde ?
Or if: why feem'ft thou fleeping to the *Good,*
And *guarding* to the *Ill?* as if the *brood*
Of beft things ftill muft Chance take in command
And not thy *Prouidence* : and *Her blinde Hand*
Thy *Benefits* erroneoufly disburfe,
Which fo let fall, ne're fall but to the *worfe* ?
Whence *fo, great crimes* commit the *Greater* fort,
And boldeft acts of fhame blaze in the *Court,*
Where *Buffones* worfhip in their *rife* of *State*
Thofe filthy *Scarabs,* whom they *Serue,* and *Hate.*
Sure things meere *backward, there* ; Honor difgracft,
And *Vertue* layd by *Fraud,* and *Poyfon,* wafte:
The *Adult'rer vp like Haman,* and fo *Sainted :*
And *Femals modefty* (as *Femals*) painted,
Loft in all reall worth : what fhall we fay ?
Things fo farre out of frame, as if the day
Were come wherein another *Phaëton*
Stolne into *Phœbus waine,* had all miffe-won
A cleane contrary way : ô powerfull *God,*
Right all amiffe, and fet the wonted period
Of *Goodneffe* in his place againe : *This deed*
Be *Vfher* to bring foorth the *Maske,* and *Weed*

Where

Where vnder, blacker things lye hid perhap,
And yet haue Hope to make a safe escape.
Of *This,* make knowne, why such an instrument
As *Weston,* a poore *Seruing-man,* should rent
The frame of *this sad-good-mans* life : did he
Stand with this *Court-bred* learned OVERBVRIE,
In strife for an *Ambasdorship* ? no, no,
His *Orbe* held no such *light* : what did he owe
The *Prophet* malice for composing *this,*
This Cynosura in neat *Poësis,*
How *Good,* and *Great* men ought, and *All,* to chuse
A *chast, fit, noble Wife,* and the abuse
Of *Strumpets* friendly shadowing in the same,
Was this his fault ? or doth there lie a flame
Yet in the embers not vnrak't, for which
He di'de so falsly ? *Heauen* wee do beseech
Vnlocke this secret, and bring all to view,
That Law may purge the bloud, Lust made vntrue.

W. S.

An Elegie consecrated to the memory of the truly worthy and learned Sir *Thomas Ouerburie* K N I G H T.

HAd not thy wrong, like to a wound ill cur'd
Broke forth in death; I had not been assur'd
Of griefe enough to finish what I write.
These lines, as those which do in cold blood fight
Had come but faintly on ; for, euer, he
That shrines a name within an *Elegie*
(Vnlesse some neerer cause do him inspire)
Kindles his bright flame at the *Funerall* fire.
Since passion (after, lessening her extent)
Is then more strong, and so more eloquent.

How powerfull is the hand of *Murther* now !
Was't not enough to see his deare life bowe
Beneath her hate ? but crushing that faire frame,
Attempt the like on his vnspotted *Fame?*
O base reuenge ! more then inhumane fact !
Which (as the *Romanes* sometime would enact
No doome for *Parricide*, supposing none
Could euer so offend) the vpright *Throne*
Of *Iustice* salues not : leauing that intent
Without a *Name*, without a *Punishment.*

Yet through thy wounded *Fame*,as thorow these
Glasses which multiply the *Species*,

We

We fee thy vertues more; and they become
So many *Statues* fleeping on thy *Tombe*.

Wherein, confinement new thou fhalt endure,
But fo; as when to make a *Pearle* more pure
We giue it to a *Doue*, in whofe wombe pent
Some time, we haue it forth moft orient.

Such is thy luftre now, that venom'd *Spight*
With her blacke Soule dares not behold thy light,
But banning it, a courfe begins to runne
With thofe that curfe the rifing of the *Sunne*.
The poyfon, that works vpwards now, fhall ftriue
To be thy faire *Fames* true *Preferuatiue*.
And witch-craft that can maske the *vpper Shine*
With no one cloud fhall blinde a raye of thine.

And as the *Hebrewes* in an obfcure pit
Their *holy Fire* hid, not extinguifh'd it,
And after time, that broke their bondage chaine
Found it, to fire their facrifice againe:
So lay thy *Worth* fomewhile, but being found,
The *Mufes Altars* plentifully crownd
With fweet perfumes, by it new kindled be
And offer all to thy deare Memorie.

Nor haue we loft thee long: thou art not gone,
Nor canft defcend into *Obliuion*.
But twice the *Sun* went round fince thy foule fled,
And only *that time* men fhall termethee dead.
Hereafter (raifd to life) thou ftill fhalt haue
An *Antidote* againft the filent Graue.

W. B. Int: Temp.

14

❧ Vpon the vntimely
Death of Sir *Thomas*
Ouerbury.

IF for to liue be but a mifery,
If by death good men gaine eternity,
Twas friendly done in robbing thee of life,
To celebrate thy nuptials with thy Wife;
So that his will no other aime intended,
But by exchange thy life fhould be amended:
Yet wert to compaffe his infatiate Luft,
He this laft friendfhip tendred to thee: truft
Whiles he difhonour'd and defam'd may die,
Iuftice and Fame, fhall crowne thy memorie.

                    B. G.   *medij Temp.*

                              In

In obitum intempeſtiuum &
lachrimabilem Illuſtiſſimi Equitis
aurati T H: O V E R B V R I magnæ
ſpei & expeɛtationis Viri.

HOw euer windie miſchiefe raiſe vp high
Darke thickning clouds, to powre vpon vs all
A tempeſt of foule rumors , which deſcry
Thy hard miſhap and ſtrange diſaſtrous fall ;
As if thy wounds were bleeding from that hand,
Which rather ſhould haue raiſd thee vp to ſtand.

Yet ſhalt thou here ſuruiue in pittying fame,
In thy ſweet Wife, in theſe moſt acute lines,
In well reputed Charaɛters of name,
And vertues tombe, which all thy honor ſhrines:
In ſpight of enuie, or the proudeſt hate,
That thu s hath ſet opinion at debate.

But for mine owne part, ſith it falls out ſo,
That death hath had her will ; I now compare
It to a wanton hand, which at a throw
To breake a boxe of pretious balme did dare:
With whoſe perfume, although it was thus ſpild,
The houſe and commers by were better filld.

Cap: *Tho: Gainsford.*

g g   A

A memoriall,
Offered to that man of virtue,
Sir *Thomas Ouerburie.*

(frame

ONce dead and twice aliue ; Death could not
A death, whofe fting could kil him in his fame.
He might haue liu'd, had not the life, which gaue
Life to his life, betraid him to his graue.
If greatnes could confift in being Good,
His Goodneffe did adde titles to his blood.
Only vnhappy in his liues laft fate,
In that he liu'd fo foone, to die fo late.
Alas whereto fhall men oppreffed truft,
When Innocence cannot protect the iuft?
His error was his fault, his truth his end,
No enemie his ruine, but his friend.
Cold friendfhip, where hot vowes are but a breath,
To guerdon poore fimplicitie with Death:
Was neuer man, that felt the fenfe of griefe
So Ouer-bury'de in a fafe beliefe:
Beliefe? ô cruell flaughter? times vnbred,
Will fay, who dies that is vntimely dead,
By treacherie, of luft, or by difgrace.
In friendfhip, 'twas but *Ouerburies* cafe;
Which fhall not more cómend his truth, then proue
Their guilt, who were his oppofites in loue.

Reft

Reſt happy Man ; and in thy ſpheare of Awe
Behold how Iuſtice ſwaies the ſword of law,
To weed out thoſe, whoſe hāds imbrew'd in blood,
Cropt of thy youth, and flower in the bud.
    Sleepe in thy Peace: thus happy haſt thou prou'd,
Thou mightſt haue dy'de more knowne,not more
                    Io: Fo: (belou'd.

Vpon S I R *Thomas Ouerbury*
the Author of this ingenious
P o e m.

H *Eſperydes* (within whoſe gardens grow
  Apples of Gold) may well thy loſſe deplore,
For in thoſe Gardens they could neuer ſhow,
A tree ſo faire of ſuch a fruitfull ſtore.
    Grace was the Root, and thou thy Selfe the Tree,
    Sweete counſells were the Berries grew on thee.

Wit was the branch that did adorne the Stocke,
Reaſon the Leafe vpon thoſe branches ſpred,
Vnder thy ſhadow did the *Muſes* flocke,
And (by Thee as a mantle couered.
    But what befell, ô too much out of kinde?
    For thou waſt blaſted by a Weſt-on winde.
                            R. Ca.
            gg 2   Of

Of S I R *Thomas Ouerburie*
his *Wife* and *Marriage*.

WHen I behold this Wife of thine, so faire,
　So far remou'd from vulgar beauties (Ayre
Being lesse bright and pure) me thinks I see
An vncloth'd Soule, by potent Alchymie
Extraught from ragged Matter. Thou hast made
A Wife more innocent then any Maide.
Eua'hs state, before the fall's, decyphered here,
And *Plato's* naked vertu's not more cleare
Such an *Idea* as scarce wishes can
Arriue at, but our Hopes must ne're attaine.
A Soule so far beyond the common Make
As scorn'd corporeall ioyning. For her sake
(Despairing else contract) Thou too turn'st Soule;
And, to enioy her faires without comptroule,
Cast'st of this bodies clog : so must all doe,
Cast Matter of, who would abstraction wooe.
　To flie so soone then (Soule) well hast thou don:
　For, in this life, such beauties are not won.
But when I call to minde thine vnripe fall,
And so sad summons to thy Nuptiall,
Either, in her, thy bold desires did taste
Forbidden fruite, and haue this Curse purchast.
Or, hauing this Elixir made thine owne
(Drawne from the remnant of Creation,)

The

The *faces* their malignant Spirits breath
To punifh thine ambitious loue with death.
Or, thy much enui'de choice hath made the reft
Of Concrete Relicts point their aymes infeft
To thy confufion. And with them feduc'de
Friendfhip (difpleaf'd to fee a Loue produc'de
Leffe carnall then it felfe) with policie
So pure and chaft a Loue to nullifie.
Yet, howfoe're, their proiect flies in fmoke, (choke.
The poyfon's cordiall , which they ment fhould
Their deeds of darknes, like the Bridall Night,
Haue ioyn'd fpirituall Louers, in defpight
Of falfe attempts: And now the wedding's donn;
When in this life, fuch fayres had not beene wonn.

E. G.

To the Booke.

THou wofull Widdow, once happie Wife,
That didft enioy fo fweete a Mate:
Who, now bereaued, is, of Life,
Vntimely wrought, through inward hate
  O Deed moft vile, to haft the end
  Of him, that was fo good a friend.

F. H.

gg 3   On

On this excellent Poem
the Wife.

LOe here the matchles patterne of a Wife,
Diſciphered in forme of Good, and Bad :
 The Bad commends the good, as Darke doth
Or as a loathed Bed a ſingle Life ;   (Light,
The Good, with Wiſdome and Diſcretion clad,
 With Modeſtie, and faire demeanour dight,
 Whoſe Reaſon doth her Will to Loue inuite.

Reaſon begot, and Paſſion bred her Loue,
Selfe-will She ſhunn'd, Fitnes the Mariage made;
 Fitnes doth cheriſh Loue, Selfe-will Debate.
Loe thus ; and in this Monument of proofe
A perfect Wife, a Worke nor Time can fade,
 Nor looſe reſpect betray to mortall Fate.
 This, none can equall; Beſt, but imitate.

R. C.

On Sir *Thomas Ouerburies* Poem the VVife.

I Am glad yet ere I die, I haue found occafion
Honeſt and iuſt; without the worlds perſwaſion
Or flatterie or briberie to commend
A woman for her goodnes; and God ſend
I may finde many more: I wiſh them well,
They are pretty things to play with: when *Eue* fell
She tooke a care that all the Wo-men kinde
That were to follow her, ſhould be as blinde
As ſhe was wilfull; and till this good Wife,
This peece of Vertue, that ne're tooke her life
From a fraile Mothers labor: Thoſe ſtand ſtill
As marginalls to point vs to our ill
Came to the world, as other creatures doe
That know no God but will ; we learnt to woe,
And if ſhe were but faire and could but kiſſe,
Twenty to one we could not chooſe amiſſe ;
And as we iudge of trees if ſtraight and tall
That may be ſound, yet neuer till the fall
Finde how the raine hath drill'd them ; So till now
We only knew we muſt loue; but not how.
But here we haue example, and ſo rare,
That if we hold but common ſenſe and care,
And ſteere by this card ; he that goes awry,
Ile boldly ſay at his Natiuitie,

gg 4   Tha

That man was feal'd a foole: yet all this good
Giuen as it is, not cloath'd in flefh and blood
Some may auerre and ftrongly twas meere ment
In way of practife, but not prefident;
Either will make vs happy men ; for he
That marrieth any way this myfterie,
Or any parcell of that benefit,
Though he take hold of nothing but the wit,
Hath got himfeife a partner for his life
Morethen a woman better then a Wife.

I. F.

Eiufdem in Eadem.

A S from a man the firft fraile Woman came,
The firft that euer made vs know our fhame,
And finde the curfe of labor ; fo againe,
Goodneffe and vnderftanding found a man
To take this fhame away ; and from him fprung
A peece of excellence without a Tongue
Becaufe it fhould not wrong vs ; yet the life
Makes it appeare a Woman and a Wife.
And this is fhe, if euer Woman fhall
Doe good heereafter ; borne to bleffe our fall.

J. F.

On Sir *Thomas Ouerburies* Poem the Wife.

WEre euery beauty, euery feuerall grace,
  Which is in Women, in one womans face,
Some courtly Gallants might, I think, come to her,
Which would not wed her, though they feem'd to
Setled affections follow not the Eye;   (woe her
Reafon and Iudgement, muft their courfe defcrie.
Pigmalions Image made of Marble ftone,
Was lik'd of all ; belou'd of him alone.
But heer's a Dame growne husbandleffe of late,
Which not a Man but wifheth were his Mate.
So faire without, fo free from fpot within,
That Earth feemes heereto ftand exempt from fin.
  Iuno vouchfafe, and *Hymen*, when I wed,
I may behold this Widdow in my Bed.

D. T.

On

On the Wife.

BEauty affords contentment to the Eye
Riches are meanes to cure a weake eſtate,
Honour illuſtrates what it commeth nie:
To marry thus men count it happy Fate.
  Vertue they think doth in theſe Emblems ſhroud,
  But triall ſhewes they are gulled with a Cloud:

Theſe are but complements ; the inward worth,
The outward cariage, geſture, wit, and grace,
Is that alone that ſets a Woman forth:
And in this Woman, theſe haue each a place.
  Were all Wiues ſuch, This age would happy be,
  But happier that of our Poſteritie.

D. T.

On the Wife.

WEl haſt thou ſaid, that womē ſhould be ſuch;
  And were they that, had but a third as much
I would be maried too, but that I know
Not what ſhe is, but ſhould be thou doſt ſhow:
  So let me praiſe thy worke, and let my life
  Be ſingle, or thy Widdow be my Wife.

X. Z.

On the Wife.

THis perfect Creature, to the Easterne vse
Liu'd, whilst a wife retir'd from common show:
Not that her Louer fear'd, the least abuse,
But with the wisest, knew it fitter so :
Since, falne a widdow, and a zealous one,
She would haue sacrifizde her selfe agen,
But importun'd to life ; is now alone,
Lou'd, woo'd, admir'd, by all wise single men.
 Which, to th'adultrous rest, that dare begin
 There vs'd temptations, were a mortall sinne.

To the Wife.

EXpos'd to all, thou wilt lesse worthy seeme
I feare : Wiues common, all men disesteeme ;
Yet some things haue a diffring Fate : some fret
We doubt in wares which are in corners set :
Hid Medalls rust, which being vs'de grow bright ;
The day more friendeth vertue then the night.
Thou though more common, then maist seem more
I only wish thou maist be vnderstood.   (good

G. R.

To the cleane contrary Wife.

Look here:& chide thofe fpirits, which maintain
 Their Empire,with fo ftrong cómand in you,
  That all good eyes, which do your follies view,
Pitty, what you for them, muft once fuftaine :
O from thofe Euills, which free Soules difdaine
  To be acquainted with,) and but perfue
  Worft Minds)from them(as hateful, as vntrue,)
By reading this, for Fames faire fake refraine :
  Who would let feed vpon her birth, the brood
  Of lightnes, Indifcretion, and the fhame
  Of fowle Incontinence, when the bafe blood
  Is careleffe only of an Honourd Name,
Be all that gentle are, more high Improou'd,
For loofe Dames are but flatter'd, neuer Lou'd.

W: Stra:

Of the choyce of a Wife.

IF I were to chufe a Woman,
As who knowes but I may marry:
I would truft the eye of no man,
Nor a tongue that may mifcarry:
  For in way of Loue and Glory
  Each tongue beft tells his owne ftory.

Firft, to make my choyce the bolder,
I would haue her childe to fuch:
Whofe free vertuous liues are older
Then Antiquitie can touch:
  For tis feldom feene, that Blood
  Giues a beauty great and good.

Yet an ancient ftocke may bring
Branches I confeffe of worth,
Like rich mantles fhadowing
Thofe defcents that brought them forth,
  Yet fuch Hills though gilded fhow
  Sooneft feele the Age of fnow.

Therefore

Of the choyce of a Wife.

Therefore to preuent such care
That repentance soone may bring,
Like Marchants I would chuse my ware,
Vse-full good, not glittering.
  He that weds for state or face,
  Buyes a Horse to lose a Race.

Yet I would haue her faire as any,
But her owne not kist away :
I would haue her free to many,
Looke on all like equall day ;
  But descending to the Sea,
  Make her set with none but me.

If she be not tall tis better ;
For that word, A goodly Woman,
Prints it selfe in such a letter,
That it leaues vnstudied no man :
  I would haue my Mistresse grow
  Onely tall , to answere No.

                                      Yet

Of the choyce of a Wife.

Yet I would not haue her lose
So much breeding, as to fling
Vnbecomming scorne on those
That must worship euery thing.
 Let her feare loose lookes to scatter,
 And loose men will feare to flatter.

Children I would haue her beare,
More for loue of name then bed :
So each childe I haue is heyre
To another maydenhead ;
 For she that in the act's afraide,
 Euery nigh'ts another maide.

Such a one, as when shees woo'd
Blushes not for ill thoughts past ;
But so innocently good,
That her dreames are euer chast ;
 For that Maide that thinkes a sin,
 Has betraide the Fort shee's in.

Of the choyce of a Wife.

In my visitation still,
I would haue her scatter feares,
How this man, and that was ill,
After protestations Teares :
 And who vowes a constant life,
 Crownes a meritorious Wife.

When the Priest first giues our hands,
I would haue her thinke but thus ;
In what high and holy bands
Heauen, like twins, hath planted vs,
 That like Aarons rod together,
 Both may bud, grow greene, and wither.

An *Elegie* in praiſe of Sir *Thomas Ouerbury and his* POEM.

T'Is dangerous to be *good :* well we may praiſe
  Honeſtie, or *Innocence ;* but who can raiſe
A powre, that ſhall ſecure't, gainſt wrongs to come,
When ſuch a *Saint* hath ſuffer'd *Martyrdome ?*
  Iniurious hands, which 'cauſe they could not get
The *gemme,* would therefore ſpoile the *cabinet.*
But, though the *cage* be broake, the *birde* is flowne
To *heauen,* her proper and ſecurer home :
Where 'mongſt a quire of *Saints,* and *Cherubins,*
Of *Angels,* *Thrones,* and *Seraphims,* ſhe ſings
Thoſe ſacred *Haleluiahs :* heauen may boaſt
T'haue got that Angell there, which we haue *loſt :*
But we ſhall ſtill complaine, for to vs *here,*
A *Saint* is more loſſe, than a *throne* is *there.*
  That *firmament* of holy *fires,* which wee
Enioyd, whilſt thou wert, by enioying thee,
Lyes now rak't vp in *aſhes* as the light
Of day, the Sun once gone, is drownd in night.
But as the *Moone,* ſometimes, the *Sun* being ſet,
Appeares, and we a new (though leſſe) light get ;
So, though our greateſt *lampe,* of vertue be,
By cruell Fate, *extinguiſhed,* in thee ;
Yet, to adde ſome freſh *oyle,* t'our *ſnuffe* of life,
Thou haſt, behind thee, left a matchleſſe *Wſfe :*
  A   Who

Who hath (fince that fad time her Husband di'de)
Bin wooed by many, for a fecond bride:
But, like a chaft religious widdow, fhe,
Hauing loft her firft mate, Scornes *bigamie*.

P. B. *medij Temp.*

A *Statue* Erected in memorie
of Sir *Thomas Ouerburie* his *Wife.*

VPon a *Marble* fram'd by th' cunning'ft hand,
In garments greene, and orient to behold,
Like a moft louely *Virgin* let her ftand
And on her head a crowne of pureft gold.
Firft let Religion, in her heart haue place
As th'ground & fountain whence all vertues fpring,
So that each thought being fanctified by Grace:
The punifhment t' efcape, that's due to finne.
Let *Beauty* (ioyn'd with modeftie) appeare
Loues obiect in her face ; and chaftitie
In her faire *eyes*, brighter then chryftall cleere
Wherein life moues, affections led *thereby.*
In her hands *charitis*, and at the right
The holy Angells let protecting be:

And

And at the left, Gods mercies ſhining bright
Diſtributing to each neceſſitie.
Let th'earth his riches yeeld to her, and more
The heauens their influence, and by the ſame
Vnto the blinde their ſight let her reſtore
Strength'ning the weake, and raiſing vp the lame.
Vnder her feete, the Diuell and darkneſſe ſet
Let Pride faſt bound in chaines behinde her lie
Baſe ſelfe-loue, not appeare in place, and let
Foule-luſt, and *Enuie* from her preſence flie.
And on her *Breaſt*, in golden letters write
Heauens beſt belou'd, earths chiefeſt delight.

He that (in's Choyce) would meete with ſuch a Wife,
Muſt vowe virginitie, and ſingle life.

On Sir *Thomas Ouerburie* and his VVIFE.

ALL right, all wrong befalls me through a Wife,
A Bad one gaue me Death, a Good one Life.

A 2   An

An E L E G I E vpon the Death
of Sir *Thomas Ouerbury* Knight
poyſoned in the Tower.

HAdſt thou like other Sirs and Knights of worth
Sickned and dyde been ſtretcht-out and laid-forth
After thy farewell Sermon, taken earth
And left no deed to praiſe thee but thy birth,
Then Ouerbury *by a paſſe of theirs*
Thou might'ſt haue tyded hence in two howers teares,
Then had we worne thy ſprigs of memory
No longer then thy friends did roſemary ;
Or then the doale was eating for thy ſake.
And thou hadſt ſunke in thy owne wine and cake,
But ſince it was ſo ordered and thought fit
By ſome who knew thy truth and fear'd thy wit
Thou ſhouldſt be poyſoned, Death hath done thee grace,
Ranckt thee aboue the region of thy place.
For none heares poyſon nam'd but makes replie
What Prince was that ? what Stateſ-man ſo did die ?
In this thou haſt outdyde an Elegie
Which were to narrow for poſteritie
And thy ſtrong poyſon which did ſeeme to kill
Working a freſh in ſome Hiſtorians quill,
Shall now preſerue thee longer ere thou rot,
Then could a Poem mixt with Antidot ;

Nor

Nor needeſt thou truſt a Herrald with thy name,
That art the voice of Iuſtice and of Fame ;
Whilſt ſinne (deteſting her owne conſcience) ſtriues
To pay the vſe and intereſt of liues
Enough of ryme, and might it pleaſe the law
Enough of bloud ; for naming liues I ſaw
He that writes more of thee muſt write of more
Which I affect not, but referre men ore
To Tyburne by whoſe Art they may define
What life of man is worth, in valewing thine.

On Sir *Thomas Ouerbury.*

THough dumbe, deafe, dead, I crie, I heare, I kil
Thus growne a Politician gainſt my will.

J. M.

A 3   An

An *Elegie* on the late *Lord William Ha-*
ward Barron of Effingham dead
the tenth of December. 1 6 1 5.

I Did not know thee Lord, nor do I ſtriue
To winne acceſſe, or grace, with Lords aliue :
The dead I ſerue, from whence nor faction can
Moue me, nor fauour : nor a greater man.
To whom no vice commends mee, nor bribe ſent
From whom no Pēnance warns, nor portion ſpent,
To theſe I dedicate as much of me
As I can ſpare from mine owne husbandrie
And till Ghoſtes walke , as they were wont to do
I trade for ſome, and doe theſe errants too.
But firſt I doe enquire, and am aſſur'd
What Trials in their Iournies they indur'd,
VVhat Certainties of Honor and of worth,
Their moſt vncertaine Life-times haue brought
And who ſo did leaſt hurt of this ſmall ſtore (forth
He is my Patron, died he rich, or poore
Firſt I will know of Fame (after his peace
VVhen Flatterie and Enuie both doe ceaſe)
Who rul'd his actions : Reaſon or my Lord?
Did the whole man relie vpon a word,
A Badge, a Title, or aboue all chance
Seem'd he as Antient as his Cogniſance.

What

What did he ? acts of mercie ; and refraine
Oppreſſion, in himſelfe, and in his Traine.
Was his eſſentiall Table, full as free
As Boaſts and Inuitations vſe to be ?
Where if his Ruſſet-friend did chance to dine,
Whether his Satten-man would fill him wine.
Did he thinke periurie as lou'd a Sinne
Himſelfe foreſworne, as if his ſlaue had been ?
Did he ſeeke Regular pleaſures, was he knowne
Iuſt Husband to one Wife, and ſhe his owne ?
Did he giue freely without pauſe, or doubt
And read petitions, ere they were worne out ?
Or ſhould his well deſeruing *Clyent* aske,
Would he beſtow a Tilting, or a Maske
To keepe need vertuous. And that done not feare
What Lady dam'd him for his abſence there ?
Did he attend the Court for no mans fall,
Wore he the ruine of no Hoſpitall.
And where he did his rich apparell don,
Put he no Widdow nor an Orphan on.
Did he loue ſimply vertue for the thing,
The King for no reſpect but for the King.
But aboue all did his Religion waite
Vpon Gods Throne, or on the chaire of ſtate.
He that is guilty of no *Quære* heere,
Out-laſts his Epitaph, out liues his Heyre.
But there is none ſuch, none ſo little bad,
Who but this negatiue goodneſſe euer had ?

Of ſuch a Lord we may expect the birth,
Hee's rather in the wombe, then on the earth.
And t'were a Crime in ſuch a publique fate
For one to liue well, and degenerate:
And therefore I am angry when a name
Comes to vpbraid the World like *Effingham.*
Nor was it modeſt in thee to depart
To thy eternall home, where now thou art;
Ere thy reproach was ready : or to die
Ere cuſtome had prepard thy calumny.
Eight daies haue paſt ſince thou haſt paid thy debt
To ſinne, and not a libell ſtirring yet
Courtiers that ſcoffe by Patent, ſilent ſit,
And haue no vſe of Slander, or of wit :
But (which is monſtrous) though againſt the tyde,
The Water-men haue neither rayld nor lide.
Of good and bad there's no diſtinction knowne,
For in thy praiſe the good and bad are one.
It ſeemes we all are couetous of Fame,
And hearing what a purchaſe of good-name
Thou lately mad'ſt, are carefull to increaſe
Our little by the holding of ſome leaſe   (crew
From thee our Land-lord, and for that th'whole
Speake now like Tenants readie to renew.
It were too ſad to tell thy pedigree,
Death hath diſordered all miſplacing thee,
Whilſt now thy Herrald in his line of heyres
Blots out thy name, and fills the ſpace with teares.
                                                    And

And thus hath conquering Death or Nature rather
Made thee prepoſtrous ancient to thy Father
Who grieues th'art ſo, and like a glorious light
Shines ore thy Hearſe. He therfore that would write
And blaze thee throughly may at onceſay all
Here lies the Anchor of our Admirall.
Let others write for glory or reward
Truth is well paid when ſhe is ſung and heard.

An

An Elegie on the Death
of the L A D Y
R v t l a n d.

I May forget to eat, to drinke, to sleepe
Remembring thee, but when I doe, to weepe
In well weigh'd lines, that men shall at thy hearse
Enuy the sorrow which brought forth my verse.
May my dull vnderstanding haue the might
Only to know her last was yesternight?
Rutland the faire is dead, or if to heare
The name of *Sydney* will more force a teare,
Tis she that is so dead; and yet there be
Some more aliue professe not Poetrie:
The Statesmen and the Lawyers of our time
Haue businesse still, yet do it not in rime:
Can she be dead, and can there be of those
That are so dull to say their prayers in prose?
It is three daies since she did feele Deaths hand
And yet this Ile not cald the Poets Land?
Hath this no new ones made, and are the old
At such a needfull time as this growne cold?
They all say they would faine, but yet they plead
They cannot write because their Muse is dead.
Heare me then speake which will take no excuse,
Sorrow can make a verse without a Muse.

Why

Why didſt thou dieſo ſoone ? O pardon me
Iknow it was the longeſt life to thee.
That ere with modeſtie was cald a ſpan
Since the Almightie left to ſtriue with man ;
Mankind is ſent to ſorrow; and thou haſt
More of the buſines which thou cam'ſt for paſt,
Then all thoſe aged Women which yet quicke
Haue quite outliu'd their owne Arithmeticke.
As ſoone as thou couldſt apprehend a griefe
There were enough to meet thee, and the chiefe
Bleſſing of women : mariage was to thee
Nought but a ſacrament of Miſerie :
For whom thou hadſt,if we may truſt to Fame,
Could nothing change about thee, but thy name.
A name which who (that were againe to do't)
Would change without a thouſand ioyes to boot
In all things elſe, thou rather leadſt a life
Like a betrothed Virgin then a Wife.
But yet I would haue cald thy Fortune kinde
If it had only tride thy ſetled minde,
With preſent croſſes ; Not the loathed thought
Of worſe to come,or paſt, then might haue wroght
Thy beſt remembrance to haue caſt an eye
Backe with delight vpon thine infancie :
But thou hadſt ere thou knewſt the vſe of teares
Sorrow laid vp againſt thou comſt to yeares,
Ere thou wert able, who thou wert to tell
By a ſad warre thy noble Father fell.

In

In a dull clime which did not vnderstand
What t'was to venture him to saue a Land;
He left two children who, for vertue, wit,
Beauty, were lou'd of all; Thee, and his wit;
Two was two few, yet death hath from vs tooke
Thee a more faultlesse issue, then his booke,
Which now the only liuing thing we haue
From him, wee'le see, shall neuer finde a graue
As thou hast done : alas would it might be,
That bookes their Sexes had as well as we,
That we might see this married to the worth
And many Poems like it selfe bring forth :
But this vaine wish Diuinitie controules,
For neither to the Angels, nor to soules,
Nor any thing he meant should euer liue
Did the wise God of Nature sexes giue;
Then with this euerlasting worke alone
We must content our selues since she is gone;
Gone like the day thou dyed'st vpon, and we
May call that backe againe as soone as thee.
  Who should haue lookt to this, where were you all
That doe your selues the helps of Nature call
Physitions ? I acknowledge you were there
To sell such words as none in health would heare
So dyde she : Curst be he who shall defend
Your Art of hastning Nature to an end.
In this you shew'd that Phisicke can but be
At best, an Art, to cure your pouertie;

You're

You're many of you Impoftors, and do giue
To ficke men potions that your felues may liue.
For that hath furfeited and cannot eate
Muft haue a medcine to procure you meate,
And that's the deepeft ground of all your skill
Vnleffe it be fome knowledge how to kill.
Sorrow and madneffe make my verfes flow
Croffe to my vnderftanding. For I know
You can do wonders ; eu'ry day I meete
The loofer fort of people in the ftreete
From defperate difeafes freed, and why
Reftore you them and fuffer her to die ?
Why fhould the State allow you Colledges
Penfions for Lectures and Anatomies ?
If all your potions, vomits, letting bloud
Can only cure the bad, and not the good ?
Which only they can doe, and I will fhow
The hidden reafon why you did not know
The way to cure her. You beleeu'd her bloud
Ran in fuch courfes as you vnderftood
By Lectures ; you beleeu'd her arteries
Grew as they do in your Anatomies.
Forgetting. that the State allowes you none
But only Whores and Theeues to practife on.
And euery paffage about them I'me fure
You vnderftood, and only them can cure,
Which is the caufe that both ——
Are noted for enioying fo long liues.

But

44

But noble bloud treades in too ſtrange a path
For your ill-got Experience ; and hath
An other way of cure. If you had ſeene
Penelope diſſected, or the Queene
Of *Sheba*, then you might haue found a way
To haue preſeru'd her from that fatall day.
As tis. You haue but made her ſooner bleſt
By ſending her to heauen, where let her reſt.
    I will not hurt the peace which ſhe ſhould haue
    By longer looking in her quiet graue.

FINIS.

THE METHOD.

*F*Irſt *of Mariage, and the effect thereof, Children.
Then of his contrary,* Luſt ; *then for his choice,
Firſt, his opinion negatiuely, what ſhould not be* : *the
Firſt cauſes in it, that is, neither* Beautie, Birth, *ncr*
Portion. *Then affirmatiue, what ſhould be, of which
kind there are foure* : Goodneſſe, Knowledge, Diſcretion, *and as a ſecond thing,* Beautie. *The firſt only
is abſolutely good* : *the other being built vpon the firſt
doe likewiſe become ſo. Then the application of that
woman by loue to himſelfe, which makes her a* Wife.
And laſtly, the only condition of a Wife, Fitneſſe.

A WIFE.

*E*Ach Woman is a *briefe* of Womankinde,
And doth in little euen as much containe,
As, in one Day and Night, all life we finde,
Of either, More, is but the ſame againe :
   God fram'd Her ſo, that to her *Husband,* She,
   As *Eue,* ſhould all the *World of Women* be.

So

A WIFE.

So fram'd he *Both*, that *neither* power he gaue
Vfe of themfelues, but by *exchange* to make:
Whence in their Face, the *Faire* no pleafure haue,
But by *reflex* of what thence *other* take.
   Our Lips in their owne Kiffe no pleafure finde:
   Toward their proper Face, our Eies are blinde.

So God in *Eue* did *perfit* Man, *begun* ;
Till then, in vaine much of himfelfe he had :
In *Adam* God created onely *one*,
Eue, and the *world to come*, in *Eue* he made.
   We are *two halfes*: whiles each frō other ftraies,
   Both barren are; *Ioyn'd, both* their *like* can raife.

At firft, both *Sexes* were in *Man* combin'de,
Man a *Shee-Man* did in his bodie breed ;
Adam was *Eues*, *Eue* Mother of Mankinde,
Eue from *Liue-flefh*, Man did from *Duft* proceed.
   One, thus made *two*, *Mariage* doth re-vnite,
   And maks them both but one *Hermaphrodite*.

Man

A WIFE.

Man did but the *well being* of his life
From *Woman* take ; her *Being* she from *Man* ;
And therefore *Eue* created was a Wife,
And at the end of all her *Sex*, began :
   Mariage their obiect is ; their *Being* then,
   And now *Perfection*, they receiue from *Men*.

Marriage ; to all whose ioyes *two parties* be,
And *doubled* are by being *parted* so,
Wherein the very *act* is Chastitie,
Whereby *two Soules* into *one Body* go.
  Which make *two one*, while here they liuing be
  And after death in their *posteritie*.

God to *each Man a priuate Woman* gaue,
That in that *Center* his *desires* might stint,
That he a *comfort like himselfe* might haue,
And that on her *his like* he might *imprint*.
  Double is Womans *vse*, part of their end
  Doth on *this Age*, part on the *next* depend.

          B   We

A WIFE.

We fill but *part of Time*, and cannot dye,
Till we the world a *frefh fupply* haue lent,
Children are Bodies fole *Eternitie* ;
Nature is *Gods*, *Art* is *Mans* inftrument.
  Now all *Mans Art* but only dead things makes
  But herein *Man* in things of *life* partakes.

For wandring *Luft* ; I know tis infinite,
It ftill *begins*, and addes not more to more.
The *guilt* is euerlafting, the *delight*,
This inftant doth not feele, of *that* before.
  The *taft* of it is only in the *Senfe*,
  The *operation* in the *Confcience*.

Woman is not *Lufts bounds,* but *Woman-kinde* ;
One is *Loues number* : who from that doth fall,
Hath loft his hold, and no *new reft* fhall finde ;
Vice hath no meane, but not to be at all ;
  A *Wife* is that *enough*, *Luft* cannot finde ;
  For *Luft* is ftill with *want*, or *too much, pinde*.

Bate

A WIFE.

Bate *luft* the Sin, my fhare is eu'n with his,
For, *Not to luft*, and to *Enioy*, is one :
And more or leffe paft, *equall* Nothing is ;
I ftill haue *one*, Luft *one at once*, alone :
   And though the Woman often changed be,
   Yet Hee's the fame without varietie.

Marriage our *luft* (as 'twere with fuell fire)
Doth, with a medicine *of the fame*, allay ;
And not *forbid*, but *rectifie defire*
My felfe I cannot chufe, *my wife* I may :
   And in the choyce of *Her*, it much doth lie,
   To mend my felfe in my pofterity.

O rather let me *Loue*, then *be in loue* ;
So let me chufe, as *Wife* and *Friend* to finde,
Let me forget her *Sex*, when I *approue*,
Beafts likeneffe lies in *fhape*, but *ours in minde* :
   Our *Soules no Sexes* haue, their Loue is cleane,
   No *Sex*, both in the *better part* are *Men*.

50

A WIFE.

But Phificke for our *luft* their *Bodies* be,
But matter fit to fhew our *Loue* vpon;
But onely *Shells* for our *pofteritie,*
Their foules were giu'n left men fhould be alone:
  For, but the *Soules Interpreters, words be,*
  Without which, *Bodies* are no Company.

That *goodly frame* we fee of flefh and blood,
Their *fafhion* is, not *weight*; it is I fay
But their *Lay-part*; but well digefted food;
Tis but twixt *Duft, and Duft, lifes middle way*:
  The woorth of it is nothing that is *feen,*
  But only that it holds a *Soule* within.

And all the carnall *Beauty* of my Wife,
Is but skin-deepe, but to *two fenfes* knowne;
Short euen of Pictures, fhorter liu'd then Life,
And yet the *loue* furuiues, that's built thereon:
  For our *Imagination,* is too high,
  For *Bodies,* when they meete, to fatisfie,

All

A WIFE.

All Shapes, all Colours are *alike* in *Night*,
Nor doth our *Touch* diftinguifh *foule or faire:*
But mans *imagination*, and his *fight*,
And thofe, but the firft weeke; by Cuftome are
    Both made alike, which diffred at *firft view*;
    Nor can that difference *abfence* much renew.

Nor can that *Beauty*, lying in the *Face*,
But meerely by *imagination* be
Enioy'de by vs, in an *inferiour place.*
Nor can that *Beauty* by *enioying we*
    Make *ours become* ; fo our *defire* growes tame,
    We changed are, but it remaines the fame.

Birth, leffe then *Beauty*, fhall my *Reafon* blinde,
Her *Birth* goes to my *Children*, not to me :
Rather had I that *aftiue Gentrie* finde,
Vertue, then *paffiue* from her Anceftry ;
    Rather in *her aliue* one vertue fee,
    Then all the reft dead in her *Pedigree.*

A W I F E.

In the Degrees, high rather be fhe plac't,
Of *Nature*, then of *Art*, and *Policie* :
Gentry is but a *relique* of Time-paft,
And *Loue* doth onely but the *prefent* fee ; (*fame*
   Things were firft made, then *words:* fhe were the
   With, or *without, that title,* or that name.

As for (the oddes of Sexes) *Portion*,
Nor will I fhun it, nor my aime it make ;
Byrth, Beauty, Wealth , are nothing worth alone,
Áll thefe I would for *good additions* take,
   Not for *Good Parts* ; thofe *two* are ill combin'd,
   Whó, any *third* thing frô *themfelues*, hath ioyn'd.

Rather then thefe, the obiect of my *Loue*,
Let it be *Good* ; when thefe with vertue go,
They (in themfelues *indifferent*,) vertues proue,
For *Good* (like fire) turnes all things to be fo.
   Gods Image, in Her *Soule*, ô let me place
   My *Loue* vpon ; not *Adams* in Her *Face*.

Good,

A W I F E.

Good, is a fairer attribute then *White*,
Tis the *mindes beauty* keepes the *other* ſweete:
That's not ſtill one, nor mortall with the light,
Nor glaſſe, nor painting can it counterfet,
   Nor doth it raiſe deſires, which euer tend
   At once, to their perfection, and their end.

By *Good* I would haue *Holy* vnderſtood,
So *God* ſhe cannot loue, but alſo *mee*,
The law requires our *words* and *deedes* be good,
Religion euen the *Thoughts* doth ſanctifie:
   And ſhe is *more* a *Maide* that *rauiſht* is,
   Then She which only doth but *wiſh amiſſe*.

Luſt only by *Religion* is withſtood;
Luſts obiect is aliue, his ſtrength within;
Moralitie reſiſts but in *cold bloud*;
Reſpect of *Credit* feareth *ſhame*, not *ſinne*.
   But no place *darke enough* for ſuch offence
   She finds, that's *watcht* by her owne *conſcience*.

B 4   Then

A WIFE.

Then may I *truſt her Body* with her *minde*,
And, thereupon ſecure, neede neuer know
The pangs of *Iealouſie*: and *Loue* doth finde
More paine to *doubt* her falſe, then *know* her ſo:
   For *Patience* is, of euills that are knowne,
   The certaine Remedie ; but *Doubt* hath none.

And be that thought *once* ſtirr'd, twill neuer die,
Nor wil the grief more milde by cuſtome proue;
Nor yet *Amendment* can it ſatisfie,
The *Anguiſh* more or leſſe, is *as our Loue* :
   This miſery doth *Iealouſie* enſue,
   That we may proue her *falſe*, but cannot *True*.

Suſpicion may the will of *Luſt* reſtraine,
But *Good* preuents from hauing ſuch a *will*,
A *Wife* that's *Good*, doth *Chaſt and more* containe,
For *Chaſt* is but an *Abſtinence* from ill :
   And in a *Wife* that's *Bad*, although the *beſt*
   Of qualities ; yet in a *Good*, the *leaſt*.

To

A WIFE.

To barre the meanes is *Care*, not *Iealousie*:
Some *lawfull* things to be auoyded are,
When they *occasion* of *vnlawfull* be :
Lust ere it hurts, is best descride a farre :
    Lust is a sinne *of two* ; he that is sure
    Of *either* part, may be of *both* secure.

Giue me next *Good*, an *vnderstanding Wife*,
By Nature *wise*, not *Learned* by much Art,
Some *Knowledge* on Her side, will all my life
More scope of conuersation impart,
    Besides, Her inborne vertue fortifie,   (why.
    They are most firmely good, that best know

A *passiue vnderstanding* to conceiue,
And *Iudgement* to discerne, I wish to finde :
Beyond that, all as hazardous I leaue ;
Learning, and *pregnant wit* in Woman-kinde,
    What it findes malleable, maketh fraile,
    And doth not adde more *ballast*, but more *saile*.

Domesticke

56

A WIFE.

Domesticke Charge doth best that *Sexe* befit,
Contiguous businesse ; so to fixe the Minde,
That *Leasure* space for *Fancies* not admit :
Their *Leasure* t'is, corrupteth *Woman-kinde*,
   Else, being plac'd from many vices free,
   They had to Heau'n a shorter cut then wee.

Bookes are a part of Mans prerogatiue,
In formall Inke they *Thoughts*, and *Voices* hold,
That we to them our solitude may giue,
And make *Time-present* trauell that of *old*.
   Our Life, *Fame* peeceth longer at the end,
   And *Bookes* it farther backward doe extend.

As *good*, and *knowing*, let her be *Discreet*,
That, to the others *weight*, doth *Fashion* bring ;
Discretion doth consider what is *Fit*,
Goodnesse but what is *lawfull* ; but the *Thing*,
   Not *Circumstances* ; *Learning* is and *wit*,
   In Men, but *curious folly without it*.

               To

A WIFE.

To keepe their Name, when 'tis in others hands,
Diſcretion askes ; their *Credit* is by farre
More *fraile* then *They* ; on likely-hoods it ſtands,
And hard to be diſproou'd, *Luſt's ſlanders* are.
   Their *Carriage*, not their *Chaſtity* alone,
   Muſt keepe their *Name* chaſte from *ſuſpition*.

Womens *Behauiour* is a ſurer barre
Then is their *No : That* fairely doth *denie*
Without *denying* ; *thereby* kept they are
Safe eu'n from *Hope* ; in part to blame is ſhee,
   Which hath *without conſent* bin only tride;
   He comes too *neere*, that comes *to be denide.*

Now ſince a *Woman* we to *Marry* are,
A *Soule* and *Body*, not a *Soule* alone ;
When one is *Good*, then be the other *Faire* ;
Beauty is *Health*, and *Beauty*, both in one ;
   Be ſhee ſo faire, as change can yeeld no gaine;
   So faire, as Shee moſt Women elſe containe,

So

A WIFE.

So Faire at leaſt let me imagine Her;
That thought to *me* is *Truth : opinion*
Cannot in matter of *opinion* erre;
With no eyes ſhall I ſee her but *mine owne*.
 And as my *Fancy Her* conceiues to be,
 Euen ſuch my Senſes both, do *Feele* and *See*.

The *Face* we may the ſeat of *Beauty* call,
In it the rellifh of the reſt doth lie,
Nay cu'n a figure of the *Minde* withall :
And of the *Face*, the *Life* mooues in the *Eye*;
 No things elſe, being *two*, ſo like we ſee,
 So like, that they, *two* but in number, be.

Beauty in *decent ſhape*, and *Colours* lies,
Colours the *matter* are, and *ſhape* the *Soule* ;
The *Soule*, which from no ſingle part doth riſe,
But from the iuſt proportion of the *whole*,
 And is a meere ſpiritnall harmonie,
 Of euery part, vnited in the *Eye*.

        Loue

A WIFE.

Loue is a kinde of *Superstition,*
Which feares the Idoll which it self hath fram'd;
Lust a Desire, which rather from his *owne*
Temper, then from the *obiect* is inflam'd ;
    Beauty is Loues *obiect* ; *Woman* Lust's; to gaine
    Loue, Loue Desires; *Lust* onely to *obtaine.*

No circumstance doth *Beautie* beautifie,
Like gracefull *fashion,* natiue *Comelinesse.*
Nay eu'n gets pardon for *Deformity* ;
Art cannot it beget, but may encrease ;
    When *Nature* had fixt *Beauty,* perfect made,
    Something she left for *Motion* to adde.

Bnt let that *Fashion* more to *Modesty*
Tend, then *Assurance* ; *Modesty* doth set
The face in her iust place, from *Passions* free,
Tis both the *Mindes,* and *Bodies Beautie* met ;
    But *Modesty,* no vertue can we see ;
    That, is the Faces onely *Chastitie.*

                          Where

A WIFE.

Where *goodneſſe* failes,twixt ill and ill *that* ſtands:
Whence tis, that *women*,though they weaker be,
And their deſires more ſtrong,yet on their hands
The *Chaſtity* of *men* doth often lie :
   Luſt would more common be then any one,
   Could it, as other ſinnes, be done *alone*.

All theſe *good parts* a *Perfect woman* make,
Adde *Loue to me*, they make a *Perfect Wife*,
Without her *Loue*, Her *Beauty* ſhould I take,
As that of *Pictures*; dead ; *That* giues it life :
   Till then, Her *Beauty* like the Sun doth ſhine
   Alike to all ; *That* makes it, onely *mine*.

And of that *Loue*, let *Reaſon Father* be,
And *Paſſion Mother* ; let it from the one
His *Being* take, the other his *Degree* ;
Selfe-loue (which ſecond Loues are built vpon)
   Will make *me* (if not *Her*) her *Loue* reſpect ,
   No Man, but fauours his owne worths effect.

                        As

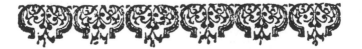

A WIFE.

As *Good*, and *wife* ; fo be fhe *Fit* for mee,
That is, To *will*-and *Not to will*, the fame,
My *Wife* is my *Adopted-felfe*, and fhee
As Mee, fo what I loue, to Loue muft frame.
    For when by Marriage, both in one concurre,
    Woman conuerts to Man, not Man to her.

F I N I S.

The Authors Epitaph.
written by himfelfe.

THe Span of my daies meafur'd, heere I reft,
    That is, my body ; but my foule, his gueft,
Is hence afcended, whither, neither Time,
Nor Faith, nor Hope, but onely loue can clime ;
Where being now enlightned, She doth know
The Truth of all, men argue off below :
    Onely this duft doth heere in Pawne remaine,
    That, when the world diffolues, fhe come again.

Characters,

OR
Wittie descriptions of the pro-
perties of sundry Persons.

A good Woman.

 Good Woman is a com-
fort, like a man. Shee
lacks of him nothing
but heat. Thence is her
sweetnes of disposition,
which meets his stout-
nes more pleasingly ; so wooll meets
yron easier then yron, and turnes resi-

C   sting

fting into embracing. Her greateft learning is religion, and her thoughts are on
her owne *Sexe*, or on men, without ca-
fting the difference. *Difhoneftie* neuer
comes neerer than her eares, and then
wonder ftops it out, and faues vertue the
labour. Shee leaues the neat *youth*, telling his *lufhious* tales, and puts backe the
Seruingmans, putting forward, with a
frowne : yet her kindnes is free enough
to be feene, for it hath no guilt about it:
and her mirth is cleare, that you may
looke through it, into vertue, but not beyond. She hath not behauiour at a certaine, but makes it to her occafion. Shee
hath fo much knowledge as to loue it,
and if fhe haue it not at home, fhee will
fetch it, for this fometimes in a pleafant difcontent fhe dares chide her *Sexe,*
though fhee vfe it neuer the worfe. Shee
is much within, and frames outwarde
things to her minde, not her minde to
them. She weares good clothes, but neuer better ; for fhe findes no degree beyond *Decencie.* Shee hath a content of
                                              her

her owne, and fo feekes not an husband,
but findes him. She is indeed moft, but
not much of defcription for fhee is direct
and one, and hath not the variety of ill.
Now fhee is giuen frefh and aliue to a
husband, and fhee doth nothing more
then loue him, for fhe takes him to that
purpofe. So his good becomes the bufineffe of her actions, and fhee doth her
felfe kindneffe vpon him. After his, her
chiefeft vertue is a good husband. For
Shee is *Hee.*

A very Woman.

A *Veric Woman*, is a dow-bakt man,
or a *Shee* ment well towards man,
but fell two bowes fhort, *ftrength*
and *vnderftanding.* Her vertue is the
hedge, *Modeftie,* that keeps a man from
climing ouer into her faults. Shee fim-
pers as if fhee had no teeth, but lips, and
fhee diuides her eyes, and keeps halfe for
C 2   her

her felfe, and giues the other to her neat
Youth. Being fet downe fhee cafts her
face into a platforme, which dureth the
meale, & is taken away with the voider.
Her draught reacheth to good man-
ners, not to thirft, and it is a part of their
myfterie not to profeffe hunger; but *Nature* takes her in priuate and ftretcheth
her vpon meat. Shee is *Marriaigcable* and
Fourteene at once ; and after fhee doth
not liue but tarrie. Shee reads ouer her
face euery morning, and fomtimes blots
out pale and writes red. She thinks fhe
is faire, though many times her opinion
goes alone, and fhe loues her glaffe, and
the knight of the Sunne for lying. Shee
is hid away all but her face, and that's
hang'd about with toyes and deuices,
like the figne of a Tauerne, to draw
Strangers. If fhee fhew more fhee preuents defire, and by too free giuing,
leaues no *Gift*. Shee may efcape from
the Seruing-man, but not from the
Chamber-maide. Shee commits with
her eares for certaine : after that fhee
                                        may

may goe for a Maide, but fhe hath been
lien with in her vnderſtanding. Her *Phi-
loſophie*, is a ſeeming neglect of thoſe,
that be too good for her. Shee's a yonger brother for her portion, but not for
her portion of wit, that comes from her
in a treble, which is ſtill too big for it;
yet her *Vantiie* ſeldom matcheth hir, with
one of her owne degree for then ſhe will
beget another creature a begger : and
commonly, if ſhee marrie better, ſhee
marries worſe. Shee gets much by the
ſimplicitie of her Sutor, and for a ieſt,
laughes at him without one. Thus ſhe
dreſſes a Husband for her ſelfe, and after
takes him for his patience, and the land
adioyning, yee may ſee it, in a Seruing-
mans freſh *Naperie*, and his Leg ſteps
into an vnknowne ſtocking. I need not
ſpeake of his *Garters*, the taſſell ſhewes it
ſelfe. If ſhe loue, ſhe loues not the Man,
but the beaſt of him. Shee is *Salomons*
cruel creature, and a mans walking-con-
ſumption : euery caudle ſhee giues him,
is a purge. Her chiefe commenda-

tion is, fhee brings a man to repentance.

　　　　Her next part.

　　Her lightneffe gets her to fwimme at
top of the table, where her wric little finger bewraies *caruing* ; her neighbours at
the latter end know they are welcome,
and for that purpofe fhee quencheth her
thirft. She trauels to and among, and fo
becomes a woman of good entertainment, for all the follie in the Countrie,
comes in cleane Linnen to vifite her: fhe
breaks to them her griefe in Suger cakes,
and receiues from their mouthes in exchange, many ftories that conclude to
no purpofe. Her eldeft Sonne is like her
howfoeuer, & that difpraifeth him beft :
her vtmoft drift is to turne him Foole,
which commonly fhee obtaines at the
yeares of difcretion. She takes a iourney
fometimes to her Neeces houfe, but neuer thinkes beyond *London.* Her *Deuoti-*
on is good clothes, they carrie her to
Church, expreffe their ftuffe and fafhion,
　　　　　　　　　　　　　　　　and

and are filent; if fhe be more deuout, fhe
lifts vp a certaine number of eyes, in ftead
of prayers, and takes the Sermon, and
meafures out a nap by it, iuft as long. She
fends Religion afore to *Sixtie*, where fhe
neuer ouertakes it, or driues it before her
againe: Her moft neceffary inftruments
are a *waiting Gentlewoman*, and a *Chamber-maide*; fhe weares her Gentlewoman
ftill, but moft often leaues the other in
her Chamber-window. She hath a little *Kennel* in her lap, and fhee fmells the
fweeter for it. The vtmoft reach of her
Prouidence, is the fatneffe of a Capon,
and her greateft enuie, is the next Gen.
tlewomans better Gowne. Her moft
commendable skill, is to make her Huf-
bands fuftian beare her Veluet. This fhe
doth many times ouer, and then is deliuered to olde Age, and a Chaire, where
euery body leaues her.

A diffem-

A *Dissembler*,

IS an essence needing a double definition, for hee is not that hee appeares.
Vnto the eye he is pleasing, vnto the
eare not harsh, but vnto the vnderstanding intricate, and full of windings: he is
the *prima materia*, & his intents giue him
forme: he dieth his meanes and his meaning into two colours, he baites craft
with humilitie, and his countenance is
the picture of the present disposition. He
winnes not by batterie, but vndermi-
ning, and his racke is smoothing. Hee
allures, is not allur'd by his affections, for
they are the brokers of his obseruation.
He knowes passion onely by sufferance,
and resisteth by obeying. He makes his
time an accomptant to his memorie,
and of the humors of men weaues a net
for occasion : the Inquisitor must looke
through his iudgement, for to the eye
only he is not visible.

A Courtier

A Courtier,

TO all mens thinking is a man, and to moſt men the fineſt : all things elſe are defined by the vnderſtan.ding,but this by the ſences; but his ſureſt marke is, that hee is to be found onely about Princes. Hee ſmells ; and putteth away much of his iudgement about the ſcituation of his clothes. He knowes no man that is not generally knowne. His wit, like the *Marigold,* openeth with the *Sunne,*and therefore he riſeth not before ten of the clocke. He puts more confidence in his words than meaning , and more in his pronuntiation than his words. *Occaſion* is his *Cupid,* and he hath but one receipt of making loue. Hee followes nothing but inconſtancie, admires nothing but beautie, honours nothing but fortune.Loues nothing. The ſuſtenance of his diſcourſe is Newes , and his cen-ſure like a ſhot depends vpon the char-
ging

ging.He is not, if he be out of Court, but fiſh-like breathes deſtruction, if out of his owne element. Neither his motion, or aſpect are regular, but hee moues by the vpper *Spheres*, and is the reflection of higher ſubſtances.

If you finde him not heere, you ſhall in *Paules*, with a picke-tooth in his Hat, a cape cloke, and a long ſtocking.

A Golden Aſſe.

IS a young thing, whoſe Father went to the Diuell ; he is followed like a ſalt bitch, and lymb'd by him that gets vp firſt ; his diſpoſition is cut, and knaues rent him like Tenter-hookes : hee is as blinde as his mother, and ſwallowes flat-terers for friends. He is high in his owne imagination ; but that imagination as a ſtone, that is raiſed by violence, deſcends naturally: when he goes, hee lookes who lookes : if hee findes not good ſtore of

vailers,

vailers, hee comes home ftiffe and feer, vntill hee bee new oyled and watered by his husbandmen. Wherefoeuer he eates he hath an officer, to warne men not to talke out of his element, and his owne is exceeding fenfible, becaufe it is fenfuall; but he cannot exchange a peece of reafon, though he can a peece of gold. Hee is naught pluckt, for his feathers are his beauty, and more then his beautie, they are his difcretion, his countenance, his All. Hee is now at an end, for hee hath had the Wolfe of vaine-glory, which hee fed, vntill himfelfe became the food.

A Flatterer.

IS *the fhadow of a Foole.* Hee is good wood-man, for hee fingleth out none but the wealthy. His carriage is euer of the coulour of his patient; and for his fake hee will halt or weare a wry necke. Hee difpraifeth nothing but pouerty,

and

and small drinke, and praiseth his grace of making water. Hee selleth himselfe, with reckoning his great Friends, and teacheth the present, how to winne his praises by reciting the others gifts : hee is ready for all imployments, but especially before Dinner, for his courage and his stomacke go together. Hee will play any vpon his countenance, and where he cannot be admitted for a counseller, he will serue as a foole. Hee frequents the court of wards and ordinaries, and fits these guests of *Togæ virilis*, with wiues or whoores. He entreth young men into acquaintance and debt books. In a word, he is the impression of the last terme, and will be so, vntill the comming of a new terme or termer.

An ignorant Glorie hunter.

IS an *insectum animal*; for he is the maggot of opinion, his behauiour is another thing from himself, & is glewed, & but

but set on. He entertaines men with re-
petitions, and returnes them their owne
words. He is ignorant of nothing, no
not of thofe things, where ignorance is
the leffer fhame. He gets the names of
good wits, and vtters them for his companions. He confeffeth vices that he is
guiltleffe of, if they be in fafhion ; and
dares not falute a man in old cloths, or
out of fafhion. There is not a publicke
affembly without him, and he will take
any paines for an acquaintance there.
In any fhew he will be one, though he
be but a whifler, or a torch bearer; and
beares downe ftrangers with the ftory
of his actions. He handles nothing that
is not rare, and defends his wardrobe,
diet, and all cuftomes, with entitling
their beginnings from Princes, great
Souldiers and ftrange Nations. He dares
fpeake more then he vnderftands, and
aduentures his words without the re-
liefe of any feconds. Hee relates battels
and skirmifhes, as from an eye witneffe,
when his eies theeuifhly beguiled a bal-
lad

lad of them. Jn a word, to make fure of
admiration, hee will not let himfelfe vn-
dreft and himfelfe, but hopes, fame and
opinion will bee the Readers of his Riddles.

- - - - - - - - - - - - - -

A Timist.

I S *a noune adiectiue of the prefent tenfe.*
He hath no more of a confcience then
Feare, and his religion is not his but the
Princes. Hee reuerenceth a Courtiers
Seruants feruant. Is firft his owne Slaue,
and then whofoeuer looketh big ; when
hee giues he curfeth, and when hee fells
he worfhips. Hee reades the ftatutes in
his chamber, and weares the Bible in the
ftreetes : hee neuer praifeth any but before themfelues or friends : and miflikes
no great mans actions during his life.
His new-yeares gifts are ready at *Alha-*
lom us, and the fute he meant to mediate
before them. He pleafeth the children of
great

great men, and promiseth to adopt
them; and his curtesie extends it selfe e-
uen to the stable. Hee straines to talke
wisely, and his modesty would serue a
Bride. Hee is grauitie from the head to
the foote; but not from the head to the
heart; you may finde what place he affecteth, for he creepes as neere it as may
bee, and as passionately courts it; if at
any time his hopes are effected, he swel-
leth with them; and they burst out too
good for the vessell. In a word, he dan-
ceth to the tune of fortune, and studies
for nothing but to keepe time.

An Amorist.

IS a certaine blasted or planet-stroken,
and is the Dog that leades blinde *Cu-*
pid; when hee is at the best, his fashion
exceedes the worth of his weight. He is
neuer without verses, and muske con-
fects; and sighs to the hazard of his buttons

tons; his eyes are all white, either to
weare the liuery of his Miſtris complexion, or to keepe *Cupid* from hitting the
blacke. Hee fights with paſſion, and
looſeth much of his blood by his wea-
pon; dreames, thence his paleneſſe. His
armes are careleſly vſed, as if their beſt
vſe were nothing but embracements. He
is vntruſt, vnbuttoned, and vngartered,
nor out of careleſneſſe, but care; his far-
theſt end being but going to bed. Sometimes he wraps his petition in neatneſſe,
but it goeth not alone; for then he makes
ſome other qualitie moralize his affection, and his trimneſſe is the grace of that
grace. Hir fauour lifts him vp, as the Sun
moiſture ; when ſhe disfauours, vnable
to hold that happineſſe, it falls downe
in teares; his fingers are his Orators, and
hee expreſſeth much of himſelfe vpon
ſome inſtrument. He anſweres not, or
not to the purpoſe ; and no maruell, for
he is not at home. He ſcotcheth time
with dancing with his Miſtris, taking vp
of her gloue, and wearing her feather;
                                    he

hee is confinde to her colour, and dares not paſſe out of the circuit of her memory. His imagination is a foole, and it goeth in a pide-coat of red and white; ſhortly, he is tranſlated out of a man into folly ; his imagination is the glaſſe of luſt, and himſelfe the traitour to his own diſcretion.

An *Affectate Traueller.*

IS a ſpeaking faſhion ; hee hath taken paines to be ridiculous, and hath ſeene more then he hath perceiued. His attire ſpeakes *French* or *Italian*, and his *gate* cryes, *Behold me.* Hee cenſures all things by countenances, and ſhrugs, and ſpeaks his owne language with ſhame and liſping: he will choake rather then confeſſe *Beere* good drinke : and his pick-tooth is a maine part of his behauiour. He chuſeth rather to be counted a *Spie*, then not a *Politician*: and maintaines his reputati-

D on

on by naming great men familiarly. He chufeth rather to tell lies, then not wonders, and talkes with men fingly: his difcourfe founds big, but meanes nothing: & his boy is bound to admire him howfoeuer. He comes ftill from great Perfonages, but goes with meane. He takes occafion to fhew Iewels giuen him in regarde of his vertue, that were bought in S. *Martines*: and not long after hauing with a *Mountbanks* method, pronounced them woorth thoufandes, enpawneth them for a few fhillings. Vpon feftiuall dayes he goes to *Court*, and falutes without refaluting: at night in an ordinary he canvaffeth the bufineffe in hand, and feemes as conuerfant with all intents and plots, as if he begot them. His extraordinary account of men is, firft to tell them the ends of all matters of confequence, and then to borrow money of them; hee offereth courtefies, to fhew them, rather then himfelfe humble. Hee difdaines all things aboue his reach, and preferreth all Countries before his owne. Hee imputeth

puteth his wants and pouertie to the ignorance of the time, not his own vnwor-
thineffe : and concludes his difcourfe
with halfe a period or a word, and leaues
the reft to imagination. In a word, his
religion is fafhion, and both bodie and
foule are gouerned by fame, hee loues
moft voices aboue truth.

***

A Wife man.

IS the trueth of the true definition of
man, that is, a reafonable creature.
His difpofition alters, he alters not. Hee
hides himfelfe with the attire of the vulgar ; and in indifferent things is content
to be gouerned by them. He lookes according to nature, fo goes his behauiour.
His minde enioyes a continuall fmooth-
neffe : fo commeth it, that his confideration is alwayes at home. He endures the
faults of all men filently, except his
friends, and to them he is the mirrour of
D 2   their

their actions ; by this meanes his peace cōmeth not from fortune, but himselfe. He is cunning in men,not to surprize but keepe his owne, and beats off their ill affected humours, no otherwise then if they were flies. Hee chuseth not friends by the subsidy-booke, and is not luxurious after acquaintance. Hee maintaines the strength of his body, not by delicacies, but temperance ; and his minde by giuing it preheminence ouer his bodie. Hee vnderstands things not by their forme, but qualities ; and his comparisons intend not to excuse, but to prouoke him higher. He is not subiect to casualties,for Fortune hath nothing to do with the minde, except those drowned in the body:but he hath diuided his soule,from the case of his soule, whose weakenesse hee assists no otherwise then commiseratinely, not that it is his, but that it is. He is thus, and will bee thus : and liues subiect neither to Time nor his frailties; the seruant of vertue, and by vertue, the friend of the highest.

A Noble

A Noble Spirit.

HAth furueyed and fortified his difpofition, and conuerts all occur
rents into experience, betweene
which experience and his reafon, there
is marriage;the iffue are his actions. Hee
circuits his intents, and feeth the end before he fhoot. Men are the inftruments
of his Art, and there is no man without,
his vfe : occafion incites him, none en-
ticeth him ; and he mooues by affection,
not for affection ; he loues glory,fcornes
fhame,and gouerneth and obeyeth with
one countenance ; for it comes from one
confideration. Hee cals not the variety
of the world chances, for his meditation
hath trauelled ouer them ; and his eye
mounted vpon his vnderftanding, feeth
them as things vnderneath. Hee couers
not his body with delicacies,norexcufeth
thefe delicacies by his body but teacheth
it, fince it is not able to defend its owne

imbecillity,

imbecility, to fhew or fuffer. Hee licenceth not his weakeneſſe, to weare Fate, but knowing reaſon to bee no idle gift of Nature, hee is the Steeres-man of his owne deſtiny. Truth is his Goddeſſe, and he takes paines to get her, not to look like her. He knowes the condition of the world, that he muſt act one thing like a-nother, and then another. To theſe hee carries his deſires, & not his deſires him; and ſtickes not faſt by the way (for that contentment is repentance) but knowing the circle of all courſes, of all intents, of all things, to haue but one center or period, without all diſtraction, he haſteth thither and ends there, as his true and naturall element. Hee doth not contemne Fortune, but not confeſſe her. Hee is no Gameſter of the world (which only complaine and praiſe her) but being onely ſenſible of the honeſty of actions, contemnes a particular profit as the excrement or ſcum. Vnto the ſociety of men he is a *Sunne*, whoſe cleereneſſe directs their ſteps in a regular motion: when hee
is

is more particular, he is the wife mans friend, the example of the indifferent, the medicine of the vitious. Thus time goeth not from him, but with him: and he feeles age more by the ſtrength of his ſoule, then the weakneſſe of his body: thus feeles he no paine, but eſteemes all ſuch things as friends, that deſire to file off his fetters and helpe him out of priſon.

An Olde Man.

IS a thing that hath bene a man in his dayes. Olde men are to bee knowne blinde-folded: for their talke is as terrible as their reſemblance. They praiſe their owne times as vehemently, as if they would ſell them. They become wrinckled with frowning and faceing youth; they admire their olde cuſtomes, euen to the eatcing of red herring, and going wetſhod. They call the thumbe vnder the girdle, Grauity; and becauſe they can

D 4　　　　hardly

hardly fmell at all, their Pofies are vnder
their girdles. They count it an ornament
of fpeech, to clofe the period with a
cough ; and it is venerable, they fay, to
fpend time in wiping their driueled
beards. Their difcourfe is vnanfwerable,
by reafon of their obftinacy: their fpeech
is much, though little to the purpofe.
Truths and lies paffe with an equall af-
firmation, for their memories feuerall is
wonne into one receptacle, and fo they
come out with one fenfe. They teach
their feruants their duties with as much
fcorne and tyranny, as fome people teach
their dogs to fetch. Their enuie is one of
their difeafes. They put off and on their
cloths, with that certainty, as if they
knew their heads would not direct them.
and therefore Cuftome fhould. They
take a pride in halting and going ftiffely,
and therfore their ftaues are carued and
tipped: they truft their attire with much
of their grauity ; and they dare not goe
without a gowne in Summer. Their hats
are brufhed to draw mens eyes off from
their

their faces ; but of all, their *Pomanders*
are worne to moſt purpoſe, for their pu-
trified breath ought not to want either a
ſmell to defend, or a dog to excuſe.

A Countrey Gentleman.

IS a thing, out of whoſe corruption the
generation of a Iuſtice of peace is produced. Hee ſpeakes ſtatutes and huſ-
bandry well enough, to make his neighbours thinke him a wiſe man ; hee is well
skilled in *Arithmeticke* or rates: and hath
eloquence inough to ſaue his two pence.
His conuerſation amongſt his Tenants is
deſperate; but amongſt his equals full of
doubt. His trauell is ſeldome farther then
the next market Towne, and his inquiſition is about the price of Corne : when
he trauelleth, he will goe ten mile out of
the way to a Couſins houſe of his to ſaue
charges ; and rewards the Seruants by
taking them by the hand when hee de-
parts.

parts. Nothing vnder a *Sub-pena* can draw him to *London* : and when hee is there, he ftickes faft vpon euery obiect, cafts his eyes away vpon gazing, and becomes the prey of euery Cut-purfe. When he comes home, thofe wonders ferue him for his Holy-day talke. If hee goe to Court, it is in yellow ftockings? and if it be in Winter in a flight tafetie cloake, and pumps and pantofles. He is chained that wooes the vfher for his comming into the prefence, where hee becomes troublefome with the ill managing of his Rapier and the wearing of his girdle of one fafhion and the hangers of another? by this time he hath learned to kiffe his hand, and make a Leg both together, and the names of Lords and Counfellours? hee hath thus much toward entertainment and courtefie, but of the laft he makes more vfe? for by the recitall of *my Lord*, hee coniures his poore countrey-men. But this is not his elemēt, he muft home againe, being like a Dor, that endes his flight in a dunghill.

A Fine

A Fine Gentleman.

IS the *Cynamon tree*, whofe barke is
more worth then his body. Hee hath
read the Booke of good manners, and
by this time each of his limbs may
read it. He alloweth of no iudge,but the
eye ; painting, boulftring, and bomba-
fting are his *Oratours* : by thefe alfo hee
prooues his induftry : for hee hath pur-
chafed legs,haire, beautie, and ftraight-
neffe,more then nature left him. He vn-
lockes maiden-heads with his language,
and fpeakes *Euphues*, not fo gracefully as
heartily. His difcourfe makes not his behauiour, but hee buies it at Court, as
Countrey men their cloathes in Birchin-
lane. Hee is fomewhat like the *Salaman-
der*, and liues in the flame of loue,which
p aines he expreffeth comically: and nothing grieues him fo much, as the want
of a Poet to make an iffue in his loue;
yet he fighs fweetly, and fpeakes lamen-
tably:

tably : for his breath is perfumed, and his words are winde. Hee is beft in feafon at Chriftmas ; for the Boares head and Reueller come together; his hopes are laden in his quality: and left Fidlers fhould take him vnprouided, hee weares pumps in his pocket : and left hee fhould take Fidlers vnprouided, he whiftles his owne Galliard. He is a Calender of ten yeares, and marriage rufts him. Afterwards he maintaines himfelfe an implement of houfhold by caruing and vfhering. For all this, he is iudiciall onely in Taylours and Barbers, but his opinion is euer ready, and euer idle. If you will know more of his acts, the Brokers fhop is the witneffe of his valour, where lyes wounded, dead, rent, and out of fafhion, many a fpruce Sute, ouerthrowen by his fantaftickneffe.

An Elder

An Elder Brother.

IS a creature borne to the beſt aduantage of things without him, that hath
the ſtart at the beginning, but loyters
it away before the ending. Hee lookes
like his Land, as heauily, and durtily, as
ſtubbornely. He dares doe any thing but
fight; and feares nothing but his Fathers
life and minority. The firſt thing hee
makes known is his eſtate; and the Load-
ſtone that drawes him is the vpper end of
the Table. He wooeth by a particular,
and his ſtrongeſt argument is the ioyn-
ture. His obſeruation is all about the faſhion, and hee commends Partlets for a
rare deuiſe. He ſpeakes no language, but
ſmels of dogs or hawkes; and his ambition flies Iuſtice-height. Hee loues to bee
commended, and hee will goe into the
Kitchin, but heele haue it. He loues glory, but is ſo lazie, as hee is content with
flattery. Hee ſpeakes moſt of the prece-
dency

dency of age, and protefts fortune the
greateft vertue. He fummoneth the olde
feruants, & tels what ftrange acts he will
doe when he raignes. He verely beleeues
houfe-keepers the beft common wealths
men; and therefore ftudies baking, brew-
ing, greafing, and fuch as the limmes of
goodneffe. He iudgeth it no fmall figne
of wifdome to talke much; his tongue
therefore goes continually his errand, but
neuer fpeeds. If his vnderftanding were
not honefter then his will, no man fhould
keepe good conceit by him; for hee
thinkes it no theft, to fell all he can to o-
pinion. His pedigree and his fathers feale-
ring, are the ftilts of his crazed difpofition. He had rather keepe company with
the dregs of men, then not to be the beft
man. His infinuation is the inuiting of
men to his houfe; and he thinks it a great
modeftie to comprehend his cheere vnder a peece of Mutton and a Rabet; if he
by this time be not knowen, he will goe
home againe : for he can no more abide
to haue himfelf concealed, then his land;
yet

yet he is as you fee good for nothing : except to make a ftallion to maintaine the race.

A *Braggadochio Welchman.*

IS the Oyfter, that the Pearle is in, for a man may be pickt out of him. He hath the abilities of the minde in *Potentia,* and *actu* nothing but boldneffe. His clothes are in fafhion before his body : and he accounts boldneffe the chiefeft vertue. aboue all men he loues an Herrald, and fpeakes pedegrees naturally. He accounts none well defcended , that call him not Couzen ; and preferres *Owen Glendower* before any of the nine Worthies. The firft note of his familiaritie is the confefsion of his valour; and fo hee preuents quarrels. He voutcheth Welch, a pure and vnconquered language, and courts Ladies with the ftory of their Chronicle. To conclude, he is precious in

in his owne conceit, and vpon S. *Dauies*
day without comparifon.

A Pedant.

HE treads in a rule, and one hand
fcannes verfes, and the other holds
his Scepter. He dares not thinke a
thought that the nominatiue cafe go-
uernes not the Verbe; and he neuer had
meaning in his life, for he trauelled onely
for words. His ambition is *Criticifme*, and
his example *Tully.* Hee vallues phrafes,
and elects them by the found, and the
eight parts of fpeech are his Seruants. To
be briefe, he is a *Heteroclite*, for he wants
the plurall number, hauing onely the fin-
gle quality of words.

A Scr·

A Seruing-man.

IS a creature, *which though bee be not
drunke, yet is not his owne man.* He
tels without asking who ownes him,
by the fuperfcription of his Liuery His
life is, for eafe and leifure, much about
Gentleman-like. His wealth enough to
fuffice Nature, and fufficient to make
him happy, if he were fure of it; for he
hath little, and wants nothing, hee va-
lues himfelfe higher or lower, as his
Mafter is. He hates or loues the Men,
as his Mafter doth the Mafter. Hee is
commonly proud of his Mafters horfes,
or his Chriftmas; he fleeps when he is
fleepy, is of his religion, only the clock
of his ftomack is fet to go an hour after
his. He feldome breakes his owne clothes. He neuer drinkes but double, for
hee muft bee pledg'd; nor commonly
without fom fhort fentence nothing to
the purpofe: and feldome abftaines till

E   he

hee come to a thirft . His difcretion is
to be carefull for his mafters credite, &
his fufficiency to marfhall difhes at a
Table, and to carue well . His neat-
neffe confifts much in his haire & outward linnen. His courting language,
vifible bawdy iefts ; and againft his
matter faile , he is alway ready furni-
fhed with a fong . His inheritance is
the Chamber-mayd, but often purcha-
feth his Mafters daughter, by reafon of
opportunity, or for want of a better: he
alwaies cuckolds himfelfe, and neuer
marries but his owne widdow . His
Mafter being appeafed, he becomes a
Retainer , and entailes himfelfe and
his pofterity vpon his heire-males for
euer.

An Hoft

IS the kernell of a Signe: or the Signe
is the fhell, & *mine Hoft* is the Snaile.
He

He confifts of double beere & fellowfhip, and his vices are the bawds of his
thirft. Hee entertaines humbly, and
giues his Guefts power, as well of himfelfe as houfe. He anfwers all mens ex-
pectations to his power, faue in the reckoning: and hath gotten the tricke of
greatneffe, to lay all miflikes vpon his
feruants. His wife is the *Cummin feede*
of his Doue-houfe; and to bee a good
Gueft, is a warrant for her libertie. He
traffiques for Guefts by mens freinds,
friends-friend, and is fenfible onely of
his purfe. In a word, hee is none of his
owne: for he neither eates, drinkes, or
thinkes, but at other mens charges and
appointments.

An Oftler

I S *a thing that fcrubbeth vnreafonably*
his horfe, reafonably himfelfe. He confifts of Trauellers, though he bee none

himfelfe. His higheft ambition is to
be *Hoft*, and the inuention of his figne
is his greateft wit : for the expreffing
wherof he fends away the Painters for
want of vnderftanding. Hee hath certaine charmes for a horfe mouth, that
he fhould not eat his hay : and behind
your backe, hee will cozen your horfe
to his face. His curry-combe is one of
his beft parts, for hee expreffeth much
by the gingling : and his mane-combe
is a fpinners card turn'd out of feruice.
He puffes and blowes ouer your horfe,
to the hazzard of a double Iugge : and
leaues much of the dreffing to the pro-
uerb of *Muli mutuo fcabient*, One horfe
rubs another. Hee comes to him that
cals lowdeft, not firft ; hee takes a broken head patiently, but the knaue hee
feeles not. His vtmoft honefty is good
fellowfhip, and he fpeakes Northerne,
what countrey man foeuer. He hath a
penfion of Ale from the next *Smith* &
Sadler for intelligence. He loues to fee
you ride, & holds your ftirrop in expectation.   **A** *good*

A good Wife

IS a mans beſt mooueable, a ſcien incorporate with the ſtocke, bringing
ſweet fruite ; one that to her husband
is more then a friend, leſſe then trouble : an equall with him in the yoake.
Calamities and troubles ſhee ſhares a-
like, nothing pleaſeth her that doth not
him. Shee is relatiue in all ; and hee
without her, but halfe himſelfe. She is
his abſent hands, eies, eares, & mouth:
his preſent and abſent All. She frames
her nature vnto his howſoeuer : the
Hiacinth followes not the *Sunne* more
willingly. Stubborneneſſe and obſti-
nacy, are hearbes that grow not in her
garden. She leaues ratling, to the goſſips of the town, and is more ſeen then
heard· Her houſhold is her charge, her
care to that, makes her ſeldome *non re-*
ſident. Her pride is but to be clenly, and
her thrift not to be prodigal. By her diſ-
E 3   cretion

cretion fhee hath children , not wan-
tons ; a Husband without her, is a mifery in mans apparell : none but fhee
hath an aged husband, to whom fhe is
both a ftaffe and a chaire. To conclude, fhee is both wife and religious,
which makes her all this.

A Melancholy man

IS a ftraier from the droue : one that
nature made fociable, becaufe fhee
made him man, and a crazed difpofition hath altered. Impleafing to all, as
all to him ; ftragling thoughts are his
content, they make him dreame wa-
king, there's his pleafure. His imagination is neuer idle, it keepes his minde
in a continuall motion, as the poife the
clocke : hee windes vp his thoughts often, and as often vnwindes them ; *Pe-
nelopes* webbe thriues fafter. Hel'e feldome bee found without the fhade of
some

some groue, in whose bottome a riuer
dwells. He carries a cloud in his face,
neuer faire weather: his outside is framed to his inside, in that hee keepes a
Decorum, both vnseemly. Speake to
him; he heares with his eyes, eares follow his mind, and that's not at leasure.
Hee thinkes businesse, but neuer does
any: he is al contemplation, no action.
Hee hewes and fashions his thoughts,
as if he meant them to some purpose,
but they proue vnprofitable, as a piece
of wrought timber to no vse. His Spirits and the Sunne are enemies; the
Sunne bright and warme, his humor
blacke and cold: varietie of foolish
apparitions people his head, they suffer
him not to breath, according to the
necessities of nature; which makes him
sup vp a draught of as much aire at
once, as would serue at thrice. Hee
denies nature her due in sleepe, and
ouer-paies her with watchfulnesse:
nothing pleaseth him long, but that
which pleaseth his owne fantasies:

E 4   they

they are the confuming euills, and euill confumptions, that confume him aliue. Laftly, he is a man onely in fhew, but comes fhort of the better part; a whole reafonable foule, which is mans chiefe preheminence, and fole marke from creatures fenfible.

A Sailor

IS a pitcht peece of reafon calkt and tackled, and onely ftudied to difpute with tempefts. He is part of his owne Prouifion, for he liues euer pickled. A fore-winde is the fubftance of his Creed; and frefh water the burden of his prayers. He is naturally ambitious, for he is euer climing: out of which as naturally hee feares; for he is euer fly-ing: time and he are euery where, euer contending who fhall arriue firft: he is well winded, for he tires the day, and out-runnes darkneffe. His life is like a *Hawkes*, the beft part mewed; and if

he

he liue till three coates, is a Maſter. He
ſees Gods wonders in the deep : but ſo
as rather they appeare his play-fel-
lowes, then ſtirrers of his zeale: nothing
but hunger and hard rockes can con-
uert him, and then but his vpper deck
neither ; for his hold neither feares nor
hopes. his ſleeps are but repreeuals of
his dangers, and when he awakes, tis
but next ſtage to dying. His wiſdome
is the coldeſt part about him, for it euer
points to the North : and it lies loweſt,
which makes his valour euery tide ore-
flow it. In a ſtorme tis diſputable, whether the noiſe bee more his, or the Elements, and which will firſt leaue ſcol-
ding ; on which ſide of the ſhip he may
bee ſaued beſt, wherether his faith be
ſtarre-boord faith, or lar-boord : or the
helme at that time not all his hope of
heauen : his keel is the Embleme of his
conſcience, till it be ſplit hee neuer re-
pents, then no farther then the land
allowes him, and his language is a new
confuſion : and all his thoughts new
                                    nations

nations : his bodie and his ſhip are both one burthen, nor is it known who ſtowes moſt wine, or rowles moſt, only the ſhip is guided, he has no ſterne : a barnacle and hee are bred together both of one nature, and tis fear'd one reaſon: vpon any but a woodden horſe hee cannot ride, and if the winde blow againſt him he dare not : he ſwarues vp to his ſeat as to a ſayle-yarde, and cannot ſit vnleſſe he beare a flag ſtaffe: if euer he be broken to the ſaddle, tis but a voyage ſtill, for he miſtakes the bridle for a bowlin, and is euer turning his horſe taile : he can pray, but tis by rote, not faith, and when he would hee dares not, for his brackiſh beleefe hath made that *ominous.* A rocke or a quick-ſand plucke him before hee be ripe, elſe hee is gathered to his friends at Wapping.

A *Soul-*

A Souldier

IS the husband-man of valour, his sword is his plough, which honor & *aqua-vitæ*, two fiery mettald iades, are euer drawing. A younger brother best becomes Armes; an elder, the thankes for them; euery heat makes him a harueft: and difcontents abroad are his Sowers: he is actiuely his Princes, but paffiuely his angers feruant. Hee is often a defirer of learning, which once arriued at, proues his ftrongeft armor: hee is a louer at all points; and a true defender of the faith of women: more wealth then makes him feeme a handfome foe, lightly he couets not, leffe is below him: he neuer truely wants, but in much hauing, for then his eafe and letchery afflict him: the word *Peace*, though in prayer, makes him ftart, and God he beft confiders by his power: hunger and cold ranke in the fame file with

with him, and hold him to a man : his
honour elſe, and the deſire of doing
things beyond him, would blow him
greater then the ſonnes of A*nack*. His
religion is, commonly, as his cauſe is
(doubtful) and that the beſt deuotion
keeps beſt quarter : he ſeldom ſees gray
haires,ſome none at all, for where the
ſword faiٍes, there the fleſh giues fire :
in charity, he goes beyond the Clergy,
for hee loues his greateſt enemy beſt,
much drinking. He ſeemes a full Stu-
dent,for he is a great deſirer of controuerſies, hee argues ſharply,and carries
his concluſion in his ſcabbard ; in the
firſt refining of mankind this was the
gold, his actions are his ammell. His
alay (for elſe you cannot worke him
perfectly)continuall duties, heauy and
weary marches, lodgings as full of
neede as cold diſeaſes. No time to argue, but to execute. Line him with
theſe, and linke him to his ſquadrons,
and he appeares a moſt rich chaine for
Princes.

                                    A *Taylor*

A Taylor

IS a creature made vp of shreds, that were pared off from *Adam*, when he was rough cast. The end of his Being differeth from that of others, and is not to serue God, but to couer sinne. Other mens pride is his best Patron, and their negligence, a maine passage to his profit. Hee is a thing of more then ordinarie iudgement: For by vertue of that, hee buieth land, buildeth houses and raiseth the lowe set roofe of his crosse legged Fortune. His actions are strong incounters, and for their notoriousnesse alwaies vpon Record. It is neither *Amadis de Gaule*, nor the Knight of the *Sunne*, that is able to resist them. A tenne groates fee setteth them on foote, and a brace of Officers bringeth them to execution. He handleth the Spanish Pike, to the hazard of many poore Egyptian vermins ; and

in

in ſhew of his valour, ſcorneth a greater Gantlet, then will couer the toppe
of his middle-finger. Of all weapons
he moſt affecteth the long Bill, & this
he will manage to the great preiudice
of a Cuſtomers eſtate. His ſpirit not-
withſtanding is not ſo much as to
make you thinke him man; like a true
mongrell, he neither bites nor barkes,
but when your backe is towards him.
His heart is a lumpe of congealed
ſnow : *Prometheus* was a ſleepe while it
was making. He differeth altogether
from God; for with him the beſt peeces are ſtil marked out for Damnation,
and without hope of recouery ſhall
be caſt downe into hell. Hee is partly
an Alchimiſt ; for hee extracteth his
owne apparell out of other mens clothes ; and when occaſion ſerueth,
making a brokers ſhop his Alembike,
can turne your ſilkes into gold , and
hauing furniſhed his neceſſities , after
a moneth or two if he be vrg'd vnto it,
reduce them againe to their proper
ſubſtance

fubftance . Hee is in part likewife an Arithmetician , cunning enough in Multiplication and addition , but can not abide fubftraction : *Summa totalis*, is the language of his *Canaan* ; *& vfq̃ ad vltimum quadrantem* , the period of all his Charitie. For any skill in *Geometrie*, I dare not commend him ; For he could neuer yet finde out the dimenfions of his owne confcience: Notwith-ftanding he hath many bottoms , it feemeth this is alwaies bottomleffe. He is double yarded , and yet his female complaineth of want of meafure. And fo, with a *Libera nos à malo*; I leaue you, promifing to amend whatfoeuer is amiffe, at his next fetting

A Puritane

IS a difeas'd peece of *Apocripha*: bind him to the Bible , and hee corrupts the whole text: Ignorance , & fat feed, are

are his Founders; his Nurſes, Railing,
Rabbies, and round breeches: his life
is but a borrowed blaſt of winde ; For
betweene two religions, as betweene
two doores, he is euer whiſtling. Truly whoſe childe he is , is yet vnknown;
For willingly his faith allowes no Father: onely thus farre his pedegree is
found, Bragger and he flouriſht about
a time firſt ; his fierie zeale keepes him
continuall coſtiue, which withers him
into his owne tranſlation, and till hee
eate a Schooleman, he is hidebound;
hee euer prayes againſt *Non Reſidents*,
but is himſelfe the greateſt diſconti-
nuer, for hee neuer keepes neere his
text: any thing that the Law allowes,
but Marriage, and March-beere, hee
murmures at ; what it diſallowes and
holds dangerous, makes him a diſci-
pline. Where the gate ſtands open,
he is euer ſeeking a ſtile: and where his
Learning ought to climbe, he creepes
through ; giue him aduice, you runne
into *Traditions*, and vrge a modeſt
                                        courſe

courſe, he cries out *Councels*. His greateſt care is to contemne obedience, his
laſt care to ſerue God, handſomely and
cleanly; He is now become ſo croſſe a
kinde of teaching , that ſhould the
Church enioine cleane ſhirts, he were
lowſie : more ſenſe then ſingle prayers
is not his; nor more in thoſe, then ſtill
the ſame petitions : from which hee
either feares a learned faith, or doubts
God vnderſtands not at firſt hearing.
Shew him a Ring, he runs backe like a
Beare; and hates ſquare dealing as al-
lied to caps, a paire of Organs blow
him out o'th Pariſh, and are the onely
gliſter-pipes to coole him. Where the
meate is beſt , there he confutes moſt,
for his arguing is but the efficacy of his
eating : good bits hee holds breedes
good poſitions , and the Pope he beſt
concludes againſt, in Plum-broth. He
is often drunke, but not as we are, tem-
porally, nor can his ſleepe then cure
him, for the fumes of his ambition
make his very Soule reele , and that
F ſmall

ſmall Beere that ſhould allay him (ſilence) keeps him more ſurfeited, and
makes his heate breake out in priuate
houſes : women and Lawyers are his
beſt Diſciples,the one next fruit, longs
for forbidden Doctrine, the other to
maintain forbidden titles, both which
he ſowes amongſt them. Honeſt hee
dare not be, for that loues order : yet
if he can be brought to Ceremonie,&
made but maſter of it, he is conuerted.

A whoore

IS a hie way to the Diuell, hee that
lookes vpon her with deſire, begins
his voiage : he that ſtaies to talke with
her, mends his pace, and who enioyes
her is at his iourneys end : Her body is
the tilted Lees of pleaſure, daſht ouer
with a little decking to hold colour:
taſt her ſhe's dead, and fals vpon the
pallate; the ſins of other women ſhew
in

in Landſcip,far off and full of ſhadow,
hers in Statue, neere hand,and bigger
in the life : ſhe prickes betimes, for her
ſtocke is a white thorne, which cut and
grafted on, ſhe growes a Medler : Her
trade is oppoſite to any other, for ſhee
ſets vp without credit, and too much
cuſtome breakes her; The mony that
ſhe gets is like a traitors, giuen only to
corrupt her, and what ſhe gets, ſerues
but to pay diſeaſes. She is euer moo'rd
in ſinne, and euer mending, and after
thirty, ſhe is the Chirurgions creature,
ſhame and Repentance are two ſtrangers to her,and only in an hoſpitall acquainted : ſhe liues a Reprobate, like
Caine, ſtill branded, finding no habi-
tation but her feares, and flies the face
of Iuſtice like a Fellon. The firſt yeare
of her trade ſhee is an Eyeſſe, ſcratches
and cries to draw on more affection :
the ſecond Soare : the third a Ramage
whoore : the fourth and fifth, ſhe's an
intermewer, preies for her ſelfe, and
ruffles all ſhe reaches; from thence to

F 2 tenne

tenne fhee beares the name of white
Whoore, for then her bloud forfakes
her with falt Rheumes, and now fhee
has mewd three coates ; Now fhee
growes weary and difeas'd together,
fauours her wing, checks little, but lies
for it, bathes for her health, & fcoures
to keepe her coole, yet ftill fhe takes in
ftones, fhe fires her felfe elfe : the next
remoue is Haggard, ftil more cunning;
and if my art deceiue mee not, more
crazie. All cares and cures are doubled
now vpon her, and line her perch , or
now fhe mews her pounces, at all thefe
yeares fhee flyes at fooles and kils too :
the next is Buffard Bawde , and there
I leaue her.

A very whore

IS a woman. She enquires out all the
great meetings , which are medi-
cines for her itching. She kiffeth o-
pen

pen mouth'd, and spits in the palmes of
her hands to make them moyst. Her
eyes are like free-booters liuing vpon
the spoyle of stragglers; and she baites
her desires with a million of prostitute
countenances, and entisements; in the
light she listneth to parlies : but in the
darke she vnderstands signes best. She
will sell her smocke for Cuffes , and so
her shooes be fine, she cares not thogh
her stockings want feet. Her modesty
is curiositie, and her smell is one of her
best ornaments. She passeth not a span
breadth. And to haue done, she is the
Cook and the meate, dressing her selfe
all day , to bee tasted with the better
appetite at night.

A meere Common Lawyer

IS the best shadow to make a dif-
creet one shew the fairer. He is a
Materia prima informed by reports,
E 3   actuated

actuated by statutes, and hath his Motion by the fauourable Intelligence of the Court. His law is alwaies furnisht with a Commission to arraigne his Conscience : but vpon iudgement giuen, he vsually sets it at large. He thinks no language worth knowing but his *Barragouin.*   Onely for that point hee hath been a long time at warres with *Priscian* for a Northerne Prouince. He imagines that by superexcellencie his profession only is learning, and that it's a prophanation of the temple to his *Themis* dedicated, if any of the liberall Arts be there admitted to offer strange incense to Her. For indeed hee is al for money. Seuen or eight yeares squires him out, some of his Nation lesse standing : and euer since the Night of his Call, he forgot much what he was at dinner. The next morning his man (in *Actu* or *potentia*) enioyes his pickadels. His Landresse is then shrewdly troubled in fitting him a Ruffe; His perpetuall badge. His loue-letters of
the

the laſt yeare of his Gentlemanſhip are
ſtuft with *Diſcontinuances* , *Remitters,*
and *Vncore priſts* : but now being ena-
bled to ſpeake in proper perſon , hee
talkes of a French hood, in ſtead of a
Iointure, wages his law , and ioines
iſſue. Then he begins to ſticke his letters in his ground Chamber window;
that ſo the ſuperſcription may make
his Squire-ſhip tranſparent. His He-
raldry giues him place before the Mi-
niſter, becauſe the Law was before the
Goſpell. Next Terme hee walkes his
hoopſleeue gowne to the Hall; there
it proclaimes him. He feeds fat in the
Reading, and till it chances to his turn,
diſlikes no houſe order ſo much , as
that the month is ſo contracted to a
fortnight. Mongſt his countrey neighbours, he arrogates as much honor for
being Reader of an Inne of Chancery, as if it had been of his owne houſe.
For they, poore ſoules, take Law and
Conſcience, Court and Chancery for
all one. He learnd to frame his Caſes

F 4   from

from putting Riddles and imitating *Merlins* Prophefies, and fo fet all the Croffe-row together by the eares. Yet his whole Lawe is not able to decide *Lucians* one olde controuerfie 'twixt *Tau* and *Sigma.* He accounts no man of his Cap and coate idle, but who trots not the Circuit. Hee affects no life or quality for it felfe, but for gaine; and that at leaft, to the ftating him in a Iuftice of peacefhip,which is the firft quickning foule fuperadded to the elementary and inanimate forme of his new Title. His Termes are his wiues vacations. Yet fhee then may vfurpe diuers Court-daies, and hath her *Re* turnes *in Menfem*, for writs of entry; often fhorter. His vacations are her Termers. But in Affife time (the circuit being long) he may haue a tryall at home againft him by *Nifi Prius.* No way to heauen, he thinkes, fo wife, as through *weft-minfter Hall*; and his Clarkes commonly through it vifit both heauen and hell. Yet then he oft
forgets

forgets his iourneis end, although hee
looke on the *Starre-Chamber*. Neither
is hee wholly deftitute of the Arts.
Grammer he hath, enough to make ter-
minations of thofe words which his
authoritie hath endenizon'd. *Rhetorike*
fome ; but fo little , that its thought a
concealement.*Logike* enough to wran-
gle. *Arithmetike* enough for the Ordi-
nals of his yeere-bookes, and number-
roles:but he goes not to *Multiplication*;
there's a Statute againft it. So much
Geometrie, that he can aduice in a *Per-
ambulatione facienda* ; or a *Rationalibus
diuifis*. In *Aftronomy* and *Aftrologie* he
is fo far feene , that by the *Dominicall*
letter, he knowes the Holy-dayes, and
finds by Calculation that *Michaelmas*
Terme will be long and dirty. Marry,
he knowes fo much in *Mufique*,that he
affects onely the moft and cunningeft
Difcords ; rarely a perfect *Concord*,efpe-
cially fong, except *in fine*. His skill in
Perfpectiue endeauours much to deceiue the eye of the Lawe, and giues
many

many falſe colours. He is ſpecially pra-
ctiſed in *Necromancy*, (ſuch a kinde as
is out of the Statute of *Primo*) by raiſing
many *dead Queſtions.* What ſufficien-
cy he hath in *Criticiſme*, the fowle Copies of his *Speciall Pleas* will tell you.

Many of the ſame coat, which are
much to be honoured, partake of diuers of his indifferent qualities, but ſo,
that *Diſcretion*, *vertue*, and ſometimes
other *good learning*, concurring and di-
ſtinguiſhing Ornaments to them, make
them as a foyle, to ſet their worth on.

A Meere Scholler.

A *Meere Scholler is an intelligible Aſſe*:
Or a ſilly fellow in blacke, that
ſpeakes Sentences more familiarly
then Senſe. The Antiquity of his
Vniuerſity is his Creed, and the excel-
lency of his Colledge (though but for
a match at Foot-ball) an Article of his
faith :

faith : he ſpeakes Latine better then his
Mother-tongue; and is a ſtranger in no
part of the world, but his own Coun-
trey:he do's vſually tell great ſtories of
himſelf to ſmal purpoſe,for they are cõ-
monly ridiculous, be they true or falſe:
his Ambition is,that hee either is, or
ſhall be a graduate : but if euer he get
a Fellowſhip, hee ha's then no fellow.
In ſpight of al *Logick* he dare ſweare &
maintaine it, that a Cuckold and a
Townſ-man are *Termini conuertibiles*,
though his Mothers Husband bee an
Alderman : he was neu beregotten (as
it ſeemes) without much wrangling ;
for his whole life is ſpent in *Pro* & *Con-
tra*:his tongue goes alwaies before his
wit, like a Gentleman-vſher,but ſome-
what faſter.That he is a compleat Gallant in all points,*Cap a pea*; witneſſe his
horſemanſhip, and the wearing of his
weapons : he is commonly long-win-
ded, able to ſpeak more with eaſe,then
any man can endure to heare with pa-
tience.Vniuerſity ieſts are his vniuerſall
discourſe,

diſcourſe, and his newes the demeanor
of the Proĉtors: his Phraſe, the apparel
of his minde, is made of diuers ſhreds
like a cuſhion, and when it goes play-
neſt, 't hath a raſh outſide, and Fuſtian
linings. The currant of his ſpeech is
clos'd with an *Ergo*; and what euer be
the queſtion, the trueth is on his ſide.
Tis a wrong to his reputation to be ignorant of any thing; and yet he knows
not that hee knowes nothing : hee
giues direĉtions for Husbandrie from
Virgils Georgicks; for Cattell from his
Bucolicks; for warlike Stratagems, from
his *Aeneides*, or *Cæſars Commentaries* :
hee orders all things by the Booke, is
skilful in all trades, and thriues in none:
he is led more by his eares then his vnderſtanding, taking the ſound of words
for their true ſenſe : and do's therefore
confidently beleeue, that *Erra Pater*
was the Father of hereticks, *Rodolphus
Agricola*, a ſubſtantiall Farmer; and
will not ſticke to auerre, that *Syſtema's
Logicke* doth excell *Keckermans* : his ill
luck

luck is not fo much in being a foole, as in being put to fuch pains to expreffe it to the world: for what in others is naturall, in him (with much adoe) is artificiall: his pouerty is his happineffe, for it makes fome men beleeue, that hee is none of fortunes fauorites. That learning which hee hath, was in Non-age put in backeward like a glifter, and 'tis now like Ware miflayd in a Pedlers packe; a ha's it, but knowes not where it is. In a word, hee is the Index of a man, and the Title-page of a Scholler, or a Puritane in morality, much in profeffion, nothing in practife.

A *Tinker*

IS a mooueable: for he hath no abiding place; by his motiõ he gathers heat, thence his chollericke nature. Hee feemes to be very deuout, for his life is a continuall pilgrimage, and
some-

sometimes in humility goes barefoot,
therein making necessity a vertue. His
house is as ancient as *Tubal Caines*, and
so is a runnagate by antiquity : yet hee
prooues himselfe a Gallant, for he carries all his wealth vpon his backe; or a
Philosopher, for hee beares all his substance about him. From his Art was
Musicke first inuented, and therefore is
hee alwayes furnisht with a song : to
which his hammer keeping tune,
prooues that he was the first founder of
the Kettle-drumme. Note that where
the best Ale is, there stands his musick
most vpon crotchets. The companion
of his trauels is some foule sunne-burnt
Queane, that since the terrible Statute
recanted Gypsisme, and is turned Ped-
leresse. So marches he al ouer England
with his bag and baggage. His conuersation is vnreproueable; for he is euer
mending. He obserues truely the Statutes, and therefore he had rather steale
then begge, in which he is vnremoue-
ably constant in spight of whips or im-
prison-

prifonment : and fo a ftrong enemy to idleneffe, that in mending one hole,he had rather make three then want work; and when hee hath done, he throwes the Wallet of his faults behinde him. Hee embraceth naturally ancient cuftomes, conuerfing in open fields, and lowly Cottages. If he vifit Citties or Townes, tis but to deale vpon the imperfeÆtions of our weaker veffels. His tongue is very voluble, which with Canting prooues him a *Linguift.* He is entertain'd in euery place, but enters no further then the doore,to auoid fufpicion. Some would take him to be a Coward; but beleeue it,hee is a Lad of mettle, his valor is commonly three or foure yards long,faftned to a pike in the end for flying off. He is very prouident, for he will fight but with one at once, and then alfo he had rather fubmit then be counted obftinate. To conclude,if he fcape Tiburne and Banbury, he dies a begger.

An

An Apparatour

IS a Chick of the egge Abuse, hatcht
by the warmth of authority : he is a
bird of rapine, and begins to prey,
and feather together. He croakes like
a Rauen againſt the death of rich men,
and ſo gets a Legacy vnbequeath'd; his
happineſſe is in the multitude of children, for their increaſe is his wealth;
and to that end, hee himſelfe yeerely
adds one. He is a cunning hunter, vn-
couping his intelligencing hounds, vnder hedges, in thickets, and corn-fields,
who follow the chaſe to City-Suburbs,
where often his game is at couert: his
quiuer hangs by his ſide, ſtuft with ſil-
uer arrowes, which he ſhootes againſt
Church-gates, and priuate mens dores,
to the hazard of their purſes & credit.
There went but a paire of ſheeres betweene him and the Purſiuant of hell,
for they both delight in ſinne, growe
richer

richer by it, and are by iuſtice appointed to puniſh it : onely the Diuell is
more cunning , for he pickes a liuing
out of others gaines. His liuing lieth in
his eyes, which (like ſpirits) he ſends
through chinkes , and key-holes , to
ſuruey the places of darkeneſſe ; for
which purpoſe he ſtudyeth the opticks,
but can diſcouer no colour but blacke,
for the pure white of chaſtity dazleth
his eyes. He is a Catholicke, for he is
euery where ; and with a Politicke, for
he transforms himſelfe into all ſhapes.
He trauels on foot to auoid idleneſſe,
and loues the Church entirely, becauſe
it is the place of his edification. He accounts not all ſinnes mortall: for fornication with him is a veniall ſinne , and
to take bribes a matter of charity : hee
is colleſtor for burnings , and loſſes at
Sea, and in caſting account, can readi-
ly ſubtraſt the leſſer from the greater
ſumme. Thus liues he in a golden age,
till death by a proceſſe, ſummons him
to appeare.

G *An*

An Almanacke-maker

IS the worſt part of an Aſtronomer :
a creature compact of figures, characters, and cyphers : out of which
he ſcores the fortune of a yeere, not ſo
profitably, as doubtfully. He is tenant
by cuſtome to the Planets,of whom he
holds the 12. Houſes by leaſe parol : to
them he payes yearely rent, his ſtudy,
and time; yet lets them out again(with
all his heart) for 40. s.*per annum*. His
life is meerely contemplatiue : for his
practiſe , tis woorth nothing , at leaſt
not worthy of credit ; & (if by chance)
he purchaſe any , he loſeth it againe at
the yeeres end,for time brings truth to
light. *Ptolomy* and *Ticho- Barche* are his
Patrŏs, whoſe volumes he vnderſtands
not, but admires ; and the rather becauſe they are Strangers , and ſo eaſier
to be credited , then controul'd. His
life is vpright, for he is alwaies looking
vpward;

vpward; yet dares beleeue nothing a-
boue *Primum mobile*, for tis out of the
reach of his *Iacobs ſtaffe*. His charity
extends no further then to mounte-
banks and Sow-gelders, to whom hee
bequeathes the ſeaſons of the yeere, to
kill or torture by. The verſes in his
Booke haue a worſe pace then euer had
Rochester Hackney : for his Proſe, 'tis
dappled with Inke-horne tearmes, and
may ſerue for an Almanacke : but for
his iudging at the vncertainty of weather, any olde Shepheard ſhall make a
Dunce of him. He would be thought
the diuels Intelligēcer for ſtoln goods :
if euer he ſteale out of that quality, as
a flie turnes to a Maggot,ſo the corruption of the cunning-man is the generation of an Empiricke : his workes flye
foorth in ſmall volumes, yet not all,for
many ride poſt to Chaundlers and Tobacco ſhops in Folio. To be briefe, he
fals 3. degrees ſhort of his promiſes;
yet is hee the Key to vnlocke Termes,
and Law-dayes, a dumbe *Mercury* to

point out high-waies, and a bayliffe of
all Marts and Faires in England. The
reſt of him you ſhall know next yeere;
for what hee will be then, hee himſelfe
knowes not.

An Hypocrite

IS a gilded *Pill*, compoſ'd of two vertuous ingredients, *Naturall diſhoneſty* and *Artificiall diſſimulation*. *Simple Fruit*, *plant* or *Drug*, he is none, but
a deformed mixture, bred betwixt *E-
uil Nature* and *falſe Art*, by a monſtrous
generation ; and may well bee put into
the reckoning of thoſe creatures that
God neuer made. In *Church* or *Com-
mon-welth*, (for in both theſe this *Mon-
grell-weed* will ſhoote) it is hard to ſay
whether he be *Phyſicke* or a *Diſeaſe*: for
hee is both, in diuers reſpects.
　　As he is gilt with an out-ſide of *Seeming purity*, or as he offreth himſelfe to
you

you to be taken downe in a cup or taste
of *Golden zeale* and *Simplicity*, you may
call him *physicke*. Nay, and neuer let
potion giue *Patient* good stoole, if being
truly tasted and rellisht, hee be not as
loathsome to the stomake of any honest man.

He is also *Physicke*, in being as com-
modious for vse, as he is odious in tast,
if the *Body* of the *company* into which he
is taken, can make true vse of him. For
the malice of his nature makes him so
Informer-like-dangerous, in taking aduantage, of any thing done or sayd:
yea, euen to the ruine of his makers, if
he may haue Benefit; that such a creature in a society makes men as carefull
of their speeches and actions, as the
sight of a known Cut-purse in a throng
makes them watchfull ouer their purses and pockets: he is also in this respect
profitable Physicke, that his conuersation being once truely tasted and dis-
couered, the hatefull foulenesse of it wil
make those that are not fully like him,

to

to purge all ſuch Diſeaſes as are ranke
in him, out of their owne liues ; as the
ſight of ſome Citizens on horſe-back,
makes a iudicious man amend his own
faults in horſemanſhip. If none of theſe
vſes can bee made of him, let him not
long offend the ſtomake of your company; your beſt way is to ſpue him out.
That he is a Diſcaſe in the body where
he liueth, were as ſtrange a thing to
doubt, as whether there be knauery in
Horſe-courſers. For, if amongſt Sheep,
the rot; amongſt Dogs, the mange; a-
mongſt Horſes, the glaunders; amōgſt
Men & VVomen the Northerne itch,
and the French Ache be diſeaſes ; an
Hypocrite cannot but be the like in all
States and Societies that breede him.
If he be a Cleargy Hypocrite, then all
manner of vice is for the moſt part ſo
proper to him, as he will grudge any
man the praɛtiſe of it but himſelfe; like
that graue Burgeſſe, who being deſired
to lend his cloathes to repreſent a part
in a Comedy, anſwered: *No, by his*
leaue,

leaue, hee would haue no body play the foole in his cloathes but himselfe. Hence are his so austere reprehēsions of drinking healths,lasciuious talke, vsury and vn-conscionable dealing; when as himself hating the profane mixture of malt & water,will by his good will let nothing come within him, but the purity of the Grape, when he can get it of anothers cost : But this must not bee done nei-ther, without a preface of seeming lothnesse, turning vp the eyes, mouing the head,laying hand on the brest,and protesting that he would not doe it,but to strengthen his body, being euen cō-sumed with dissembled zeale, and te-dious and thanklesse babling to God and his Auditors. And for the other vices, do but venture the making your selfe priuate with him, or trusting of him, & if you come off without a fauor of the aire which his soule is infected with, you haue great fortune. The far-dle of all this ware that is in him, you shall commonly see carried vpon the

G 4   backe

backe of thefe two beafts, that liue within him, *Ignorance* and *Imperiouf-neffe* : and they may well ferue to carry other vices, for of themfelues they are infupportable. His *Ignorance* acquites him of all fcience, humane or diuine, and of all Language, but his mothers; holding nothing pure, holy or fincere, but the fenfeleffe collections of his owne crazed braine, the zealous fumes of his inflamed fpirit, and the endleffe labors of his eternall tong; the motions wherof, when matter and words faile,(as they often doe)muft be patched vp, to accomplifh his foure houres in a day at the leaft, with long and feruent *hummes*. Any thing elfe, either for language or matter he cannot abide, but thus cenfureth : *Latine*, the language of the *Beaft* ; *Greeke*, the tongue wherin the heathen Poets wrot their fictions; *Hebrue*, the fpeech of the *Iewes*, that crucified Chrift : *Controuerfies* doe not edifie, *Logicke* and *Philofophy*, are the fubtilties of *Sathan*, to deceiue

ceiue the *Simple*. Humane ſtories *profane*, and not ſauouring of the *Spirit* :
In a word, all decent and ſenſible
forme of Speech & perſwaſion (thogh
in his owne tongue) vaine *Oſtentation*.
And all this is the burthen of his *Ignorance* : ſauing that ſometimes *Idleneſſe* will put in alſo, to beare a part of
the baggage.

His other *Beaſt Imperiouſneſſe*, is yet
more proudly loaden, it carrieth a
burthen, that no cords of *Authoritie*,
Spirituall nor *Temporall* ſhould binde,
if it might haue the full ſwindge : No
Pilate, no *Prince* ſhould cōmand him :
Nay, he will command them, and at
his pleaſure cenſure them, if they will
not ſuffer their eares to bee fettered
with the long chaines of his tedious
collations, their purſes to be emptied
with the inundations of his vnſatiable
humour, and their iudgements to bee
blinded with the muffler of his *zealous
Ignorance*. For this doth he familiarly
inſult ouer his *Maintainer* that breedes
him,

him, his *Patrone* that feedes him, and in time ouer all them that will suffer him to set a foote within their doores, or put a finger in their purses. All this, and much more is in him, that abhorring *Degrees* & *Vniuersities*, are reliques of *Superstition*, hath leapt from a Shopboord, or a Cloke-bag, to a Deske, or Pulpit, and that like a Sea-god in a *Pageant*, hath the rotten laths of his culpable life, and palpable ignorance, couered ouer with the painted cloth of a pure gown, and a night-cap; and with a false Trumpet of *Fained zeale*, draweth after him some poore *Nimphes* and *Madmen*, that delight more to resort to darke Caues and secret places, then to open and publike assemblies. The *Lay-Hypocrite*, is to the other a *Champion, Disciple* and *Subiect*; and will not acknowledge the tythe of the *Subiection*, to any *Miter*; no, not to any *Scepter*, that he will do to the hook and crooke of his zeale-blinde Shepheard. No *Iesuites* demand more blinde and absolute

lute obedience from their vaffals; no
Magiftrates of the *Canting* fociety,
more flauiſh fubiection from the members of that trauelling ſtate, then the
Clerke *Hypocrites* expect from theſe
lay Pupils. Nay, they muſt not onely
be obeyed, fedde, and defended, but
admired too : and that their Lay followers doe as fincerely, as a ſhirtleſſe
fellow with a Cudgell vnder his arme
doth a face-wringing *Ballet-finger*; a
water-bearer on the floore of a Play-
houſe, a wide-mouth'de *Poet*, that
ſpeaks nothing but bladders and bum-
baſt. Otherwiſe, for life and profeſſi-
on, nature and Art, inward and outward, they agree in all, like *Canters* and
Gypfies: they are all *zeale*, no *knowledge* :
all purity, no humanity : all fimplicity,
no honefty : and if you neuer truſt
them, they will neuer deceiue you.

A Maque-

A *Maquerela*, *in plaine English a Bawd*

IS an old *Char-cole*, that hath beene burnt her selfe, and therefore is able to kindle a whole greene Coppice. The burden of her song is like that of *Frier Bacons* Head ; *Time is, Time was, and Time is past*: in repeating which, she makes a wicked brazen face, & weepes in the cuppe, to allay the heate of her *Aqua-vitæ*. Her teeth are falne out ; mary her nose, and chin, intend very shortly to be friends, and meet about it. Her yeares are sixty and odde : that she accounts her best time of trading; for a *Bawde* is like a Medlar, shee's not ripe, till shee be rotten. Her enuy is like that of the Diuell, to haue all faire women like her ; and because it is impossible they should catch it being so young, shee hurries them to it by diseases. Her *Parke* is a villanous barren ground ; and all the Deere in it are
Rascall :

Characters. 139

Rascall : yet poore Cotagers in the Countrey (that knowe her but by heare-say) thinke well of her; for what she inclofes to day, she makes *Common* to morrow. Her goods and her selfe are all remou'd in one fort, onely shee makes bold to take the vpper hand of them, and to be Carted before them; the thought of which, makes her shee cannot indure a poffet, becaufe it puts her in mind of a Bafon. She fits continually at a rackt Rent; efpecially, if her *Landlord* beare office in the Parifh: for her moueables in the houfe; (befides her quicke cattell) they are not worth an *Inuentory*, onely her beds are moft commonly in print : shee can eafily turne a fempftreffe, into a waiting gentlewoman, but her Warde-robe is moft infectious, for it brings them to the *Falling-fickneffe*: she hath only this one shew of *Temprance*, that let a Gendeman fend for tenne pottles of wine in her houfe, hee shall haue but tenne quarts; and if he want it that way, let

him

him pay for't, and take it out in ſtewde prunes. The Iuſtices Clark ſtands many times her very good friend : and workes her peace with the Iuſtice of *Quorum.* Nothing ioyes her ſo much, as the comming ouer of *Strangers,* nor daunts her ſo much as the approach of Shroue-tueſday. In fine, not to foule more paper with ſo foule a ſubieƈt, hee that hath paſt vnder her , hath paſt the *Equinoƈtiall ;* Hee that hath ſcap't her, hath ſcap't worſe then the *Calenture.*

A Chamber-maide.

SHe is her miſtreſſes ſhe Secretary, and keeps the box of her teeth, her haire,& her painting very priuate. Her induſtry is vp-ſtaires, and downeſtaires like a Drawer : and by her dry hand you may know ſhe is a ſore ſtarcher. If ſhe lye at her Maſters beds feet, ſhe is quit of the *Greeneſickeneſſe* for euer;

uer ; For fhee hath terrible dreames
when fhe is awake, as if fhe were troubled with the *night Mare.* She hath a
good liking to dwell ith Countrey, but
fhe holds *London* the goodlieft Forreft
in *England*, to fhelter a great belly. She
reads *Greenes* works ouer and ouer, but
is fo carried away with *the Myrrour of
Knighthood*, fhe is many times refolu'd
to run out of her felfe, and become a
Lady Errant. If fhe catch a clap, fhe
diuides it fo equally betweene the Mafter and the Seruingman, as if fhe had
cut out the getting of it by a Threed :
onely the knaue *Sumner* makes her
bowle booty, and ouer-reach the Mafter. The pedant of the houfe, though
he promife her marriage, cannot grow
further inward with her, fhe hath paide
for her credulity often, and now grows
weary. Shee likes the forme of our
marriage very well, in that a woman is
not tyed to anfwere to any Articles
concerning queftion of her Virginity :
Her minde, her body, and clothes,

are

are parcels loofely tackt together, and for want of good vtterance, fhe perpetually laughes out her meaning. Her Miftris and fhee helpe to make away *Time*, to the idleft purpofe that can be, either for loue or money. In briefe, thefe *Chambermaides* are like Lotteries: you may draw twenty, ere one worth any thing.

A Precifian.

TO fpeake no otherwife of this *varnifht rottenneffe* then in truth & verity he is, I muft define him to be a demure Creature, full of orall Sanctity, and mentall impietie; a faire obiect to the eye, but ftarke nought for the vnderftanding : or els a violent thing, much giuen to contradiction. He will be fure to be in oppofition with the *Papift*, though it be fometimes accompanied with an abfurdity;
like

like the Ilanders neere adioining vnto *China*, who falute by putting off their fhooes, becaufe the men of *China* do it by their hats. If at any time he faft, it is vpon Sunday, and he is fure to feaft vpon Friday. He can better offord you tenne lyes, then one oath, and dare commit any finne guilded with a pretence of fanctitie. He will not ftick to commit fornication or Adulterie, fo it be done in the feare of God, and for the propagation of the godly; and can finde in his hart to lye with any whore, faue the whore of *Babylon*. To fteale he holds it lawfull, fo it be from the wicked and Ægyptians. He had rather fee *Antichrift*, then a picture in the Church window : and chufeth fooner to be halfe hanged, then fee a legge at the name of *IESVS*, or one ftand at the *Creede*. He conceiues his prayer in the kitchin, rather then in the Church, and is of fo good difcourfe, that hee dares challenge the *Almighty* to talke with him *ex tempore*. He thinks euery

H   Orga-

Organiſt is in the ſtate of damnation, and had rather heare one of *Robert wiſdoms Pſalmes*, then the beſt *Hymne* a *Cherubin* can ſing. He will not breake winde without an *Apologie*, or asking forgiueneſſe, nor kiſſe a Gentlewoman for feare of luſting after her. He hath nicknamde all the Prophets and Apoſtles with his Sonnes, and begets nothing but *Vertues* for Daughters. Finally hee is ſo ſure of his ſaluation, that he will not change places in heauen with the *Virgin Mary*, without boote.

An Innes of Court man.

HE is diſtinguiſhed from a Scholler by a paire of ſilke ſtockings, and a Beauer Hat, which makes him contemne a Scholler as much as a Scholler doth a Scholemaſter. By that he hath heard one mooting, and ſeen two plaies, he thinkes as baſely of the
Vniuerſity

Vniuerfity, as a young *Sophifter* doth of
the *Grammer-fchoole.* He talkes of the
Vniuerfity, with that ftate, as if he were
her Chauncellour; finds fault with al-
terations, and the fall of *Difcipline*,
with an *It was not fo when I was a Stu-
dent*; although that was within this
halfe yeare. He will talke ends of *Latine*, though it be falfe, with as great
confidence, as euer *Cicero* could pro-
nounce an Oration, though his beft
authors for't, be *Tauerns* & *Ordinaries.*
He is as farre behinde a *Courtier* in his
fafhion, as a Scholler is behinde him :
and the beft grace in his behauiour, is
to forget his *acquaintance.*

Hee laughes at euery man whofe
Band fits not well, or that hath not a
faire fhoo-ty, and he is afhamed to be
feene in any mans company that
weares not his clothes well. His very
effence he placeth in his out-fide, and
his chiefeft prayer is, that his reuenues
may hold out for Taffata cloakes in the
Summer, and veluet in the Winter.

For his recreation, hee had rather go to a Citizens Wife, then a Bawdy-houfe, onely to faue charges : and hee holds Fee-taile to bee abfolutely the beft tenure. To his acquaintance hee offers two quarts of wine, for one hee giues· You fhall neuer fee him me-lancholie, but when hee wants a new Suite, or feares a Seriant : At which times only, he betakes himfelfe to *Ploy-don*. By that hee hath read *Littleton*, he can call *Solon*, *Licurgus*, and *Iufti-nian*, fooles, and dares compare his Law to a *Lord Chiefe-iuftices*.

A meere Fellow of an Houfe.

HE is one whofe Hopes cõmon-ly exceed his fortunes, & whofe mind foares aboue his purfe. If he hath read *Tacitus*, *Guicchardine*, or *Gallo-Belgicus*, he contemns the *late lord Treafurer*, for all the ftate-policie hee had;

had; and laughs to thinke what a foole he could make of *Salomon*, if hee were now aliue. Hee neuer weares new cloaths, but againſt a commencement or a good time, and is commonly a degree behind the faſhion. Hee hath ſworne to ſee *London* once a yeare, though all his buſines be to ſee a play, walke a turne in *Paules*, and obſerue the faſhion. He thinkes it a diſcredit to bee out of debt, which hee neuer likely cleeres, without reſignation money. He will not leaue his part he hath in the priuiledge ouer young Gentlemen, in going bare to him, for the Empire of *Germany* : He prayes as heartily for a ſealing, as a *Cormorant* doth for a deare yeare : yet commonly hee ſpends that reuenue before he receiues it.

At meales, he ſits in as great ſtate ouer his *Penny-Commons*, as euer *Vitellius* did at his greateſt Banquet : and takes great delight in comparing his fare to my Lord *Mayors*.

H 3   If

If he be a leader of a *Faction* , hee thinkes himſelfe greater then euer *Cæſar* was, or the *Turke* at this day is. And he had rather looſe an Inheritance then an Office, when hee ſtands for it.

If hee be to trauell, he is longer furniſhing himſelfe for a fiue miles iourney, then a ſhip is rigging for a ſeuen yeares voyage. Hee is neuer more troubled, then when he is to maintaine talke with a Gentle-woman : wherein hee commits more abſurdities , then a clowne in eating of an egge.

Hee thinkes himſelfe as fine when he is in a cleane band, and a new paire of ſhooes, as any Courtier doth, when hee is firſt in a New-faſhion .

Laſtly, hee is one that reſpects no man in the *Vniuerſitie*, and is reſpected by no man out of it.

A

A worthy Commander in the warres

IS one that accounts learning the nourifhment of military vertue, and layes that as his firft foundation. He neuer bloudies his fword but in heat of battell ; and had rather faue one of his owne Souldiers, then kill ten of his enemies. He accounts it an idle, vaine-glorious, and fufpected bounty, to bee full of good words; his rewarding therfore of the deferuer arriues fo timely, that his liberality can neuer be fayd to be gouty handed. He holds it next his Creed, that no Coward can be an honeft man, and dare die in't. Hee doth not think his body yeelds a more fprea-ding fhadow after a victory then before; and when he lookes vpon his enemies dead body, tis with a kinde of noble heauineffe, not infultation; hee is fo honourably mercifull to women in

H 4 furpri-

furprifall, that onely, that makes him an excellent Courtier. He knowes the hazards of battels, not the pompe of Ceremonies, are Souldiers beſt Theaters, & ſtriues to gaine reputation not by the multitude, but by the greatnes of his aċtions. He is the firſt in giuing the charge, and the laſt in retiring his foot. Equall toile he endures with the Common Souldier, from his example they all take fire, as one Torch lights many. He vnderſtands in warre, there is no meane to erre twice; the firſt, and leaſt fault beeing ſufficient to ruine an Army: faults therfore he pardōs none, they that are prefidents of diforder, or mutiny, repaire it by being examples of his *Iuſtice.* Befiege him neuer ſo ſtriċt-ly, ſo long as the ayre is not cut from him, his heart faints not. He hath learned afwel to make vfe of a viċtory as to get it, and in purfuing his enemy like a whirle-wind carries all afore him; being affured, if euer a man will benefit himfelfe vpon his foe, then is the time, when

when they haue loft force, wifedome,
courage and reputation. The goodneffe of his caufe is the fpeciall motiue
to his valour ; neuer is he knowne to
flight the weakeft enemy that comes
arm'd againft him in the hand of *Iuftice*.
Hafty and ouermuch heat he accounts
the *Step-dame* to all great actions, that
wil not fuffer thē to thriue; if he cannot
ouercome his *enemy* by force, he does
it by *Time*. If euer he fhake hands with
warre, hee can dye more calmely then
moft Courtiers, for his continuall dangers haue been as it were fo many me-
ditations of death; hee thinkes not out
of his owne calling, when he accounts
life a continuall warfare, and his prayers then beft become him when armed
Cap a pea. He vtters them like the great
Hebrew Generall, on horfebacke. Hee
cafts a fmiling cōtempt vpon *Calumny*,
it meets him as if *Glaffe* fhould encounter *Adamant*. He thinkes warre is neuer to be giuen ore, but on one of thefe
three conditions : an affured *peace*, ab-
folute

folute *victory*, or an honeft *death*. Laftly, when peace folds him vp, his filuer
head fhould leane neere the golden
Scepter, and die in his *Princes* bofome.

A *vaine-glorious Coward* in Command

IS one that hath bought his place, or
come to it by fome Noble-mans let
ter : hee loues a life dead payes, yet
wifhes they may rather happen in his
Company by the fcuruy, then by a battell. View him at a mufter, and he goes
with fuch noife, as if his body were the
wheelebarrow that carried his iudgement rumbling to drill his Souldiers.
No man can worfe define betweene
Pride and noble *Courtefie* : hee that falutes him not fo farre as a Piftol carries
leuel, giues him the *difguft* or *affront*,
chufe you whether. He traines by the
booke,

book, and reckons fo many poſtures of
the Pike and Musket, as if hee were
counting at Noddy. When he comes
at firſt vpon a Camiſado,he lookes like
the foure windes in painting, as if hee
would blow away the enemy ; but at
the very firſt onſet ſuffers feare & trem-
bling to dreſſe themſelues in his face
apparantly. He ſcorns any man ſhould
take place before him : yet at the en-
tring of a *breach*, he hath been ſo hum-
ble-minded, as to let his Lieutenant
lead his Troopes for him. He is ſo ſure
armed for taking hurt, that he ſeldome
does any: and while hee is putting on
his Armes, he is thinking what ſumme
hee can make to ſatisfie his ranſome.
He wil rail openly againſt all the great
Commanders of the aduerſe party,yet in
his owne conſcience allowes them for
better men : ſuch is the nature of his
feare, that contrary to all other filthy
qualities, it makes him thinke better of
another man then himſelfe. The firſt
part of him that is ſet a running, is his
Eye-

Eye-sight: when that is once struck with terrour, all the *Costiue Physicke* in the world cannot stay him ; if euer he doe any thing beyond his own heart,tis for a *Knighthood,* and he is the first kneeles for't without bidding.

A Pyrate

TRuely defined, is a *bold Traitor,* for he fortifies a castle against the King. Giue him Sea-room in neuer so smal a vessel; & like a witch in a sieue, you would think he were going to make merry with the Diuel. Of all callings his is the most desperate,for he wil not leaue off his theeuing thogh he be in a narrow prison, and look euery day (by tempest or fight) for execution. He is one plague the Diuel hath added, to make the Sea more terrible then a storme; and his heart is so hardned in that rugged element, that hee

cannot

cannot repent, though hee view his
graue (before him) continually open :
he hath ſo little his own, that the houſe
he ſleepes in is ſtolne; all the neceſſities
of life he filches, but one : he cannot
ſteale a ſound ſleepe, for his troubled
conſcience : He is very gentle to thoſe
vnder him, yet his rule is the horribleſt
tyranny in the world : for hee giues licence to all rape, murder, and cruelty
in his owne example : what he gets, is
ſmall vſe to him, onely liues by it, (ſom-
what the longer) to do a little more ſeruice to his belly; for hee throwes away
his treaſure vpon the ſhore in riot, as if
he caſt it into the Sea. Hee is a *cruell*
Hauke that flies at all but his own kind :
and as a *Whale* neuer coms a-ſhore, but
when ſhee is wounded; ſo hee, very ſeldome, but for his neceſſities. He is the
Marchants booke, that ſerues onely to
reckon vp his loſſes ; *a perpetuall plague*
to noble traffique, the *Hurican of the*
Sea, & the *Earth-quake of the Exchange.*
Yet for al this giue him but his pardon,
                                    and

and forgiue him reſtitution, hee may
liue to knowe the inſide of a Church,
and die on this-ſide Wapping.

An ordinarie Fencer

IS a fellow, that beſide ſhauing of
Cudgels, hath a good inſight into
the world, for he hath long been
beaten to it. Fleſh and bloud hee is like
other men; but ſurely nature meant
him *Stockfiſh* : his and a Dancing-
ſchoole are inſeparable adiunĉts; and
are bound, though both ſtinke of ſweat
moſt abominably, neither ſhall complaine of annoiance : three large ba-
uins ſet vp his Trade, with a bench;
which (in the vacation of the after-
nooue) hee vſes for his day-bed; for a
firkin to piſſe in, hee ſhall be allowed
that, by thoſe make *Allom* : when hee
comes on the Stage at his Prize, hee
makes a leg ſeauen ſeuerall waies, and
                              ſcrambles

fcrambles for mouey, as if he had been borne at the *Bathe* in *Somerfet-fhire* : at his challenge hee fhewes his mettalf; for contrarie to all rules of Phyficke,he dare bleed , though it be in the dog-daies : hee teaches *Diuelifh* play in's Schoole, but when he fights himfelfe, he doth it in the feare of a good Chri-ftian. He compounds quarrels among his Schollers, and when hee hath brought the bufines to a good vpfhot, he makes the reckuoning. His wounds are feldom aboue skind-eep; for an in-ward brufe , Lamb-ftones and fweet-breads are his only *Sperma Ceti,* which he eats at night, next his heart fafting : ftrange Schoole-mafters they are, that euery day fet a man as farre backward as he went forward; and throwing him into a ftrange pofture, teach him to threfh *fatisfaction* out of *iniury.* One figne of a good nature is, that he is ftill open breafted to his friends, for his foile,and his doublet, weare not aboue two buttons : and refolute he is, for he

fo

fo much fcorns to take blowes, that he
neuer weares *Cuffes* : and he liues better contented with a little, then other
men; for if he haue two eyes in's head,
he thinks Nature hath ouerdone him.
The Lord *Mayors* triumph makes him
a man, for that's his beft time to flourifh.   Laftly, thefe Fencers are fuch
things, that care not if all the world
were ignorant of more letters then only to read their Patent.

A *Puny-clarke.*

HE is tane from *Grammar-fchoole*
halfe codled, and can hardly
fhake off his dreames of bree-
ching in a twelue-month. He is a Far-
mers fonne, and his fathers vtmoft ambition is to make him an *Atturney*. He
doth itch towards a Poet, and greafes
his breeches extremely with feeding
without a napkin. He ftudies falfe dice
                                        to

to cheat Coftermongers, and is moft chargeable to the butler of fome *Inne of Chancerie*, for piffing in their greene pots. He eats Ginger-bread at a Play-houfe; and is fo fawcie, that he venters fairely for a broken pate at the banque-ting houfe, and hath it. He would ne-uer come to haue any wit, but for a long *vacation*, for that makes him be-thinke him how hee fhall fhift another day. He prayes hotly againft fafting; and fo he may fup wel on friday nights, he cares not though his mafter be a Pu-ritan. He practifes to make the words in his *Declaration* fpread, as a Sewer doth the difhes at a Niggards Table; a Clark of a fwooping *Dafh*, is as com-mendable as a Flanders horf of a large taile. Though you be neuer fo much delai'd, you muft not call his Mafter knaue; that makes him goe beyond himfelfe and write a Challenge in Court hand; for it may bee his owne another day. Thefe are fome certaine of his *liberall faculties* but in the

I   Ternie

Terme time, his *Clog* is a *Buckrom bag.* Laftly, which is great pitty, hee neuer comes to his full growth, with bearing on his fhoulder the finfull burden of his Mafter at feuerall Courts in *Weft-minfter.*

A Foote-man,

LEt him be neuer fo wel made, yet his Legs are not matches, for he is ftil fetting the beftfoot forward He wil neuer be a ftaid man, for he has had a running head of his owne, euer fince his child-hood. His mother (which, out of queftion, was a light heel'd wench) knew it, yer let him run his race, thinking age would reclaime him from his wilde courfes. He is very long winded; and, without doubt, but that he hates naturally to ferue on horf-backe, hee had proued an excellent trumpet. He has one happineffe aboue

al the reſt of the Seruingmen, for when
he moſt ouer-reaches his Maſter, hee's
beſt thought of. He liues more by his
own heat then the warmth of clothes;
and the waiting-woman hath the greateſt fancy to him when hee is in his
cloſe trouſes. Gardes he weares none ;
which makes him liue more vpright
then any groſſe-gartered Gentleman-
vſher. Tis impoſſible to drawe his picture to the life, cauſe a man muſt take
it as he's running; only this, Horſes are
vſually let bloud on S. *Steuens* day : on
S. *Patricks* he takes reſt, and is drencht
for all the yeere after.

A Noble and retired Houſe-keeper,

IS one whoſe bounty is limited by
reaſon, not *oſtentation* : and to make
it laſt, he deales it diſcreetly, as wee
ſowe the *furrow*, not by the ſacke, but

by the handfull.His word and his meaning neuer ſhake hands and part, but
alway goe together. Hee can ſuruay
good, and loue it, and loues to doe it
himſelfe, for it owne ſake, not for
thankes. Hee knowes there is no ſuch
miſerie as to out-liue good name; nor
no ſuch follie as to put it in praĉtiſe.His
minde is ſo ſecure, that *thunder* rockes
him a ſleepe, which breaks other mens
ſlumbers. *Nobilitie* lightens in his eies;
and in his face and geſture is painted,
The god of Hoſpitalitie. His great houſes beare in their front more durance,
then ſtate; vnleſſe this adde the greater ſtate to them, that they promiſe to
out-laſt much of our new phantaſticall
building. His *heart* neuer growes old,
no more then his *memorie* : whether at
his booke, or on horſebacke,he paſſeth
his time in ſuch noble exerciſe, a man
cannot ſay,any time is loſt by him : nor
hath he only *yeares*, to approue he hath
liued till hee be old, but *vertues*. His
thoughts haue a *high aime*, though
their

their dwelling be in the *Vale of an humble heart*; whence, as by an *Engine* (that raifes water to fall, that it may rife the higher) he is heightned in his humility. The *Adamant* ferues not for all Seas, but his doth; for he hath , as it were , put a gird about the whole world, and founded all her *quick-fands*. He hath this hand ouer *Fortune*, that her iniuries, how violent or fudden foeuer, they do not daunt him; for whether his time call him to liue or dye, he can do both nobly:if to fall,his defcent is breaft to breaft with vertue; and euen then, like the *Sunne* neere his Set, he fhewes vnto the world his *cleareft countenance.*

***

I 3   *An Intru-*

An Intruder into fauour

IS one that builds his reputation on
others infamy : for flaunder is
moſt commonly his morning prayer.
His paſſions are guided by *Pride*, and
followed by *Iniuſtice*. An inflexible anger againſt ſome poore ſutor, he falſly
calles a *Couragious conſtancy*, and thinks
the beſt parr of grauity to conſiſt in a
ruffled forehead.   He is the moſt fla-
uiſhly ſubmiſſe ;   though enuious to
thoſe are in better place then himſelfe;
and knowes the Art of words ſo well,
that (for ſhrowding diſhoneſty vnder
a faire pretext) he ſeemes to preſerue
mud in Chryſtall.   Like a man of a
kinde nature , he is firſt good to himſelfe ; in the next file , to his French
Tailor, that giues him all his perfecti-
on:for indeed, like an *Eſtridge*, or *Bird
of Paradiſe*, his feathers are more
worth then his body. If euer hee doe
                                   good

good deede (which is very feldome)
his owne mouth is the *Chronicle* of it,
leaſt it ſhould die forgotten. His whole
body goes all vpon *ſcrewes*, and his
face is the *vice* that moues them. If his
Patron be giuen to muſicke, hee opens
his chops, and *ſings*, or with a wrie
necke falles to tuning his inſtrument:
if that faile, hee takes the height of his
Lord with a Hawking pole. He followes the mans fortune, not the man:
ſeeking thereby to increaſe his owne.
He pretends he is moſt vndeſeruedly
enuied, and cries out, remembring the
game, *Cheſſe*, that a Pawne before a
King is moſt plaid on. Debts he owes
none, but ſhrewd turnes, and thoſe he
paies ere he be ſued. He is a flattering
Glaſſe to conceale age, and wrinkles.
He is *Mountains Monky*, that climbing
a tree, and skipping from bough to
bough, giues you backe his face; but
come once to the top, he holdes his
noſe vp into the winde, and ſhewes
you his tayle: yet all this gay glitter

ſhewes

shewes on him, as if the Sunne shone in a puddle; for hee is a small wine that will not last, and when he is falling, he goes of himselfe faster then misery can driue him.

A faire and happy Milke-mayd,

IS a Countrey Wench, that is so far from making her selfe beautifull by Art, that one looke of hers is able to put *all face Physicke* out of countenance. She knowes a faire looke is but a *dumb Orator* to commend vertue, therefore mindes it not. All her excellencies stand in her so silently, as if they had stolne vpon her without her knowledge. The lining of her apparel (which is her selfe) is far better then outsides of *Tissew*: for though she be not arraied in the spoile of the *Silke-worme*, shee is deckt in *innocence*, a far better wearing. She doth not, with lying long a bed,
spoile

spoile both her *complexion* and *Conditions*; nature hath taught her,too *Immoderate sleepe is ruft to the Soule* : she rises therefore with *Chaunticleare*, her Dames Cocke, and at night makes the *Lambe* her *Courfew*. In milking a Cow, and straining the Teates through her fingers,it seemes that so sweet a Milkepresse makes the Milke the whiter, or sweeter; for neuer came *Almond Gloue or Aromatique Oyntment* on her Palme to taint it. The golden eares of corne fall andkisse her feete when she reapes them, as if they wisht to be bound and led prisoners by the same hand fell'd them. Her breath is her owne,which sents all the yeare long of *Iune*, like a new made Hay-cocke. She makes her hand hard with labour, and her heart soft with pittie : and when winter euenings fall early (sitting at her merry wheele) shee sings a defiance to the giddy *wheele of Fortune*. She doth all things with so sweet a grace, it seemes *ignorance* will not suffer her to doe ill,

being

beeing her minde is to doe well. She
beſtowes her yeares wages at next
faire; and in chooſing her Garments,
counts no brauery i'th' world like decencie. The *Garden* and *Bee-hiue* are
all her *Phyſicke* and *Chyrurgery*, and ſhe
liues the longer for't. Shee dares goe
alone, and vnfold ſheep i'th' night, and
feares no manner of ill, becauſe ſhee
meanes none : yet to ſay truth, ſhee is
neuer alone, for ſhee is ſtill accompanied with old *ſongs*, *honeſt thoughts*, and
prayers, but ſhort ones; yet they haue
their efficacy, in that they are not
pauled with inſuing idle cogitations.
Laſtly, her dreames are ſo chaſte, that
ſhe dare tell them : onely a Fridaies
dreame is all her *ſuperſtition* : that ſhee
conceales for feare of anger. Thus
liues ſhe, and all her care is ſhee may
dye in the *Spring-time*, to haue ſtore of
flowers ſtuck vpon her winding ſheet.

An Arrant Horfe-courfer

HAth the trick to blowe vp Horf-
flefh, as a Butcher doth Veale,
which fhall wafh out againe in
twice riding twixt *waltham* & *London.*
The Trade of Spurre-making had decayed long fince, but for this vngodly
tyre-man. He is curft all ouer rhe foure
ancient High-wayes of England;none
but the blind men that fel fwitches i'th'
Road are beholding to him. His Stable is fill'd with fo many Difeafes, one
would thinke moft part about Smithfield were an Hofpitall for Horfes, or a
flaughter-houfe for the common hunt.
Let him furnifh you with a Hackney,
'tis as much as if the Kings Warrant
ouer-tooke you within ten miles to ftay
your iourney. And though a man can
not fay, he cozens you directly ; yet a-
ny Oftler within ten miles, fhould he
be

be brought vpon his Booke-oath , will affirme hee hath layd a bayt for you. Refolue when you firft ftretch your felfe in the ftirrops, you are put as it were vpon fome Vfurer, that will neuer beare with you paft his day. He were good to make one that had the Collick alight often,and (if example will caufe him)make vrine; let him only for that fay,*Gramercy Horfe*.For his faile of hor-fes, he hath falfe couers for all manner of Difeafes, only comes fhort of one thing (which he defpaires not vtterly to bring to perfection to make a horfe goe on a wodden legge and two crut-ches. For powdring his eares with *Q*uickfiluer, and giuing him fuppofito-ries of liue Eeles he's expert. All the while you are a cheaping he feares you will not bite;but he laughs in his fleeue when he hath cozened you in earneft. French-men are his beft Chapmen,he keeps amblers for them on purpofe, and knowes he can deceiue them very eafily. He is fo conftant to his Trade,
that

that while he is awake, he tires any man
he talkes with, and when hee's asleepe
he dreams very fearefully of the pauing
of Smithfield, for he knowes it would
founder his occupation.

A Roaring Boy

HIs life is a meere counterfet Patent: which neuertheles, makes
many a Countrey Iustice trem-
ble. *Don Quixotes water Milles* are stil
Scotch Bagpipes to him. Hee sendes
Challenges by word of mouth : for he
protests (as hee is a Gentleman and a
brother of the Sword) hee can neither
write nor read. He hath runne through
diuers parcels of Land, and great houses, beside both the Counters. If any
priuate quarrell happen among our
great Courtiers, he proclaimes the *businesse*, thats the word, the *businesse*; as
if the vnited forces of the *Romish Ca-
tholickes*

tholickes were making vp for *Germany*.
Hee cheats young Guls that are newly
come to Towne; and when the keeper
of the Ordinary blames him for it, he
anfwers him in his own Profeffion, that
a *woodcocke* muft bee pluckt ere he bee
dreft. Hee is a *Superuifor* to Brothels,
& in them is a more vnlawfull reformer
of vice, then Prentifes on Shroue-tuef-
day. He loues his Friend, as a Coun-
fellor at Law loues the veluet Breches
he was firft made Barrefter in, hee'll be
fure to weare him thread-bare ere hee
forfake him. He fleepes with a Tobac-
co-pipe in's mouth; and his firft praier
i'th' morning is, hee may remember
whom he fell out with ouer-night. *Sol-*
dier he is none, for hee cannot diftinguifh 'tweene *Onion feede* and *Gunpow-*
der : if he haue worne it in his hollow
tooth for the Tooth-ach, and fo come
to the knowledge of it, that's all. The
Tenure by which he holds his meanes,
is an eftate at Will; and thats borrowing . Land-lords haue but foure
Quarter-

Quarter-dayes; but he three hundred and odde. Hee keeps very good *Company*; yet is a man of no *reckoning*: and when he goes not drunke to bed, hee is very fick next morning. He commonly dies like *Anacreon*, with a Grape in's throat; or *Hercules*, with fire in's marrow. And I haue heard of fome (that haue fcap't hanging) begg'd for *Anatomies*, onely to deterre men from taking *Tobacco*.

———————

A drunken Dutch-man refident in England

IS but Quarter-Mafter with his wife. He ftinkes of Butter, as if hee were noynted all ouer for the Itch. Let him come ouer neuer fo leane, and plant him but one Moneth neere the Brew-howfes in S. *Catherines*, and hee'l bee puft vp to your hand like a bloate Herring. Of all places of pleafure, he loues

loues a Common Garden, and (with
the Swine of the Parifh) had neede be
ringed for rooting. Next to thefe hee
affects Lotteries naturally ; and bequeathes the beft prize in his Will a-
forehand; when his hopes fall , hee's
blanke. They fwarme in great Tene-
ments like flies : fixe Houfe-holds will
liue in a Garret. Hee was wont (onely
to make vs fooles)to buy the Foxe skin
for three pence, and fell the taile for a
fhilling. Now his new Trade of brew-
ing Strong-waters makes a number of
mad-men. He loues a Welch-man extreamly for his Diet and Orthography;
that is, for pluralitie of confonants and
cheefe. Like a Horfe, hee's onely guided by the mouth : when hee's drunke,
you may thruft your hand into him
like an Ele-skinne,and ftrip him, his infide outwards. Hee hoordes vp faire
gold, and pretends 'tis to feethe in his
Wiues broth for a confumption, and
loues the memory of King *Henry* the 8
moft efpecially for his old Soueraigns.
He

He ſaies wee are vnwiſe to lament the decay of Timber in England : for all manner of buildings or Fortification whatſoeuer, hee deſires no other thing in the world, then Barrels and Hoppoles. To conclude, the onely two plagues he trembles at, is ſmall Beere, and the Spaniſh Inquiſition.

A Phantaſtique.

An Improuident young Gallant.

THere is a confederacy between him and his clothes, to be made a puppy: view him wel, & you'll ſay his Gentry ſits as ill vpon him, as if he had boght it with his pény. He hath more places to ſend money to, then the Diuell hath to ſend his Spirits : and to furniſh each Miſtriſſe, would make him runne beſide his wits, if hee had any to loſe. Hee accounts baſhfulneſſe the

wicked'ft thing in the world; and therfore ftudies Impudence. If all men were
of his minde, all honefty would be out
of fafhion: he withers his Cloathes on
the Stage, as a Sale-man is forc't to do
his futes in Birchin-lane; and when the
Play is done, if you marke his rifing,
tis with a kinde of walking Epilogue
betweene the two candles, to know if
his Suite may paffe for currant: he ftudies by the difcretion of his Barber, to
frizle like a Baboone: three fuch would
keepe three the nimbleft Barbers in th'
towne, from euer hauing leafure to
weare net-Garters: for when they
haue to doe with him, they haue many Irons in th'fire. He is trauelled, but
to little purpofe; onely went ouer for
a fquirt, and came backe againe, yet
neuer the more mended in his conditions, 'caufe he carried himfelfe along
with him: a Scholler he pretends himfelfe, and fayes he hath fweat for it: but
the truth is, he knowes *Cornelius*, farre
better then *Tacitus*: his ordinary fports
are

are Cock-fights; but the moſt frequent, horſe-races, from whence hee comes home drie-foundred, Thus when his purſe hath caſt her calfe,he goes down into the Country,where he is brought to milk and white cheeſe like the *Swit-zers.*

A BVTTON-MAKER of Amſterdam,

IS one that is fled ouer from his *Conſcience*;and left his wife and children vpon the Pariſh.For his knowledge, he is meerely a *Horne-booke* without a *Chriſt-croſſe* afore it, and his zeale conſiſts much in hanging his Bible in a Dutch button : hee cozens men in the purity of his cloathes: and twas his only ioy when he was on this ſide, to bee in Priſon : he cryes out, tis impoſſible for any man to be damn'd, that liues in his Religion, and his equiuocation is

K 2   true

true: fo long as a man liues in't, he cannot; but if he die in't, there's the question. Of all Feafts in the yeere, hee accounts S.*Georges* Feaft the prophaneft,
becaufe of St. *Georges* Croffe, yet fomtimes he doth *facrifice* to his own belly;
provided, that he put off the Wake of
his owne natiuitie, or wedding, til *good
Friday*. If there bee a great feaft in the
Towne, though moft of the wicked (as
he cals them) be there, hee will be fure
to be a gueft, and to out-eat fixe of the
fatteft *Burgers*: he thinkes, though he
may not pray with a *Iew*, hee may eate
with a *Iew:* he winkes when hee prayes,
and thinks he knowes the waie fo now
to heauen, that hee can finde it blinde-
fold. Latine he accounts the language
of the *Beaft* with feuen heades; & when
he fpeakes of his owne Countrie, cries
he is fled out of *Babel.*Laftly, his deuotion is *Obftinacy*; the only folace of his
heart,*Contradiction*; and his maine end
Hypocrifie.

A diftafter

A Diſtaſter of the Time

IS a *winter Graſhopper* al the yeer lõg that looks back vpon *Harueſt*, with a leane paire of cheeks, neuer ſets forward to meete it : his malice ſuckes vp the greateſt part of his own venome, & therewith impoiſoneth himſelfe : and this ſickeneſſe riſes rather of *ſelfe-opinion*, *or ouer-great expectation*; ſo in the conceit of his owne ouer-worthineſſe, like a *Coiſtrell*, he ſtriues to fill himſelfe with winde, and flyes againſt it. Any mans aduancement is the moſt capital offence that can bee to his malice : yet this enuy, like *Phalaris Bull*, makes that a torment, firſt for himſelfe, hee prepared for others : hee is a *Day-bed for the Diuell* to ſlumber on; his bloud is of a yellowiſh colour : like thoſe that haue bin bitten by *Vipers*:& his gaule flowes as thick in him as oyle, in a poyſon'd ſto

K 3   macke.

macke. He infects all focietie, as thunder fowres wine : war or peace, dearth
or plenty, make him equally difconten-
ted. And where he findes no caufe to
taxe the State , he defcends to raile a-
gainft the rate of falt butter. His wifhes
are *whirle-winds*; which breath'd forth,
returne into himfelfe , and make him a
moft giddy & tottering veffell. When
he is awake, and goes abroad, he doth
but walke in his fleepe , for his vifitati-
on is directed to none; his bufineffe is
nothing. Hee is often dumbe-madde,
and goes fetter'd in his owne entrailes.
Religion is commonly his pretence of
difcontent, though he can be of all religions; therefore truly of none. Thus
by vnnaturallizing himfelfe , fome
would think him a very dangerous fellow to the State, but he is not greatly
to be fear'd : for this deiection of his,
is onely like a rogue that goes on his
knees and elbowes in the mire , to further his begging.

a

A meere Fellow of a House

EXamines all mens carriage but his owne; and is so kinde natured to himselfe, hee findes fault with all mens but his owne. He weares his apparell much after the fashion ; his meanes will not suffer him come too nigh : they afford him *Mock-veluet*, or *Satinisco*; but not without the Colledges next leases acquaintance : his inside is of the selfe same fashion, not rich: but as it reflects from the glasse of selfe-liking, there *Crœsus* is *Irus* to him. He is a *Pedant* in shew, though his title be *Tutor* ; and his *Pupils*, in broader phrase, are *schole-boyes*. On these he spends the false gallop of his tongue ; and with senselesse discourse towes them along, not out of ignorance. He shewes them the rinde, conceales the sappe: by this meanes he keepes them the longer, himselfe the better. He hath learn't to cough, and

K 4 spit,

ſpit and blow his noſe at euery period, to recouer his memorie : and ſtudies chiefely to ſet his eyes and beard to a new forme of learning. His Religion lies in waite for the inclination of his Patron; neither ebbes nor flowes, but iuſt ſtanding water, betweene *Prote-ſtant* and *Puritane.* His dreames are of pluralitie of Benefices and non-reſi-dency; and when he riſes, acts a long Grace to his looking glaſſe. Againſt hee comes to bee ſome great mans Chaplaine, hee hath a habite of bold-neſſe, though a very Coward. Hee ſpeakes Swords, Fights *Ergo's* : his paſe on foote is a meaſure; on horſe-backe a gallop : for his legs are his owne, though horſe and ſpurres are borrowed. He hath leſſe vſe then poſ-ſeſſion of Bookes. He is not ſo proud, but he will call the meaneſt Author by his name; nor ſo vnskill'd in the He-raldry of a ſtudy, but hee knowes each mans place. So ends that fellowſhip, and begins an other.

A

A meere Petifogger

IS one of *Sampſons Foxes*:He ſets men together by the eares, more ſhamefully then *Pillories*; & in a long vacation his ſport is to go a Fiſhing *with the Penall ſtatutes.* He cannot erre before Iudgement, and then you ſee it, onely *Writs of error* are the *Tariers* that keep his *Client* vndoing ſomewhat the longer. He is a veſtrie-man in his Pariſh, and eaſily ſets his neighbours at variance with the *Vickar,* when his wicked *counſell* on both ſides is like weapons put into mens hands by a *Fencer,* whereby they get blowes, hee money. His honeſty and learning bring him to *Vnder-ſhrif-ſhip*;which hauing thriſe runne through, he do's not feare the *Lieutenant* a'th'Shire : nay more, he feares not God. *Cowardiſe* holds him a good Common-wealthes man ; his pen is the plough, and parchment the

Soyle,

Soyle, whence he reapes both Coyne
and Curſes. He is an *Earthquake*, that
willingly will let no ground lye in
quiet. Broken titles make him whole;
to haue halfe in the County breake
their Bonds, were the onely libertie of
conſcience : He would wiſh (though
he be a *Browniſt*) no neighbour of his
ſhould pay his tithes duly, if ſuch Sutes
held continuall Plea at *Weſtminſter*. He
cannot away with the reuerend Ser-
uice in our Church, becauſe it ends
with *The peace of God*. He loues blowes
extreamely, and hath his *Chyrurgions*
bill of all rates, from head to foote, to
incenſe the fury : he would not giue a-
way his yeerely beatings for a good
peece of mony. He makes his Wil in
forme of a Law-caſe, full of quiddits,
that his friends after his death (if for
nothing elſe, yet) for the vexation of
Lawe, may haue cauſe to remember
him. And if hee thought the Ghoſts
of men did walke againe (as they report in time of Popery) ſure he would
hide

hide some single mony in *Westminster-Hall,* that his spirit might haunt there. Onely with this , I will pitch him o're the Barre, and leaue him ; That his fingers itch after a Bribe , euer since his first practising of Court-hand.

An Ingrosser of Corne.

THere is no vermine in the Land like him ; he slanders both Heauen and Earth with pretended Dearths, when there's no cause of scarsity. His hording in a deere yeere, is like *Erisicthons* Bowels in *Ouid: Quodque vrbibus esse , quodq̓ satis poterat populo, non sufficit vni.* Hee prayes dayly for more inclosures, and knows no reason in his Religion, why we should call our fore-fathers dayes, *The time of ignorance,* but onely because they sold Wheat for twelue pence a bushell. He wishes that *Danske* were at the *Moloccos;*

cos; and had rather be certaine of some
forraine inuasion, then of the setting vp
of the Stilyard. When his Barnes and
garners are ful (if it be a time of dearth)
he wil buy halfe a bushell i'th' Market
to serue his Houshold : and winnowes
his Corne in the night, lest, as the chaff
throwne vpon the water, shew'd plenty
in *AEgypt*; so his (carried by the wind)
should proclaime his abundance. No
painting pleases him so wel, as *Pharaohs*
dreame of the seauen leane Kine, that
ate vp the fat ones; that hee has in his
Parlour, which he will describe to you
like a motion, and his comment ends
with a smothered prayer for the like
scarsitie. Hee cannot away with Tobacco; for hee is perswaded (and not
much amisse) that tis a sparer of bread-
corne; which he could finde in's heart
to transport without Licence : but
weighing the penaltye, hee growes
mealy-mouth'd, and dares not. Sweet
smels hee cannot abide; wishes that the
pure ayre were generally corrupted :
nay,

nay, that the spring had lost her fragrancy for euer, or wee our superfluous sense of smelling (as he tearmes it) that his corne might not be found mustie. The Poore he accounts the Iustices intelligencers, and cannot abide them: he complains of our negligence of discouering new parts of the World, only to rid them from our Climate. His Sonne, by a certaine kinde of instinct, he bindes Prentise to a Taylor, who all the terme of his Indenture hath a deare yere in's his bellie, and rauins bread extreamly : when hee comes to be a freeman (if it be a Dearth) he marries him to a Bakers daughter.

A Diuellish Vsurer

IS sowed as *Cummin* or *Hemp-seede*, with curses; and he thinks he thriues the better. Hee is better read in the *Penall Statutes*, then the Bible; and his euill Angell perswades him, hee shall
sooner

ſooner be ſaued by them. Hee can be no mans friend; for all men hee hath moſt intereſt in, hee vndo's : and a double-dealer hee is certainly; for by his good will he euer takes the forfeit. Hee puts his money to the vnnaturall Act of generation; and his Scriuener is the ſuperuiſor Bawd to t. Good Deeds he loues none, but Seal'd and Deliuered; nor doth he wiſh any thing to thriue in the Countrey, but Bee-hiues; for they make him waxe rich. He hates all but Law-Latine; yet thinkes he might bee drawne to loue a Scholler, could he reduce the yeare to a ſhorter compaſſe, that his vſe-money might come in the faſter: he ſeems to be the ſon of a Iailor, for all his eſtate is moſt heauy & cruell bonds. He doth not giue, but ſel daies of payment; and thoſe at the rate of a mans vndoing: he doth only feare, the day of Iudgement ſhould fall ſooner, then the paiment of ſome great ſum of money due to him : hee remoues his lodging when a Subſidy comes; and if

hee

he be found out, and pay it, hee grum-
bles Treafon; but tis in fuch a deformed
filence, as Witches rayfe their Spirits
in. Grauitie he pretends in all things,
but in his priuate Whore; for hee will
not in a hundreth pound take one light
fixe-pence; and it feemes hee was at
Tilbury Campe, for you muft not tell
him of a *Spaniard*. Hee is a man of no
confcience; for (like the *Iakes-farmer*
that fwounded with going into Buck-
lersbury) hee falls into a cold fweat, if
hee but looke into the Chauncerie:
thinkes in his Religion, wee are in the
right for euery thing, if that were abo-
lifht: hee hides his money, as if hee
thought to finde it againe at laft day,
and then begins old trade with it. His
clothes plead prefcription; and whether they or his body are more rotten,
is a queftion: yet fhould hee liue to be
hang'd in them, this good they would
doe him, The very Hangman would
pittie his cafe. The Table he keeps is
able to ftarue twenty tall men; his feruants

uants haue not their liuing, but their
dying from him,and that's of Hunger.
A fpare Dyet he commends in al men,
but himfelfe : he comes to Cathedrals
onely for loue of the finging boyes,be-
caufe they looke hungry. He likes our
Religion beft, becaufe tis beft cheape ;
yet would faine allow of Purgatorie,
'caufe 'twas of his Trade, and brought
in fo much money:his heart goes with
the fame fnaphance his purfe doth, tis
feldome open to any man : friendfhip
hee accounts but a word without any
fignification;nay, he loues al the world
fo little, that, and it were poffible, hee
would make himfelfe his owne Execu-
tor :for certaine, hee is made Admini-
ftrator to his own good name,while he
is in perfect memorie, for that dyes
long afore him; but he is fo farre from
being at the charge of a Funerall for it,
that hee lets it ftinke aboue ground.
In conclufió, for Neighbourhood,you
were better dwell by a contentious
Lawyer. And for his death, tis rather
Surfet,

Surfet, the Pox, or Defpaire; for feldom
fuch as he dye of Gods making, as honeft men fhould doe.

A Water-Man

IS one that hath learnt to fpeake well
of himfelfe; for alwaies hee names
himfelfe, *The firft man.* If he had betane
himfelfe to fome richer Trade, hee
could not haue chos'd but done well:
for in this (though it be a meane one)
he is ftill plying it, and putting himfelfe
forward. He is euermore telling ftrange
newes; moft commonly lyes. If he be
a Sculler, aske him if he be married,
hee'l equiuocate and fweare hee's a fin-
gle man. Little truft is to be giuen to
him, for he thinks that day he does beft
when he fetches moft men ouer. His
daily labour teaches him the Arte of
diffembling; for like a fellow that rides
to the Pillorie, he goes not that way he
L   lookes:

lookes : hee keepes ſuch a bawling at
weſtminſter , that if the Lawyers were
not acquainted with it, an order would
be tane with him. When he is vpon the
water, he is Fare-company : when he
comes aſhore, he mutinies ; and contrary to all other trades , is moſt ſurly
to Gentlemen, when they tender payment. The Play-houſes only keep him
ſober; and as it doth many other Gallants, make him an afternoones man.
London-Bridge is the moſt terribleſt
eye-ſore to him that can be.   And to
conclude , nothing but a *great Preſſe*,
makes him flye from the Riuer ;
nor any thing , but a great
Froſt , can teach him
any good man-
ners.

A Re-

A Reuerend Iudge

IS one that defires to haue his greatnes,only meafur'd by his goodneffe:
his care is to appeare fuch to the people, as he would haue them be ; and to
be himfelfe fuch as hee appeares ; for
vertue cannot feeme one thing,and be
another : hee knowes that the hill of
greatneffe yeeldes a moft delightfull
profpeÄ,but withall that it is moft fub-
ieÄ to lightning, and thunder:and that
the people, as in ancient *Tragedies,* fit
and cenfure the aÄions of thofe are in
authority : he fquares his owne therefore, that they may farre bee aboue
their pity : he wifhes fewer Lawes,fo
they were better obferu'd : and for
thofe are MulÄuarie, he vnderftands
their inftitution not to be like briers or
fpringes, to catch euery thing they lay
hold of; but like Sea-marks (on our
dangerous *Goodwin*) to auoid the fhip-

wracke of ignorant paſſengers : hee hates to wrong any man; neither hope, nor deſpaire of preferment can draw him to ſuch an exigent : he thinks him-ſelfe then moſt honorably ſeated, when hc giues mercie the vpper hand : hee rather ſtriues to purchaſe good name then land; and of all rich ſtuffes for-bidden by the Statute, loathes to haue his Followers weare their clothes cut out of bribes and extortions. If his Prince call him to higher place, there he deliuers his minde plainly, and free-ly, knowing for truth, there is no place wherein diſſembling ought to haue leſſe credit, then in a Princes Councel. Thus honour keeps peace with him to the graue, and doth not (as with many) there forſake him, and goe backe with the Heralds : but fairely ſits ore him, and broods out of his memorie, many right excellent Common-wealths men.

A ver-

A vertuous Widdow

IS the Palme-tree, that thriues not af
ter the supplanting of her husband.
For her childrens sake she first marries, for shee married that she might
haue children, and for their sakes shee
marries no more. She is like the purest
gold, onely imployde for Princes med-
dals, she neuer receiues but one mans
impression; the large iointure moues
her not, titles of honor cannot sway hir.
To change her name, were (she thinks)
to commit a sinne should make her
asham'd of her husbands calling; she
thinks she hath traueld all the world in
one man; the rest of her time therfore
she directs to heauen. Her maine superstition is, she thinks her husbands
ghost would walke, should she not per-
forme his Will: she would do it, were
there no Prerogatiue Court. She giues
much to pious vses, without any hope

to merit by them:and as one Diamond
fashions another; so is she wrought into works of Charity, with the dust or
ashes of her husband. She liues to see
her selfe full of time; being so necessarie for earth,God calles her not to heauen, till she be very aged: and euen
then, though her naturall strength faile
her,she stands like an ancient *Pyramid*;
which the lesse it growes to mans eye,
the neerer it reaches to heauen : this
latter Chastitie of Hers, is more graue
and reuerend, then that ere shee was
married; for in it is neither hope, nor
longing,nor feare, nor ielousie. Shee
ought to be a mirrour for our youngest
Dames, to dresse themselues by, when
she is fullest of wrinkles. No calamity
can now come neere her, for in suffering the losse of her husband, shee accounts all the rest trifles : she hath laid
his dead body in the worthiest monument that can be : Shee hath buried it
in her owne heart. To conclude, shee
is a Relique, that without any superstition

tion in the world, though she will not
be kist, yet may be reuerenc't.

An ordinary widdow

IS like the Heralds Hearse-cloath; she
serues to many funerals, with a very
little altering the colour. The end of
her Husband begins in teares; and the
end of her teares beginnes in a Husband. She vses to Cunning women to
know how many Husbands thee shall
haue , and neuer marries without the
consent of sixe midwiues. Her chiefest
pride is in the multitude of her Sui-
tors; and by them she gaines : for one
serues to draw on another, and with
one at last she shootes out another, as
Boyes doe Pellets in Elderne Gunnes.
She commends to them a single life, as
Horsecoursers doe their Iades, to put
them away. Her fancy is to one of the
biggest of the Guard, but Knighthood

L 4 makes

makes her draw in a weaker Bow. Her
seruants, or kinsfolke, are the Trumpe-
peters that summon any to this com-
bat : by them she gaines much credit,
but looseth it againe in the old Pro-
uerbe : *Fama est mendax.* If she liue to
be thrice married, she seldome failes to
cozen her second Husbands Credi-
tors. A Church-man shee dare not
venture vpon; for she hath heard widdowes complaine of dilapidations :
nor a Soldier, though he haue Candle-
rents in the City, for his estate may be
subiect to fire : very seldome a Lawyer,
without he shew his exceeding great
practise, & can make her case the better : but a Knight with the olde rent
may doe much, for a great comming
in is all in all with a Widdow : euer
prouided, that most part of her Plate
and Iewels (before the wedding) lye
conceal'd with her Scriuener. Thus
like a too-ripe Apple, shee falles of her
selfe : but he that hath her, is Lord but
of a filthy purchase, for the title is
crack't.

crackt. Laftly, while fhe is a widdow, obferue euer, fhee is no Morning woman: the euening, a good fire and fack, may make her liften to a Husband: and if euer fhe be made fure, tis vpon a full ftomake to bed-ward.

A Quackfaluer

IS a Mountebanke of a larger bill then a Taylor; if he can but come by names enow of Difeafes, to ftuffe it with, tis all the skill hee ftudies for. Hee tooke his firft being from a Cunning woman, and ftole this blacke Art from her while he made her Seacoale fire. All the difeafes euer fin brought vpon man, doth he pretend to be Curer of; when the truth is, his maine cunning is Corne-cutting. A great plague makes him; what with railing againft fuch, as leaue their cures for feare of infection, and in friendly breaking
king

king Cakebread, with the Fifh-wiues
at Funerals, he vtters a moft abomina-
ble deale of mufty *Carduus*-water, and
the Conduits cry out, All the learned
Doctors may caft their Caps at him.
He parts ftakes with fome Apothecary in the Suburbes, at whofe houfe hee
lyes : and though he be neuer fo familiar with his wife, the Apothecarie
dare not (for the richeft Horne in his
fhop)difpleafe him. All the Mid-wiues
in the towne are his intelligencers; but
Nurfes and young Marchants Wiues
(that would faine conceiue with child)
thefe are his Idolaters. Hee is a more
vniuft Bone-fetter. then a Dice-ma-
ker; hath put out more eyes then the
fmall Pox; made more deafe then the
Cataracts of *Nilus*; lamed more then
the Gout; fhrunke more finewes, then
one that makes Bow-ftrings; and kild
more idly, then Tobacco. A Magi-
ftrate that had any way fo noble a fpirit, as but to loue a good horfe well,
would not fuffer him to bee a Farrier.
His

His difcourfe is vomit; and his ignorance, the ftrongeft purgation in the
world : to one that would be fpeedily
cured, he hath more delaies, and dou-
bles then a Hare, or a Law-fuite : hee
feekes to fet vs at variance with nature,
and rather then hee fhall want difeafes
he'le beget them. His efpeciall practife
(as I fayd afore) is vpon women; labours to make their mindes ficke, ere
their bodies feele it, and then there's
worke for the Dog-leach. He pretends
the cure of mad-men; and fure hee
gets moft by them, for no man in
his perfect witte would meddle with
him.   Laftly, he is fuch a Iuggler with
Vrinals, fo dangeroufly vnskilfull, that
if euer the Cittie will haue recourfe to
him for difeafes that neede purgation,
let them imploy him in fcouring
More-ditch.

A Can-

A Canting Rogue.

T Is not vnlikely but hee was begot
by fome intelligencer vnder a
hedge; for his minde is wholy giuen
to trauell. He is not troubled with making of Iointures: he can diuorce himfelfe without the fee of a Proctor, nor
feares he the crueltie of ouerfeers of his
Will. Hee leaues his children all the
world to Cant in, and all the people
to their fathers His Language is a
Conftant tongue; the Northerne
fpeech differs from the South, Welch
from the Cornifh : but Canting is generall, nor euer could be altered by
cōqueft of the *Saxon*, *Dane*, or *Norman*.
He will not beg out of his limit though
hee ftarue; nor breake his oath if hee
fweare by his *Salomon*, though you
hang him : and hee payes his cuftome
as truely to his Graund Rogue, as tribute is payd to the great Turke. The
March

March Sunne breedes agues in others
but hee adores it like the *Indians*; for
then begins his progreſſe after a hard
winter. Oſtlers cannot endure him, for
he is of the infantry, and ſerues beſt
on foote. He offends not the Statute a-
gainſt the exceſſe of apparell, for hee
will goe naked, and counts it a volun-
tarie pennance. Forty of them lie in a
Barne together, yet are neuer ſued vpon the ſtatute of Inmates. If he were
learned, no man could make a better
deſcription of *England*; for he hath
traueld it ouer and ouer. Laſtly,
hee bragges, that his great
houſes are repair'd to his
hands, when Chur-
ches go to ruine:
and thoſe are
priſons.

A French

A French Cooke

HE learnt his trade in a Towne of Garrifon neere famifh't, where he practifed to make a little goe farre; fome driue it from more anti-quity, and fay *Adam* (when he picke fallets) was of his occupation.He doth not feed the belly, but the Palate : and though his command lie in the kitchin (which is but an inferiour place) yet fhall you finde him a very fawcy com-panion. Euer fince the warres in *Na-ples*, hee hath fo minc't the ancient and bountifull allowance, as if his na-tion fhould keep a perpetuall diet. The Seruingmen call him the laft relique of Popery, that makes men faft againft their Confcience. He can be truly faid to be no mans fellow but his Mafters : for the reft of his feruants are ftarued by him. Hee is the prime caufe why

Noble-

Noblemen build their houses so great, for the smalnes of their Kitchin, makes the house the bigger : and the Lord calles him 'his Alchymist that can extract gold out of hearbs, rootes, mushroomes or any thing : that which hee dresses wee may rather call a drinking, then a meale : yet is he so full of variety, that he brags, and truely, that hee giues you but a taste of what hee can do: he dare not for his life come amóg the Butchers; for sure they would quarter and bake him after the English fashion; hee's such an enemy to Beefe and Mutton.   To conclude, he were onely fit to make a funerall feast, where men should eat their victuals in mourning.

A Sexton

A Sexton

IS an ill-willer to humane nature. Of all Prouerbs, hee cannot endure to heare that which fayes Wee ought to liue by the quicke, not by the dead. He could willingly all his life time bee confinde to the Church-yard ; at leaſt within fiue foote on't : for at euery Church ſtile, commonly ther's an Ale-houſe ; where let him bee found neuer ſo idle pated, hee is ſtill a graue drunkard. Hee breakes his faſt heartilieſt while he is making a graue , and fayes the opening of the ground makes him hungry. Though one would take him to be a ſlouen, yet he loues cleane linnen extreamely , and for that reaſon takes an order that fine holland ſheets bee not made wormes meate. Like a nation cald the *Cuſani*, he weeps when any are borne, and laughes when they die : the reaſon ; hee goes by Burials
not

not Chriftnings : hee will hold argument in a Tauerne ouer Sacke, till the Diall and himfelfe bee both at a ftand : he neuer obferues any time but fermon time, and there he fleepes by the hourglaffe. The rope-maker payes him a penfion, and hee paies tribute to the Phyfitian; for the Phyfitian makes work for the Sexton; as the Rope-maker for the Hang-man. Laftly, he wifhes the Dogge-dayes would laft all yeere long: and a great plague is his yere of Iubile.

A Iefuite

IS a larger Spoone for a Traytor to feed with the Diuell, then any other Order : vnclafpe him, and hee's a gray Wolfe, with a golden Starre in the fore-head : fo fuperftitioufly hee followes the Pope, that hee forfakes Chrift, in not giuing *Cæfar* his due. His vowes feeme heauenly; but in medling

M   with

with State-bufineffe, he feemes to mix
heauen and earth together.   His beft
Elements, are Confeffion & Penance:
by the firft, he finds out mens inclinati-
ons; and by the latter, heapes wealth
to his Seminary.   He fprang from *Ig-*
natius Loiola, a *Spanish* Souldier; and
though hee were found out long fince
the inuention of the Canon, 'tis thoght
he hath not done leffe mifchiefe.   Hee
is a falfe Key to open Princes Cabinets
and pry into their Counfels;and where
the Popes excommunicatiõ thunders,
hee holds it no more finne the decrow-
ning of Kings, then our Puritanes doe
the fuppreffion of Bifhops.   His order
is full of all irregularity and difobedi-
ence; ambitious aboue all meafure; for
of late dayes, in *Portugall* and the *In-*
dies,he reiected the name of Iefuit,and
would bee called Difciple.   In *Rome*,
and other countries that giue him freedome, hee weares a Maske vpon his
heart; in England he fhifts it, and puts
it vpon his face.   No place in our Cli-
                                       mate

mate hides him fo fecurely as a Ladies
Chamber : the modefty of the *Purfe-
uant* hath onely forborne the bed, and
fo mift him.   There is no Difeafe in
Chriftendome, that may fo properly
be call'd *The Kings Euill*. To conclude,
would you know him beyond Sea ? In
his Seminary, hee's a Foxe; but in the
Inquifition, a Lyon Rampant.

An excellent Aftor.

WHatfoeuer is commendable
in the graue Orator, is moft
exquifitly perfeft in him; for
by a ful and fignificant aftion of body,
he charmes our attention : fit in a full
Theater, and you will thinke you fee
fo many lines drawen from the circumference of fo many eares, whiles the
Aftor is the *Center*. He doth not ftriue
to make nature monftrous, fhe is often
feene in the fame Scæne with him, but

neither on Stilts nor Crutches; and for his voice tis not lower then the prompter; nor lowder then the Foile and Target. By his action hee fortifies morall precepts with example; for what wee fee him perfonate, wee thinke truely done before vs a man of a deep thoght might apprehend, the Ghofts of our ancient *Heroes* walk't againe, and take him (at feueral times) for many of thē. He is much affected to painting, and tis a queftion whether that make him an excellent Player, or his playing an exquifite Painter. He addes grace to the Poets labours: for what in the Poet is but ditty, in him is both ditty and muficke. He entertaines vs in the beft leafure of our life, that is betweene meales, the moft vnfit time either for ftudy or bodily exercife. The flight of Hawkes aud chafe of wilde beafts, either of them are delights noble : but fome thinke this fport of men the worthier, defpight all *calumny*. All men haue been of his occupation : and indeed,

deed, what he doth fainedly, that doe others effentially : this day one plaies a Monarch, the next a priuate perfon. Heere one Acts a Tyrant, on the morrow an Exile : A Parafite this man to night, to morrow a Precifian, and fo of diuers others. I obferue, of all men liuing, a worthy Actor in one kinde is the ftrongeft motiue of affecti-on that can be : for when he dies, wee cannot be perfwaded any man can doe his parts like him. But to conclude, I value a worthy Actor by the corrupti-on of fome few of the quality, as I wold doe gold in the oare; I fhould not minde the droffe but the purity of the mettall.

M 3   *A Franklin*

A *Franklin.*

HIs outfide is an ancient Yeoman of England, though his infide may giue armes (with the beft Gentleman) and ne're fee the Herald. There is no truer feruant in the houfe then himfelfe. Though he be Mafter, he faies not to his feruants, go to field, but let vs goe; and with his owne eye, doth both fatten his flocke, and fet forward all manner of husbandry. He is taught by nature to be contented with a little; his own fold yeelds him both food and raiment : hee is pleafd with any nourifhment God fends , whileft curious gluttonie ranfacks, as it were, *Noahs Arke* for food, only to feed the riot of one meale. He is nere knowne to goe to Law; vnderftanding, to be Law-bound among men, is like to bee hide-bound among his beafts; they thriue not vnder it : and that fuch men

sleep

ſleep as vnquietly, as if their pillowes were ſtuft with Lawyers pen-kniues. When hee builds, no poore Tenants cottage hinders his proſpećt : they are indeed his Almes-houſes, though there be painted on them no ſuch ſuperſcription. Hee neuer ſits vp late, but when he hunts the Badger, the vowed foe of his Lambes : nor vſes he any crueltye, but when he hunts the Hare, nor ſubtilty but when he ſetteth ſnares for the Snite, or pitfals for the Blacke-bird; nor oppreſſion, but when in the month of Iuly, he goes to the next riuer, and ſheares his ſheep. Hee allowes of honeſt paſtime, and thinks not the bones of the dead any thing bruiſed, or the worſe for it, though the Countrey Laſſes dance in the Church-yard after Euen-ſong. Rocke-Monday, and the Wake in Summer, ſhrouings, the wakefull ketches on Chriſtmas Eue, the Hoky, or Seed-cake, theſe he yerely keeps, yet holds thē no reliques of Poperie. Hee is not ſo inquiſitiue after

newes deriued from the priuie clofet,
when the finding an eiery of Haukes
in his own ground,or the foaling of a
Colt come of a good ftraine, are ty-
dings more pleafant, more profitable.
He is Lord paramount within himfelf,
though hee hold by neuer fo meane a
Tenure; and dyes the more conten-
tedly(though he leaue his heire yong)
in regard he leaues him not liable to a
couetous Guardian. Laftly, to end
him; he cares not when his end comes;
hee needs not feare his Audit, for his
Quietus is in heauen.

A Rymer

IS a fellow whofe face is hatcht all
ouer with impudence, and fhould he
bee hang'd or pilloried tis armed for
it. Hee is a Iuggler with words, yet
practifes the Art of moft vncleanly
con-

conueyance. He doth boggle very often; and becaufe himfelfe winkes at
it, thinks tis not perceiued : the maine
thing that euer he did, was the tune he
fang to. There is nothing in the earth
fo pitifull, no not an Ape-carrier, he is
not worth thinking of, and therefore I muft leaue him as nature left him; a Dung-
hill not well layd
together.

The

The Character of a
happy life.

By Sir. H. W:

How happy is he borne or taught,
That serueth not anothers will;
whose Armour is his honest thought,
And silly Truth his highest skill.

whose passions not his Masters are,
whose soule is still prepar'd for death:
Vntyed vnto the world with care
Of Princely loue, or vulgar breath.

who hath his life from rumors freed,
whose conscience is his strong retreit:
whose state can neither flatterers feed,
Nor ruine make accusers great.

who

who enuieth nonë whom chance doth raiſe,
Or vice : who neuer vnderſtood,
How deepeſt wounds are giuë with praiſe,
Not rules of ſtate, but rules of good.

who GOD doth late and early pray,
More of his grace, then gifts to lend;
who entertaines the harmeleſſe day,
with a well choſen Booke or Friend.

This man is free from ſeruile bands,
Of hope to riſe, or feare to fall;
Lord of himſelfe, though not of Lands :
And hauing nothing, he hath All.

Certaine

CERTAINE EDICTS
from a Parliament in *Eutopia*;
Written by the Lady
Southwell.

INprimis, Hee that hath no other
worth to cōmend him then a good
Suite of Apparell, ſhall not dare to
woe a Lady in his owne behalfe, but
ſhall be allowed to carry the Hierogli-
phike of his friends affection.

Item, that no foule-fac'd Lady ſhall
raile on her that is fairer, becauſe ſhe is
fairer; nor ſeeke by blacke calumniati-
on to darken her fame, vnleſſe ſhee be
her corriuall.

Item, that no man may intitle himſelfe by the matchles name of a friend,
that loues vpon condition, vnleſſe hee
be a Schoole-maſter.

Item, that no Lady, which modeſtly
keeps

keeps her houſe for want of good clothes to viſit her Goſſips, ſhall profeſſe contempt of the worlds vanity, vnleſſe ſhe ſee no hope of the tides returning.

Item, that no Banckrupt Knight, that to ſet vp ſhop againe becoms Paraſite or Buffone to ſome great Lord, ſhall euer after ſweare by his honour; but by his Knight-hood he may.

Item, that no Lady that vſeth to paint ſhall finde fault with her painter that hath not counterfeted her picture faire enough, vnleſſe ſhe will acknowledge her ſelfe to be the better counterfetter.

Item, that no man, whoſe vaine loue hath beene reiected by a vertuous Lady, ſhall report that he hath refuſed & caſt her off, vnleſſe he will take the baſe lying fellow by the next aſſailant, ſo reiected, without any further quarrell.

Item, that no Lady ſhal court her looking glaſſe, paſt one houre in a day, vnleſſe ſhe profeſſe to be an Inginer.

Item, that no *Quarter-waiter* ſhall feed on cheeſe three quarters of a yeere

to

to feaſt on fatten one quarter, without *Galens* aduice, and the Apothecaries bill to be written by a Taylor.

Item, that wench that is ouer-enamored of her ſelfe, and thinks all other ſo too, ſhall be bound to carry a burden of Birdlime on her backe, and ſpinne at a Barne-dore to catch fooles.

Item, he that ſweareth when hee loſeth his money at dice, ſhall challenge his damnation by the way of purchaſe.

Item, no Lady that ſilently ſimpereth for want of wit, ſhall be call'd modeſt.

Item, no fellow that begins to argue with a woman, & wants wit to encounter her, ſhal think he hath redeemd his credit by putting her to ſilence with ſome laſciuious diſcourſe, vnleſſe hee were white for *william*, and greene for *Sommer.*

Item, no woman that remaineth conſtant for want of aſſault, ſhall be called chaſte.

Item,

*Item,*he that professeth vertuous loue to a woman, and giues ground when his vanity is reiected, shall haue his bels cut off and flie for a haggard.

*Item,*she that respecteth the good o-pinion of others, before the Beeing of good in her selfe, shall not refuse the name of an Hipocrite;and she that em-ploies al her time in working trappings for her selfe, the name of spider : and she that sets the first quest of enquiry a-mongst her gossips for new fashions, shal not refuse a stitcher for her second husband.

Item, He that hath reported a Lady to be vertuous,for the which he profes-seth to loue her, yet vnder hand com-menceth a base suit, and is disdained; shall not on this blow which his owne vice hath giuen him,out of policy raile suddenly on her, for feare he be noted for a vicious foole : but to his friend in priuate he may say that his iudgement was blinded by her cunning disguise, & that he finds her wauering in goodnesse

neſſe, and in time he ſhall openly profeſſe to raile on her; but with ſuch a
modeſty forſooth, as if he were loth to
bring his iudgement into queſtion;nor
would he doe it, but that hee preferres
truth euen out of his owne reach.

NEWES

NEVVES
FROM ANY WHENCE.

Oʀ,

OLD TRVTH, VNDER A SVP-
pofall of Noueltie.

Occafioned by diuers Effayes, and priuate
paffages of *wit*, betweene fundrie Gentlemen vpon that fubiect.

Newes from Court.

 T is thought heere
that there are as
great miferies be-
yond happineffe,
as a this fide it, as
being in loue. That
truth is euery
mans by affenting. That time makes
euery thing aged, and yet it felfe was

N   223   neuer

neuer but a minute olde. That, next
fleepe, the greateft deuourer of time
is bufineffe:the greateft ftretcher of it,
Paſſion: the trueft meafure of it, *Contemplation*. To be faued, alwaies is the
beft plot : and vertue alwaies cleeres
her way as fhee goes. *Vice* is euer be-
hind-hand with it felfe. That *wit* and
a *woman* are two fraile things, and both
the frailer by concurring. That the
meanes of begetting a man, hath more
increaft mankind then the end. That
the madneffe of Loue is to be ficke of
one part, and cured by another. The
madneffe of Iealoufie, that it is fo dili-
gent, and yet it hopes to lofe his labor.
That all VVomen for the bodily part,
are but the fame meaning put in diuers wordes. That the difference in
the fenfe is their vnderftanding. That
the wifedome of *Action* is *Difcretion* ;
the knowledge of *contemplation* is
truth:the knowledge of action is men.
That the firft confiders what fhould
be, the latter makes vfe of what is,
That

That euery man is weake in his owne
humours. That euery man a little beyond himsefe is a foole. That affecta-
tion is the more ridiculous part of folly then ignorance. That the matter
of greatneſſe is compariſon. That
God made one world of *Subſtances*;
Man hath made another of *Art* and
Opinion. That Money is nothing but
a thing which *Art* hath turned vppe
trumpe. That cuſtome is the ſoule of
circumſtances. That cuſtome hath ſo
farre preuailed, that *Truth* is now the
greateſt newes. Sir, *T. Ouer.*

Anſwere to the Court Newes.

THat *Happineſſe* and *Miſerie* are
Antipodes. That *Goodneſſe* is not
Felicitie, but the rode thither. That
Mans ſtrength is but a viciſſitude of
falling and riſing. That onely to re-
fraine ill, is to be ill ſtill. That the plot-

of Saluation was laid before the plot
of *Paradise*.   That enioying is the
preparatiue to contemning.   That hee
that seekes opinion beyond merite,
goes iust so farre backe.   That no man
can obtaine his desires; nor in the
world hath not to his measure.   That
to studie, men are more profitable
then bookes.   That mens loues are
their afflictions.   That Titles of Honor, are rattles to still ambition.   That
to be a King, is *Fames Butte*, and feares
Quiuer.   That the soules of Women
and Louers, are wrapt in the port-
manque of their senses.   That imagination is the end of man.   That wit is
the webbe, and wisedome the woofe
of the cloth; so that womens soules
were neuer made vp.   That enuie
knowes what it will not confesse.   That
Goodnesse is like the Art *Prospectiue*:one
point Center, begetting infinite rayes.
That Man, Woman, and the Diuell,
are the three degrees of comparison.
That this Newes holds number, but
                                               not

not weight, by which couple all things receiue forme.

Countrey Newes.

THat there is moſt heere, for it gathers in going. That reputation is meaſured by the Acre. That Pouerty is the greateſt diſhoneſty. That the pittie of *Alaſſe poore ſoule*, is for the moſt part miſtaken. That Roſt Beefe is the beſt ſmell. That a Iuſtice of peace is the beſt relique of Idolatrie. That the Allegory of Iuſtice drawne blinde, is turned the wrong way. That not to liue to heauenly is accounted great wrong. That wiſedome deſcends in a race. That we loue Names better then perſons. That to hold in Knights ſeruice, is a ſlipperie ſeruice. That a Papiſt is a new word for a Traitor. That the duty of Religion is lent, not pay'd. That the reward is loſt in the want of humilitie. That the Puritane

tane perfecution is as a clowde that
can hide the glory of the light, but not
the day. That the emulation of the
Englifh and *Scots* to be the *Kings* Countrey-men, thruft the honour on the
welch. That a Courtier neuer at-
taynes his felfe-knowledge, but by report. That his beft Embleme is a
Hearne-dogge. That many great men
are fo proud, that they know not their
owne Fathers. That Loue is the taile-
worme. That a woman is the effect
of her owne firft fame. That to remember, to know, and to vnder-
ftand, are 3. degrees not vnderftood.
That Countrey ambition is no vice, for
there is nothing aboue a man. That
fighting is a Seruing-mans valor: Martyrdome their Mafters. That to liue
long, is to fill vp the dayes wee liue.
That the zeale of fome mens Religion
reflects from their Friends. That the
pleafure of vice is indulgence of the
prefent, for it endures but the acting.
That the proper reward of goodnes is
from

from within the externall is pollicy.
That good and ill is the croſſe and pile
in the aime of life.   That the Soule is
the lampe of the body, Reaſon of the
Soule, Religion of Reaſon, Faith of
Religion, Chriſt of Faith.   That circumſtances are the Atomies of policy,
Cenſure the being, Aĉtion the life, but
ſucceſſe the Ornament. That Authority preſſeth downe with weight, and
is thought violence: policy trips vp the
heeles, & is called the dexterity. That
this life is a throng in a narrow paſſage,
hee that is firſt out, findes eaſe, hee in
the middle worſt hemm'd in with troubles, the hindmoſt that driues both out
afore him, though not ſuffering wrong,
hath his part in doing it.   That God
requires of our debts, a reckoning, not
payment.   That Heauen is the eaſieſt
purchaſe, for we are the richer for the
disburſing. That liberality ſhould
haue no obieĉt but the poore, if our
mindes were rich.   That the myſtery
of greatneſſe is to keepe the inferiour

N 4   ignorant

ignorant of it . That all this is no
Newes to a better wit. *That the City
cares not what the Countrey thinkes.*

SIR. T. R.

Newes from the very Countrey.

THat it is a Fripery of Courtiers,
Marchants, and others, which
haue been in fashion, and are very neere worne out. That Iustices of
Peace haue the felling of vnderwoods,
but the Lords haue the great fals. The
Iesuits are like Apricockes, heretofore,
here and there one succour'd in a great
mans house, and cost deere; now you
may haue them for nothing in euery
cottage. That euery great Vice is a
Pike in a Pond, that deuoures vertues,
and lesse vices. That it is wholsomest
getting a stomacke by walking on your
owne ground : and the thriftiest laying
of

of it at anothers Table. That debtors
are in *London* close prisoners, and here
haue the liberty of the house. That
Atheists in affliction, like blinde beggers, are forced to aske, though they
know not of whom. That there are
(God be thanked) not two such Acres
in all the Countrey, as the *Exchange* &
westminster-Hall. That onely Christ-
mas Lords know their ends. That
Women are not so tender fruit, but
that they doe as well, and beare as well
vpon Beds, as plashed against walles.
That our carts are neuer worse imploi-
ed, then when they are wayted on by
Coaches. That Sentences in Authors, like haires in horse taile, concur
in one root of beauty and strength, but
being pluckt out one by one, serue only
for Springes and Snares. That both
want and abundance, equally aduance
a rectified man from the world, as cot-
ton and stones are both good casting
for an Hawke. That I am sure there is
none of the forbidden fruit left, because
wee

we doe not all eat thereof. That our beſt three-pilde miſchiefe comes from beyond the ſea, and rides poſt through the country, but his errand is to Court. That next to no wife & children , your owne are the beſt paſtime , anothers wife and your children worſe , your wife & anothers children worſt. That Stateſmen hunt their fortunes, and are often at default : Fauorites courſe her, and are euer in view. That intemperance is not ſo vnwholſome heere; for none euer ſaw Sparrow ſicke of the poxe. That heere is no trechery nor fidelity, but it is becauſe heere are no ſecrets. That Court-motions are vp and downe; ours circular : theirs like ſquibs cannot ſtay at the higheſt , nor returne to the place which they roſe from, but vaniſh and weare out in the way : Ours like Mil-wheeles, buſie without changing place; they haue peremptory fortunes; wee viciſſitudes.

I. D.

Anſwere

Anſwere to the very Countrey
Newes.

IT is a thought,that man is the Cook
of time, and made dreſſer of his own
fatting. That the fiue Senſes are
Cinque-ports for temptation, the
traffique ſinne, the Lieutenant *Sathan*,
the cuſtome-tribute, ſoules. That
the Citizens of the high Court grow
rich by ſimplicitie ; but thoſe of *Lon-*
don, by ſimple craft. That life, death,
and time, do with ſhort cudgels dance
the Matachine. That thoſe which
dwell vnder the *Zona Torrida*,are troubled with more damps, then thoſe of
Frigida. That *Policie* and *Superſtition*
hath of late her maſque rent from her
face, and ſhee is found with a wry
mouth and a ſtinking breath, and thoſe
that courted her hotly,hate her now in
the ſame degree, or beyond. That
Nature too much louing her owne, becomes

becomes vnnaturall and foolifh. That
the foule in fome is like an egge, hatched by a young Pullet,who often rigging from her neft,makes hot and cold
beget rottennefle, which her wanton
youth will not beleeue, till the faire
fhell being broken, the ftinke appeareth to profit others, but cannot her.
That thofe are the wife ones,that hold
the fuperficies of vertue,to fupport her
contrary, all-fufficient. That cle-
mency within and without is the nurfe
of rebellion. That thought of the
future is retyred into the Countrey,
and time prefent dwells at Court.
That I liuing neere the Church-yard,
where many are buried of the Peft, yet
my infe-ction commeth from *Spaine,*
and it is feared it will difperfe further
into the Kingdome.

A. S.

Newes to the Vniuersitie.

A Mere Scholler is but a liue book
Action doth expresse knowledg
better then words; so much of
the soule is lost as the body cannot vtter. To teach, should rather be an effect, then the purpose of learning. Age
decaies nature, perfects Art : therefore
the glory of youth, is strength; of the
gray head, wisedome; yet most con-
demne the follies of their owne infancy, runne after those of the worlds,
and in reuerence of antiquitie will
beare an old error against a new truth.
Logicke is the *Heraldrie* of Arts, the ar-
ray of Iudgment, none it selfe, nor any
Science without it : where it and learning meete not, must be either a skilful
ignorance, or a wilde knowledge. Vnderstanding cannot conclude out of
moode and figure. Discretion containes *Rhethorique*; the next way to
learne

learne good words, is to learne fenfe;
the neweft *Philofophy* is foundeft, the
eldeft *Diuinitie* : *Aftronomie* begins in
Nature, ends in Magicke. There is
no honeftie of the bodie without
health, which no man hath had fince
Adam. Intemperance that was the firft
mother of ficknefle, is now the daughter. Nothing dyes but qualities. No
kinde in the world can perifh without
ruine of the whole. All parts helpe
one another (like States) for particular
intereft : So in Arts which are but tran-
flations of nature, there is no found
pofition in any one, which, imagine
falfe, there may not from it be drawne
ftrong conclufions, to difproue all the
reft. Where one truth is granted, it
may bee by direct meanes brought to
confirme any other controuerted.
The foule and bodie of the firft man,
were made fit to bee immortall together : we cannot liue to the one, but we
muft dye to the other. A man and a
Chriftian are two creatures. Our
per-

perfection in this World is vertue; in the next knowledge; when we shall read the glory of God in his own face.

Newes from Sea.

THat the best pleasure is to haue no obiect of pleasure, & vniformity is a better prospect thē variety. That putting to Sea is change of life, but not of condition; where risings and falls, Calmes, and crosse-gales are yours, in order and turne; fore-windes but by chance. That it is the worst winde to haue no winde, and that your smooth fac'd Courtier, deading your course by a calme giues greater impediment, then an open enemies crossegale. That leuitie is a vertue, for many are held vp by it. That it's nothing so intricate and infinite, to rigge a ship as a woman, and the more either is fraught, the apter to leake. That to

pumpe

pumpe the one, and ſhreeue the other,
is alike noyſome. That ſmall faults
hibituated, are as dangerous as little
leakes vnſound; and that to puniſh
and not preuent, is to labour in the
pumpe, & leaue the leake open. That
it is beſt ſtriking Sayle before a ſtorme,
and neceſſarieſt in it. That a little
time in our life is beſt, as the ſhorteſt
cut to our Hauen is the happieſt voyage. That to him that hath no Hauen, no winde is friendly; and yet it is
better to haue no Hauen, then ſome
kinde of one. That expedition is
euery where to be bribed but at Sea.
That gaine workes this miracle, to
make men walke vpon the water; and
that the ſound of Commoditie drowns
the noiſe of a Storme, eſpecially of an
abſent one. That I haue once in my
life out-gone night at Sea, but neuer
darkneſſe; and that I ſhall neuer wonder to ſee a hard world, becauſe I haue
liued to ſee the Sunne a bankrupt, being ready to ſtarue for cold in his perpetuall

petuall prefence. That a mans companions are (like fhips) to be kept in diftance, for falling foule one of another; onely with my friend I will clofe. That the faireft field for a running head is the Sea, where he may runne himfelfe out of breath, and his humour out of him. That I could carry you much further, and yet leaue more before then behinde, and all will bee but *via Nauis*, without print or tracke, for fo is morall inftruction to youthes watrifh humour. That though a Shippe vnder Saile be a good fight, yet it is better to fee her moor'd in the Hauen. That I care not what become of this fraile Barke of my flefh, fo I faue the paffenger. And heere I caft Anchor.

W. S.

P   Forreine

Forren Newes of the yeere. 1 6 1 6.

From France.

IT is deliuered from *France*, that the choyce of friends there, is as of their Wiues: thofe that being new, are hard and harfh, proue beft: the moft pleafing are leaft lafting. That an enemy fierce at the firft onfet, is as a torrent tumbling downe a mountaine; a while it beares all before it: haue but that whiles patience, you may paffe it dry foote. That a penetrating iudgement may enter into a mans minde by his bodies gate; if this appeare affected, apifh and vnftable; a wonder if that be fetled.

That vaine glory, new fafhions, and the *French* difeafe, are vpon termes of quitting

quitting their Countries Alleadgeance
to be made free Denisons of *England*.
That the wounds of an ancient enmi-
ty haue their scarres, which cannot bee
so well closed to the sight, but they will
lie open to the memory . That a
Princes pleasurable vices, vshered by
authoritie, and waited on by conni-
uence, sooner punish themselues by
the subiects imitation . then they can
bee reformed by remonstance or correction ; so apt are all ill examples to
rebound on them that giue them. That
Kings heare truth oftener for the tellers,
then their owne aduantage.

From Spaine.

THat the shortest cut to the riches.
of the *Indies*, is by their contempt.
That who is feared of most, feares most
That it more vexeth the proud, that
men despise them, then that they not

feare them . That greatnes is fruitfull
enough, when other helpes faile, to beget on it felfe deftruction . That it is a
groffe flattering of tyred crueltie , to
honeft it with the tittle of clemencie.
That to eat much at other mens coft,
and little at his owne , is the wholefo-
meft and moft nourifhing diet, both in
Court and Country . That thofe are
apteft to domineere ouer others , who
by fuffering indignities haue learned
to offer them . That ambition like a
fillie Doue flies vp to fall downe, it
mindes not whence it came, but whither it will . That euen Galley-flaues,
fetting light by their captiuitie , finde
freedome in bondage . That to bee
flow in military bufineffe, is to bee fo
courteous as to giue the way to an enemy . That lightning and greatneffe
more feare then hurt.

From

From Rome.

THat the Venereall(called veniall) ſin is to paſſe in the ranke of Cardinall vertues ; and that thoſe ſhould be held henceforth his Holineſſe beneficiall friends, that ſinne vpon hope of pardon. That where vice is a Satecommodity, he is an offender that often offendes not. That Iewes and Curtezans there, are as beaſts that men feed, to feed on. That for an Engliſhman to abide at *Rome*, is not ſo dangerous as report makes it ; ſince it ſkilles not where we liue;ſo we take heed how we liue. That greatneſſe comes not downe by the way it went vp,there being often found a ſmall diſtance betweene the higheſt and the loweſt Fortunes. That rackt authority is oft leſſe at home then abroad regarded, while things that ſeeme,are (commonly)more a farre off then at hand feared.

From Venice

THat the moſt profitable Banke, is the true vſe of a mans ſelfe, whiles ſuch as grow mouldy in idlenes, make their houſes their Tombes, and die. before their death . That many dangerous ſpirits lie buried in their wants which had they meanes to their mindes would dare as much as thoſe that with their better Fortunes ouer top them. That profeſſed Curtezans, if they bee any way good , it is becauſe they are openly badde. That frugalitie is the richeſt treaſure of an eſtate, where men feede for hunger , cloath for cold and modeſtie, and ſpend for Honour, Charity and Safety.

Grom

From Germany.

THat the infe&ious vice of Drun-
ken-good-fellowſhip , is like to
ſticke by th at Nation as long as the
multitude of Offenders ſo benums the
ſenſe of offending , as that a common
blot is held no ſtaine . That diſcreti-
ons muſt be taken by weight , not by
tale : who doth otherwiſe , ſhall both
proue his owne to light , and fall ſhort
of his reckoning. That feare and a nice
fore-caſt of euery ſleight danger , ſeldome giues either faithfull or fruitfull
counſell. That the Empire of *Germany* , is not more great then that ouer a
mans ſelfe.

From the Low Countries.

THat one of the fureft grounds of a mans liberty is, not to giue another power ouer it . That the moft dangerous plunge wereto to put thine enemie , is defperation while forcing him to fet light by his owne life, thou makeft him mafter of thine. That neglected danger lights fooneft and heauieft. That they are wifeft , who in the likelihoode of good , prouide for ill . That fince pittie dwelles at the next doore to miferie , he liueth moft at eafe that is neighboured with enuy . That the euill fortune of the wars, as well as the good, is variable.

Newes

Newes from my Lodging.

THat the beſt proſpect is to looke inward . That it is quietter ſleeping in a good conſcience then a whole skinne . That a ſoule in a fat body lies ſoft, and is loath to riſe . That he muſt riſe betimes who would coſen the Diuell . That *Flatterie* is increaſed, from a pillow vnder the elbow , to a bed vnder the whole body. That *Policie* is the vnſleeping night of reaſon . That he who ſleepes in the cradle of ſecuritie , ſinnes ſoundly without ſtarting . That guilt is the Flea of the conſcience . That no man is throughly awaked, but by affliction. That a hang'd Chamber in priuate, is nothing ſo conuenient as a hang'd Traitour in publike . That the religion of *Papiſtrie*, is like a curtaine, made to keepe out the light . That the life
of

of moſt Women is walkeing in their ſleepe, and they talke their dreames. That Chambering is counted a ciuiller qualitie, then playing at tables in the Hal, though ſeruing-men vſe both. That the beſt bedfellow for all times in the yeare, is a good bed without a fellow. That he who tumbles in a calme bed, hath his tempeſt within. That he who will riſe, muſt firſt lie downe and take humilitie in his way. That ſleepe is deaths picture drawne to life, or the twi-light of life and death. That in ſleepe we kindely ſhake death by the hand; but when we are awaked, wee will not know him. That often ſleepings are ſo many trials to die, that at laſt we may doe it perfectly. That few dare write the true newes of their Chamber: and that I haue none ſecret enough to tempt a ſtrangers curioſitie, or a Seruants diſcouerie.

God giue you good morrow.

B. R.

Newes of my morning Worke

THat to be good, the way is to be moſt alone, or the beſt accompanied. That the way to heauen is miſtaken for the moſt Melancholywalke. That the moſt feare the worlds opinion, more then Gods diſpleaſure. That a Court-friend ſeldome goes further then the firſt degree of Charitie. That the Diuell is the perfecteſt Courtier. That innocency was firſt cozen to man, now guiltineſſe hath the neereſt alliance. That ſleepe is deaths Leger Embaſſadour. That time can neuer be ſpent: wee paſſe by it and can not returne. That none can bee ſure of more time then an inſtant. That ſinne makes worke for repentance or the Diuell. That patience hath more power then afflictions. That euery ones memory is diuided into two parts: the part looſing
all

all is the Sea, the keeping part is Land.
That honefty in the Court liues in perfecution , like proteftants in Spaine.
That predeftination and conftancy are
a like vncertaine to be iudged of. That
reafon makes loue the Seruing-man.
That vertues fauour is better then a
Kings fauorite . That being ficke begins a fuit to God, being well, poffes-
feth it. That helth is the Coach which
carries to Heauen, fickeneffe the poft-
horfe. That worldly delights to one
in extreame fickeneffe , is like a high
candle to a blinde man. That abfcence
doth fharpen loue, prefence ftrégthens
it ; that the one brings fuell , the other
blowes it till it burnes cleere: that loue
often breakes friendfhip , that euer en-
creafeth loue. That conftancy of women , and loue in men , is alike rare.
That Art is trueths Iugler . That falf-
hood playes a larger part in the world
then trueth. That blind zeale and lame
knowledge are a like apt to ill. That
fortune is humbleft where moft con-
temned

temned. That no porter but resoluti-
on keepes feare out of mindes, That
the face of goodnesse without a body is
the worst wickednesse. That womens
fortunes aspire but by others powers.
That a man with a female wit is the
woorst *Hermaphrodite*. That a man
not worthy beeing a friend, wrongs
himselfe by beeing in acquaintance.
That the worst part of ignorance, is
making good and ill seeme alike. That
all this is newes onely to fooles.

Mist. B.

Newes from the lower end
of the Table.

IT is said among the folke here, that
if a man die in his infancy, hee hath
onely broke his fast in this world : if
in his youth, hee hath left vs at dinner.
That it is bedtime with a man at three
score and ten : and hee that liues to a
hun-

hundred, yeeres hath walked a mile after supper. That the humble minded
man makes the loweft curtefie . That
grace before meat, is our electiō before
we were:grace after meat our faluation
when we are gone. The foule that halts
betweene two opinions, fals betweene
two ftooles. That a foole at the vpper
end of the table , is the breade before
the falt. He that hates to be reproo-
ued, fits in his owne light. Hunger is
the cheapeft fawce, and nature the
cheapeft gueft. The fenfible man and
the filent woman are the beft difcour-
fers . Repentance without amendment, is but the fhifting of a foule trencher. He that tells a lie to faue his credit, wipes his mouth with his fleeue to
fpare his napkin . The tongue of a ie-
fter is the fiddle that the harts of the
company dance to. The tongue of a
foole carues a peece of his heart to e-
uery man that fits next him . A filent
man is a couered meffe. The contented man onely is his owne caruer. He
that

that hath many friends eates too much
falt with his meate. That wit without
difcretion cuts other men meate and
his owne fingers. That the foule of a
choliericke man fits euer by the fire-
fide. That patience is the lard of the
leane meat of aduerfitie. The Epicure
puts his money into his belly, and the
Mifer his belly into his purfe. That the
beft company makes the vpper end of
the table, and not the faltfeller. The
fuperfluity of a mans poffeffions is the
broken meate that fhould remaine to
the poore. That the enuious keepes
his knife in his hand, and fwallowes his
meate whole. A rich foole among the
wife is a gilt empty bowle amongft the
thirftie. Ignorance is an infenfible
hunger. The water of life is the beft
wine. He that robs mee of my inuention bids himfelfe welcome to another
mans table, and I will bid him welcom
when he is gone. The vaine glorious
man piffeth more then he drinks. That
no man can drinke an health out of the
cup

cup of blessing. To surfet vpon wit, is more dangerous then to want it. He that's ouercome of any passion is dry drunk. Tis easier to fill the belly of faith then the eye of reason. The rich glutton is better fed then taught. That faith is the elbow for a heauie soule to leane on. He that sinnes that he may repent, surfets that hee may take phisicke. He that riseth without thankesgiuing, goes away and owes for his ordinary . Hee that beginnes to repent when he is old, neuer washed his hands till night. That this life is but one day of three meales , or one meale of three courses: childe-hood, youth and old age. That to suppe well, is to liue well: and that's the way to sleepe well . That no man goes to bed till he dies , nor wakes till he be dead. And therefore.

Goodnight to you heere,
and good morrow heereafter.

I. C.

Newes

Newes from the Church.

IT was thought heere, that the world was made for man, and not man for the world, and that therefore they take a croſſe courſe that lye downe there. That thoſe that will not riſe, their ſouls muſt, and carry their bodyes to iudgement, That we haue ſpent one inheritance already, and are prodigall of this. That there is no hope beyonde mercy, and that this is that time; the next is of Iuſtice. That Chriſt when hee went away, left good ſeede in his Church; and when he comes againe, he ſhall finde Chriſtians, but not faith. That the Diuell hath got vpon vs, the ſame way that hee did at the firſt, by drawing ſhadowes ouer ſubſtances, as he did the body ouer the ſoule. That *Proteſtants* weare the name of Chriſt for a Charme, as *Papiſts* doe the Croſſe. That States vſe it, the Clergy liue by

Q   it

it, the People follow it, more by a ſtreame, then one by one. That all are religious rather then ſome, That euery one lookes to another, but not to himſelfe. That they goe ſo by throngs to Heauen, that it is to bee feared they take the broader way. That the Church is in the world, like a Ship in the Sea; the elect in the Church, like *Ionas* amongſt the Mariners. That to mend this, is to cheate the Diuell, to turne man the right ſide outward, and ſet the ſoule foremoſt againe. That the ſoule may be too ranke too, if wee looke not to it: and ſo a *Puritane* often times meets a *Papiſt* in ſuperſtition another way. That to binde from and to indifferent things, is equall, though it be thought otherwiſe. That ſome, out of a good meaning haue fallen this way into a vice. That theſe faults are more ſubtill; and therefore leſſe perceiued, and leſſe to be blamed; but as dangerous as the other, if they take heede. That the rule is in all thingss

the

the body and the foule muſt goe to ge-
ther, but the better before. That wee
haue contended ſo long about the body of Religion, that ſome men thought
it was dead: That ſo *Atheiſts* are
come into the Church, and that it will
be as hard to caſt them out as Diuels.
That thoſe which haue thus broken
the peace of *Ieruſalem* , are obliged to
ſatisfaction; and thoſe which firſt gaue
them cauſe of amendment. That they
are a good medicine one for another,
and both a good Compoſition. That
a pure *Biſhop* is the beſt gouernment, if
the pride on both ſides would let them
know it. That all Controuerſies for
the moſt part , leaue the trueth in the
middle , and are factious at both
ends. That the Church hath
this good by them , they cleanſe the
way for others, but not for themſelues.
That ſinceritie, in the cauſe of trueth, is
more worth then learning . That too
much, and too little knowledge , haue
made the world mad . That we haue a

Q 2   ſhorter

shorter cut to it, and a surer way then
Drake had ouer the world, if wee could
find it out. That euery man is a briefe
of the whole; and as he is so, he is greater then a King. That euery King is a
briefe of his Land, and hee hath a *Pat-*
terne of the gouernment of it alwayes
about him. That as the honour that
he giues vnto his Nobles and Counsel-
lours is a charge; so is that which God
giues him. That as he requires an
account, so he must giue. That he is
the Image of God in his kingdome, as
man is in the World. That therefore
the Subiects ow him obedience, as the
Creatures doe Man. That those that
will not obey, are neither good Subiects, nor good men. That to obey,
well, is as great a thing as to gouerne,
and more mens duties. That those
that thinke not so, know not the Chri-
stians part, which is to suffer. That
though States bee naught, if they professe Religion, they may deliuer many
men safe to Heauen, though they goe
                                    not

not themselues, and so they are like
bad Ministers. That this is Gods vse of
both, and of the world too, to conuey
his elect to their place. That the outward face of the Church hath but the
same vse, and the Elect are the Church
them selues. That they are the Temple of the holy ghost, and therefore
ought to plucke downe their Idols, and
set vp God there. That the Idolles of
these times, are Couetousnesse, pride,
Gluttony, wantonnesse, Heresies, and
such like admiration and seruing of our
selues. That we must make all time
an occasion of amendment, because
the Diuell makes it an occasion to
tempt. That he is a Spirit, and therefore is cunninger then we. That there
is no way to resist him, but by the Spirit of God, which is his Master. That
this is the gift of God, which he giueth
to all that are his. That it is en-
creased by the word. and held by humility and prayer. That Faith is the effect of it, and workes the assurance.

That

That thus the vnderſtanding and will, which is the whole ſoule of man, is made vp againe, and ſanctifies the body. That ſo wee are the members of Chriſt. That our Head is in Heauen, as a pawne, that where he is, we ſhall bee. That there is no opinion but knowledge ; for it is the Science of ſoules and God the Teacher.

Newes from the Bed.

THat the bed is the beſt Rendevou of mankinde, and the moſt neceſſarie ornament of a Chamber. That Souldiers are good antiquaries in keeping the olde faſhion, for the firſt bed was the bare ground. That a mans pillow is his beſt Counſeller. That *Adam* lay in ſtate, when the heauen was his canopie. That the naked trueth is, *Adam* and *Eue* lay without ſheets. That they were either very innocent very ignorant, or very impudent,

they

they were not afhamed the heauens fhould fee them ly without a couerlet. That it is likly *Eue* ftudied Aftronomie, which makes the pofteritie of her Sex euer fince to lye on their backs. That the circumference of the bed is nothing fo wide as the conuex of the heauens, yet it containes a whole world. That the fiue Senfes are the greateft fleepers. That a flothfull man is but a reafonable Dormoufe. That the Soule euer wakes to watch the bodie. That a iealous man fleeps dog-fleep. That fleepe makes no difference betweene a wife man and a foole. That for all times fleep is the beft bedfellow. That the deuill and mifchiefe euer wake. That loue is a dreame. That the prepofterous hopes of ambitious men are like pleafing dreames, fartheft off when awake. That the bed payes *Venus* more cuftome then all the world befide. That if dreames and wifhes had beene all true, there had not been fince Poperie, one Maide to make a Nun of.

Q 4   That

That the fecure man fleeps foundly, and is hardly to be awak't. That the charitable man dreames of building Churches, but ftarts to thinke the vngodlier Courtier will pull them downe againe. That fleepers were neuer dangerous in a ftate. There is a naturall reafon, why Popifh Priefts chufe the bed to confeffe their women vpon, for they hold it neceffarie, that humiliation fhould follow fhrift. That if the bed fhould fpeake all it knows, it would put many to the blufh. That it is fit the bed fhould know more then paper.

R. S.

Newes from Shipbord.

THat Repentance without amendment, is like continuall pumping, without mending the leake. That he that liues without Religion, fayles with out a compaffe. That the wantonneffe of of a peacefull Common-wealth, is like the playing of the Porpesse before a storme. That the foole is Sea-ficke in a Calme, but the Wifemans stomacke endures all weathers. That paffions in a foole are Ordinance broken loofe in a storme, that alter their propertie of offending others and ruine himfelfe. That good Fortunes are a foft quick-fand, aduerfitie a rocke; both equally dangerous. That vertue is in pouertie a ready rigg'd Ship that lyes windbound. That good fafhion in a man is like the Pilot in a Shippe, that doth moft with leaft force. That a Fooles tongue is like the buye of an Ankor, you fhall find his heart by it wherefoeuer it lyes. Wifedome makes vfe of the croffes of this world, as a skilfull Pylot of Rocks for Sea-marks to faile by.

H. R.

Newes from the Chimney corner.

THat wit is Brufhwood, Iudgement Timber: the one giues the greateft
flame,

flame , the other yeelds the durableſt heate , and both meeting makes the beſt fire. That Bawds and Atturneyes are Andyrons that hold vp their Clyents till they burne each other to aſhes they receiue warmth by theſe; theſe by them their deſtruction. That a Wiſerich-man is like the backe or ſtocke of the Chimney, and his wealth the fire, it owne neede, but to reflect the heat to others good. That Houſe-keeping in England is falne from a great fire in a hot ſummers day , to boughes in the Chimney all winter long. That mans reaſon in matter of faith is Fire, in the firſt degree of his aſcent flame, next ſmoake, and then nothing. A young fellow falne in loue with a Whore, is ſaid to be falne a ſleepe in the Chimney corner. Hee that leaues his friend for his wench, forſakes his bed to ſit vp and watch a coale. That the couetous rich man only freezes before the fire. That Choller is an ill gueſt that piſſes in the Chimney for want of a Chamber pot.

That

That chaste Beautie is like the bellowes, whose breath is cold, yet makes others burne. That hee that expounds the Scriptures vpon the warrant of his owne spirit only, layes the brands together without tongues, and is sure (at least) to burne his owne fingers. That the louer keeps a great fire in's house all the yeere long. That deuotion, like fire in frostie weather, burnes hottest in affliction. That such Fryers as flie the world for the trouble of it, lye in bed all day in winter to spare firewood. That a couetous man is a dog in a wheele, that toyles to roast meat for other mens eating. The Pagans worshipping the Sunne are said to holde their hands to the Glo-worme in steade of a coale for heat. That a wise mans heart is like a broad hearth that keeps the coales (his passions) from burning the house. That good deeds, in this life, are coales raked vp in embers, to make a fire next day.

A couetous man.

THis man would loue honour and a-
dore God if there were an L. more
in his name ; He hath cophind vp his
soule in his chifts before his body; He
could wish he were in *Mydas* his taking
for hunger on condition he had his chy-
micall qualitie : At the grant of a new
subsidie he would gladly hang himselfe
were it not for the charge of buying a
Rope and beginnes to take money vppon vse when he hears of a priuie seale.
His morning prayer is to ouerlooke his
bagges whose euery parcel begets his a-
doration. Then to his studies which are
how to coufen this tennant,begger that
Widdow or to vndoe some Orphane,
Then his bonds are veiwed , the wel-
knowen dayes of payment con'de by
hart, and if he euer pray it is some one
may breake his day that the beloued
forefeiture may be obtained . His vse is
doubled and noe one sixpence begot or
                                    borne

borne but prefently by an vntimely thrifte it is getting more, His chimney, muft not be acquainted with fire for feare of mifchance, but if extremitie of cold pinch him he gets him heat with looking on, and fometime remoouing his aged wood-pile which he meanes to leaue to many difcents till it hath out-liued all the woods of that countrey, He neuer fpends candle but at Chrift-mas (when he has them for new-yeeres gifts) in hope that his feruants will breake glaffes for want of light which they doublie pay for in their wages; His actions are guilty of more crimes then any other mens thoughts and he con-ceaues no finne which he dare not act faue only luft, from which he abftaynes for feare he fhould be charged with keeping Baftards, once a yere he feafts the reliques of which meale fhall ferue him the next quarter In his talk he rails againft eating of breakfafts drinkeing betwixt meals, and fweares he is impo-uerifhed with paying of tythes. He had
rather

haue the frame of the world fall then the price of corne; If he chance to tra-uell he curfes his fortune that his place bindes him to ryde and his faithfull cloackbag is fure to take care for his kuifion. His nights are as troublefome as the dayes euerie rat awakes him out of his unquiet fleepes ; If he haue a Daughter to marrie he wifhes he were in Hungarie or might follow the cuftome of that countrey that all her portion might be a wedding gowne. If he fall ficke he had rather die a thoufand deaths then pay for any Phificke, and if he might haue his choice he would not goe to heauen but on condition he may put money to vfe there. In fine he liues a drudge, dyes a wretch that leaues a heap of pelfe(which fo many carefull hands had fcraped together) to haft after him to Hell and by the way it lodges in a Lawyers purfe.

The

The proud man.

IS one in whom pride is a qualitie that condemnes euery one besides his master, who when he weares new cloaths thinks himselfe wrong'd if they be not obseru'd imitated and his discretion in the choice of his fashion and stuffe, aplauded when he vouchsafes to blesse the ayre which his presence; he goes as neare the wall as his Sattin suite will giue him leaue and euery passenger he viewes vnder the eye browes, to obserue whether he vayles his bonnet low enough which he returnes with an Imperious Nod ; He neuer salutes first, but his farewell is perpetuall. In his attyre he is effeminate, euerie haire knowes his owne station which if it chance to loose, it is, checkt in againe with his pocket combe. He had rather haue the whole common wealth out of order then the least member of his

much

Muchatoe and choofes rather to loofe his patrimonie then to haue his band rufled at a feaft; if he be not placed in the higheft feat, he eates nothing, howfoeuer he drinkes to no man, talkes with no man for feare of familiaritie, He profeffeth to keepe his ftomacke for the Pheafant or the Quaile and when they come he can eate little he hath beene fo cloyed with them that yeere although they be the firft he faw. In his difcourfe he talkes of none but priuie counfellours and is as prone to belie their acquaintance as he is a Ladyes fauours, if he haue but twelue pence in his purfe he will giue it for the beft roome in a play houfe; He goes to Sermons, onely to fhow his cloathes and if on other inferiour dayes he chance to meete his friend he is forry he fees him not in his beft fuite.

A Prifone

A Prison.

IT fhould be Chrifts Hofpitall, for moft of your wealthy citizens are good benefactours to it and yet it can hardly be fo, becaufe fo few in that are kept vpon almes. Charityes houfe and this are built many miles a funder. One thing notwithftanding is heere prayfe-worthy, for men in this perfecution cannot chufe but prooue good chriftians in that they are a kinde of Martyres, and fuffer. And yet it is fo curfed a peece of land that the fonne is afhamed to be his fathers heyre in it. It is an infected peft-houfe all the yeere long : the plague fores of the law and difeafes heere wholely raigning. The Surgeons are Atturneyes and Pettifoggers, who kill more, then they cure. Lord haue mercy vppon vs may well ftand ouer thefe doores, for debt is a moft dangerous and catching citie

pefti-

peſtilence. Some take this place for the
walkes in moorefields , (by reaſon the
mad men are ſo neere) but the croſſes
heere and there are not alike. No it is
not halfe ſo ſweete an ayre , for it is
the dunghill of the law, vpon which is
throwne the ruynes of gentry, and the
Naſty heapes of voluntary decayed
Bankerupts : by which meanes it coms
to be a perfect meddal of the Iron age,
ſythence nothing but Iengling of keyes,
rattling of ſhackles , Boults and grates
are here to be heard. It is the horſe of
Troy in whoſe wombe are ſhut vp all
the mad Greekes that are men of action. *Nullum vacuum* (vnleſſe in priſoners bellyes) is here truely to be proo-
ued. One excellent effect is wrought
by the place it ſelfe for the arranteſt
coward breathing being poſted hither
comes in three dayes to an admirable
ſtomacke , does any man deſire to
learne muſicke? euery man heere ſings
Lachrymæ at firſt ſight : and is hardly
out , he runnes diuiſion vpon euery
note,

note, And yet (to their commendati-
ons be it ſpoken none of them for all
that diuiſion) doe trouble the Church.
They are noe Anabaptiſts, if you aske
vnder what Horizon this clymate lyes
the Bermudas and it, are both vnder
one and the ſame height. And whereas
ſome ſuppoſe that this Iland (like that)
is haunted with deuils it is not ſo, for
thoſe deuils (ſo talked of and feared)
are non elſe but hoggiſh Iaylours.hither
you neede not ſayle, for it is a ſhip of it
ſelfe: the maſters ſide is the vpper deck;
They in the common Iayle ly vnder
hatches and helpe to ballaſſe it: Intricate caſes are the tacklings. executi-
ons the Ancors, capiaſſes, the Cables,
chancery Bills the huge ſailes, A long
tearme, the maſt, law the helme, A
Iudge the Pylot, a councell the Purſer,
an Atturney the Boatſwayne, his flee-
ting clerke the Swabber, Bonds, the
waues, Outlawryes, guſts, The ver-
dicts of Iuries rough windes, extents
the Rockes, That ſplit all in peeces.

Or if it be not a Shippe, yet this and a Ship differ not much in the Building the one is a moouing mifery, the other a ftanding. The firft is feated on a Spring the fecond on Pyles. Either this place is an Embleme of a Bawdy houfe or a Bawdy houfe of it, for nothing is to be feene (in any Roome) but Scuruy Beds and bare walles. But not fo much to difhonour it) it is an vniuerfity of poore Schoolers, in which three Artes are chiefly ftudyed. To pray, to curfe, and to write letters.

A Prifoner.

IS one that hath beene a monyed man and is ftill a very clofe fellow, whofoeuer is of his acquaintance, let them make much of him, for they fhall finde him as faft a friend as any in England : he is a fure man and you know where to finde him. The corruption of a Banckerupt is commonly the generation

tion of this creature, he dwelles on the back-fid of the world, or in the Suburbs of focietie , and liues in a Tenement which he is fure none will goe about to take ouer his head . To a man that walkes abroad he is one of the antipodes, that goes on the top of the world, and this vnder it . At his firft comming in he is a peece of new coyne, all fharking old prifoners lye fucking at his purfe an old man and he are much alike, neither of them both go farre, They are ftill angry, and peeuifh and they fleepe little. He was borne at the fall of Babell , the confufion of languages is onely in his mouth . All the vacations he fpeakes as good englifh, as any man in England : and in tearme times he breakes out of that , hopping one-leg'd pace into a racking trot of Iffues, Billes replications, reioynders demurs querrels *fubpenas &c.* able to fright a fimple country fellow , and make him beleeue he coniures , whatfoeuer his complexion was before, it

turne

turne (in this place)to choller or deepe
melancholy ſo that he needs euery
howre to take phiſicke to looſe his body for that (like his eſtate) is very foule
and corrupt aud extremely hard bound
The taking of an execution of his ſtomacke giues him fiue or ſix ſtooles and
leaues his body very ſolible . The with-
drawing of an aɕion is a vomite. He
is no ſound man; And yet an vtter Bar-
reſter (nay a ſeriant of the caſe) will
feede heartely vppon him , he is very
goood picking meate for a lawyer:
The Barber Surgeons may(if they will)
beg him for an Anatomy after he hath
ſuffered execution;an excellent leɕua-
rie may be made vpon his body: he is a
kinde of dead carcas,creditors,lawyers
and Iailours, deuoure it,creditors picke
out his eyes with his owne teares,Law-
yers flea him of his owne skinne and
lap him in partchment,and Iaylours are
the *Promethean* vultures that gnaw his
very heart.He is a bondſlaue to the law
and (albeit he were a ſhop-keeper in
London

London) yet he cannot write himſelfe
a free man. His religion is of fiue or
ſix collours, this day he prays thatGod
may turne the hearts of his creditours,
And to morrow he curſeth the houre
that euer he ſaw them. His apparrell
is daubd commonly with ſtatute late,
the ſuite it ſelfe of durance and the hoſe
full of long Paynes : He hath many o-
ther laſting ſuites which he himſelfe
is neuer able to weare out for they
weare out him. The zodiaque of his
life is like that of the Sunne (mary
not halfe ſo glorious ; It beginnes in
Aries and endes in Piſces. Both heade
and feete are all the yeare long in trou-
bleſome and laborious motions and
weſtminſter hall is his ſpheare. He liues
betwene the two Tropiques (Cancer &
Capricorne) and by that meanes is in
Double danger (of crabbed creditours)
for his purſe , and hornes for his heade
if his wiues heeles be light . If he be a
gentleman he alters his armes ſo ſoone
as he comes in. Few (here carrie feilds

R 4   or

or argent , but whatsoeuer they bare
before here the giue only Sables whiles
he lyes by it he;traueling ore the Alpes
and the hearts of his creditours are the
snowes that ly vnmelted in the middle
of sommer. He is an Almanacke out of
date: none of his dayes speakes of faire
weather . Of all the files of men he
marcheth in the last and comes limp-
ing , for he is shot and is no man of this
world , vnlesse he be fetcht of nobly.
He hath lost his way & being benight-
ted strayed into a wood full of wolues&
nothing so hard as to get away without
being deuoured he that walkes frõ sixe
to sixe in Pawles goes still but a coytes
cast before this man.

A Creditour.

IS a man that torments men for their
good conditions he is one of Deuca-
lions sonnes begotten of a stone, The
marble image in the Temple Church
that ly cros-legd doe much resemble
him sauing that his is a little more
crosse, he weares a forefeited band vnder

der that part of his girdle where his thumbe ſticks with as much pride as a welchman does a leeke on Saint *Dauids* day: and quarrels more and longer a-bout it. he is a catchpoles mornings draught for the newes that ſuch a gal-lants come yeſternight to towne, draw-es both muſcadell out of him & monie to. He ſayes the Lords prayers back-wards or (to ſpeake better of him) he hath a pater-noſter by himſelfe. And that particle forgiue vs our debts as we forgiue others &c : he either quite lea-ues out, or elſe leapes ouer that. It is a dangerous Rub in the alley of his con-ſcience. He is the bloud hound of the law and hunts counter very ſwiftly and with great iudgement. He hath a quick-ſent to ſmell out his gayne and a good deep mouth to purſue it yet neuer opens but when he bytes and bytes not but he killes or at leaſt drawes blood and then he pincheth moſt doggedly. He is a lawyers moyle and the onely Beaſt vpon which he ambles ſo often

to Weftminfter and a lawyer is his
God Almighty in him onely he trufts,
to him he flyes in all his troubles, from
him he feekes fuccour, to him he prays
that he may by his meanes ouercome
his enemies. him does he worfhip both
in the Temple and abroad, and hopes
by him and good Angels to profper in
all his actions. A Scriuener is his farrier and helpes to recouer all his difea-
fed and maymed obligations. Euery
Tearme he fets vp a Tenters in Weft-
minfter Hall vpon which he rackes and
ftretches gentlemen like englifh broad
cloth beyond the ftaple of the wooll till
the threeds cracke, and that caufeth
them with the left wet to fhrinke and
prefently to weare bare ; Marrie he
handles a citizen (at leaft if him felfe
be one) like a peece of Spanifh cloth
giues him onely a touch and ftraynes
him not too hard , knowing how apt
he is to breake himfelfe , and then he
can cut nothing out of him but fhreds,
to the one he comes like Tamberlaiue
with

with his blacke and bloudy flags , But
to the other his white one hangs out.
And (vpon the pearle) rather then
faile he takes ten groates i'th pound
for his ranfome and fo lets him march
away with bagge and baggage.
From the beginning of Hillary to the
end of Michaelmas his purfe is full of
quick filuer and that fets him running
from Sunne-rife to Sunne-fet vp fleet
ftreete and fo to the chancery, from
thence to Weft-minfter,then backe to
one court after that to another, then to
Atturney then to a counfellour, and in
euery of thefe places he melts fome of
his fat (his monie) in the vacation he
goes to graffe and gets vp his flefh a-
gaine which he bates as you haue hard
If he were to be hangd vnleffe he could
be faued by his booke he cannot for his
heart call for a Pfalme of mercy.He is a
knaue trapbaited with parchment and
wax,the fearefull myce he catches are
debtors with whom fcratching Atturneyes like cats play a good while and
then

then mouze them, The belly is an vn-
fatiable creditour but man worfe.

A Sarieant.

WAs once taken (when he bare
office in his parrifh) for an honeft man the fpawne of a decayed fhop-
keeper begets this fry, out of that dunghill is the Serpents egge hatched. It is a
deuill made fometimes out of on of the
twelue companies and does but ftudie
the parte and rehearfe on earth to be
perfect when he comes to act it in hell,
that is his ftage. The hangman and he
are twinnes;onely the Hangman is the
elder brother and he dying without
iffue (as commonly he does for non but
a rope makers widdow will marry
him) this then inherites , his habite
is a long Gowne made at firft to couer
his knauerie but that growing to monftrous he now goes in buffe, his confcience and that being both cut out of
one hyde and are of one toughneffe.
The counter gate is his kennall the
whole

whole citie his Parris Garden the misery of poore men (but especially of bad
liuers) are the offales on which he feeds.
The deuill calles him his white fonne,
he is fo like him that he is the worfe for
it. And he takes after his father, for
the one torments bodyes as faft as the
other tortures foules. Money is the
cruft he leapes at, cry a ducke a ducke
and he plunges not in fo eagerly as at
this. The dogs chaps water to fetch nothing elfe, he hath his name for the
fame qualitie for Serieant is *Quafi* R:
fee Argent looke you Rogues here is
money. He goes muffled like a theefe
and carryes ftill the markes of one, for
he fteales vpon a man cowardly,plucks
him by the throate makes him ftand,
and fleeces him. In this they differ,the
theefe is more valiant & more honeft,
his walks in terme time are vp fleete-
ftreete, at the end of tearme vp hole-
burne and fo to tyburne the gallowes
are his purlues in which the hangman
and hee are the quarter rangers,the one
turnes

turnes of and the other cuts downe, all the vacation he lyes Imbogude behinde the lettice of fome blinde drunken baudy alehoufe, &if he fpy his prey out he leapes like a freebooter and ryffles or like a bandog worryes. No officer to the citie keepes his oath fo vpright he neuer is forfworne for he fweares to be true varlet to the citie and he continues fo to his dying day. Mace which is fo comfortable to the ftomack in all kind of meates turnes in his hand to mortall poyfon, this Rauen picks not out mens eyes as others doe, all his fpite is at their fhoulders and you were better to haue the night more ride you then this Incubus. When any of the furyes in Hell dy, this *Cacodæmon* hath the reuerfion of his place. He will venture as defperatly vpon the Pox as any roaring Boy of thē all. For when he arrefts a whore himfelf puts her in cōmon bail at his owne peril, and fhe paies him foundly for his labour vpō on of the fhe riefes cuftards he is not fo greedy nor fo

fharpe

ſharpe ſet as at ſuch a ſtew pot. The citie (is by the cuſtome) to feede him
with good meat,as they ſend dead horſes to their hounds onely to keepe them
both in good heart, for not onely thoſe
cures at the doghouſe but theſe within
the walls are to ſerue in their places, in
in their ſeuerall hunting. He is a citizens birdlyme and where he houlds he
hanges.

This Yeoman.

IS the Hanger that a ſargeant weares by his ſide it is a falſe dye of the
ſame bale but not the ſame cut , for it
runnes ſome-what higher and does
more miſchiefe. It is a tumbler to dryue
in the conyes. He is yet but a bungler &
knows not how to cut vp a man without
tearing but by a patterne, one tearme
fleſhes him or a fleet-ſtreet breakefaſt.
The deuill is but his father in law and
yet for the loue he beares him he will
leaue

leaue him as much as if he were his owne childe. And for that caufe (in fteade of prayers) he does euery morning at rhe countergate aske him blef-fing and thryues the better in his acti-ons all the day after. This is the hooke that hangs vnder water to chok thefifh and his farieant isthe quil aboue water which pops downe fo foone as euer the bate is fwallowed. It is indeed an otter and the more terrible deftroyer of the two. This counter rat hath a tayle as long as his fellows but his teeth are more fharpe and he more hungry becaufe he does but fnap and hath not his full halfe fhare of the booty the eye of this wolfe is as quicke in his heade as a cutpurfes in a throng, and as nimble is he at his bufineffe as a hangman at an execution. His office is as the dogs to worrie the fheep firft, or driue them to the fhambles. The butcher that cuts his throat fteps out afterwards and that's his Sarieant. His liuing lyes with in the citie but his confcience lies buri-ed

ed in one of the holes of a counter
This Eele is bread too out of the mud
of a Bankerupt and dyes commonly
with his guts ript vp, or els a sudden
stab sends him of his last errant. He will
very greedily take a cut with a sword,
and suck more Siluer out of the wound
then his Surgean shall. His beginning
is detestable, his courses desperate,
and his end damnable.

A Iaylour.

IS a creature mistaken in the making,
for he should be a Tyger. But the
shape being thought too terrible, it is
couered and he weares the vizor of a
man : yet retaynes the qualities of his
former fiercenes, currishnes, and raue-
ning. Of that red earth of which man
was fashioned, This peece was the
basest of the rubbish which was left,
and throwne by came a Iaylour, Or if
God had something els to doe then to
regard such trash, his discent, is then
more ancyent, but more Ignoble, for

S   then

then he comes of the race of those Angels, that fell with Lucifer from heauen, whither he neuer (or very hardly)
teturnes, Of all his Bunches of keyes
not one hath wards to open that doore.
For a Iaylours soule stands not vpon
those two Pillors that support heauen,
(Iustice and mercy) it rather sits vpon
those two footestooles of hell, wrong
and cruelty. He is a Iudges slaue, a prisoner's his. In this they differ he is a voluntary one, the other compeld. He
is the hangman of the law with a lame
hand, and if the law gaue him all his
limbes perfect he would strike those on
whom he is glad to fawne. In fighting
againſt a debtor he is a creditours second, But obserues not the lawes of the
Duello, for his play is fowle, and on
all base aduantages. His conscience
and his shakles hangs vp together and
are made very neere of the same mettle
sauing that the one is harder then the
other and hath one propertie aboue
Iron for that neuer melts. He diſtills
                              money

mony out of the poores tears, & grows
fat by their curſes, No man comming
to the praƈticall part of hell: can diſ-
charge it better, becauſe here he does
nothing but ſtudie the theorique of it.
His houſe is the piƈture of hell, and the
originall of the letters Pattents of his
office ſtand exemplifyed there. A
chamber of lowſie beds is better worth
to him then the beſt acre of corne-land
in England. Two things are hard to
him (nay almoſt impoſſible) viz: To
ſaue all his priſoners that none euer e-
ſcape and to be ſaued himſelfe. His
eares are ſtopt, to the cryes of others,
and Gods to his; and good reaſon, for
lay the life of man in one ſcoale, and
his fees on the other, he will looſe the
firſt to find the ſecond. He muſt looke
for no mercy (if he deſires iuſtice to
be done him for he ſhewes none, And
I thinke he cares the leſſe, becauſe he
knowes heauen hath no neede of Iaylours. The doores there want no por-
ters, for they ſtand euer open. If it were

S 2   poſſible

poſſible for all creatures in the world, to ſleep euery night. He only and a Tyrant cannot. That bleſſing is taken from them , and this curſe comes in the ſteade, to be euer in feare , and euer hated what eſtate can be worſe.

What a Charaƈter is.

IF I muſt ſpeake the Schoole-maſters language I will confeſſe that Charaƈter comes of this infinitiue moode χαράσσω which ſignifieth to ingraue, or make a deepe Impreſſion. And for that cauſe, a letter (as A. B.) is called a Charaƈter.

Thoſe Elements which we learne firſt , leauing a ſtrong ſeale in our memories.

Charaƈter is alſo taken for an Egiptian Hierogiphicke , for an impreſſe, or ſhorte Embleme; in little comprehending much.

To

To square out a Character by our English leuell, it is a picture (reall or personall) quaintlie drawne in various collours, all of them heightned by one shadowing.

It is a quicke and soft touch of many strings, all shutting vp in one musicall close: It is wits descant on any plaine song.

FINIS.

THE TWELFTH IMPRESSION,

PAGES V2-V8ᵛ

Paradoxes, as they were spoken in a Maske, and presented *before his Maieslie at* White-hall.

Masculine.

1 HE *cannot be a Cuckold that weares a Gregorian.* — *For a Perriwig cannot fit such a head.*

2 *A Knight of the long Robe is more honourable then a Knight made in the field.* — *For Furres are deerer then Spurs.*

3 *A Drunkard is a good Philosopher.* — *For hee thinkes aright : the world goes round.*

4 *The Deuill cannot take Tobacco through his Nose.* — *For Saint Dunston seard vp that with his tongs.*

5 *A Shoomaker is the fittest man in the parish to make a Constable.* — *For hee (virture officij) may put a man into the stocks & ease him at last.*

6 *A Prisoner is the best Fencer.* — *For hee euer lies at a close ward.*

7 *An elder brother may be a wise man.* — *For hee hath wherewithall to purchase experience at any rate.*

8 *Burgomasters ought not to weare furre Gownes at midsummer.* — *For they may so bring in the sweating sicknesse.*

9 *A Cutpurse is the surest trade.* — *For his worke is no sooner done, but his money is in his hand.*

Feminine.

10 *It is better to marry a widdow then a maid.* — *For* Causa patet.

11 *Downe-*

11 *Downeright language is the best to winne a woman.*

For plaine dealing is a Iewell, and there is no Ladie but desires to haue her.

12 *If a woman with childe long to lie with another man, her husband must consent.*

For if hee will not, she will doe it without him.

13 *A painted Ladie best fits a Captaine.*

For so both may fight vnder their colours.

14 *Rich widdowes were ordained for yonger brothers.*

For they being borne to no lands must plough in another mans soile.

15 *Tis dangerous to marry a widow.*

For she hath cast her Rider.

16 *It is good for a young Popish wench to marry an old man.*

For shee shallbe sure to keepe all fasting nights-

17 *A dangerous secret is safely kept in a womans bojome.* — *For no wise man will search for it there.*

18 *A woman of learning & tongues is an admirable creature.* — *For a Star-ling that can speake is a present for an Emperor.*

19 *A great Lady should not weare her owne haire.* — *For that is too meane, as a coat of her owne spinning.*

20 *A faire womans Necke should stand awrie.* — *For so shee lookes as if she look't for a kisse.*

21 *Women loue fish better then flesh.* — *For they will haue place whatsoeuer they pay for it*

Newter.

22 *An Vsurer is the best Christian.* — *For* Quantum nummorum in arca, tantum habet, & fidei.

23 *The*

23 The best bodies should weare the meanest habits.

For painted-cloths were made to hide bare walles.

24 It is better to be a begger then to be a Merchant.

For all the world lies open to his trafique, and yet hee payes no Custome.

25 Tis more safe to bee drunke with the Hop, then with the Grape.

For a man should bee more inward with his Countreyman then with a stranger.

26 A man deepe in debt should be as deepe in drinke.

For Bacchus cancels all manner of obligations.

27 Players houses are more necessarie in a well gouern'd Common-wealth, then schooles.

For men are better taught by example, then precept.

28 Tauernes are more requisite in a Countrey then Academies.

For it is better that the multitude were louing then learned.

29 *A Tobacco-Shop and a Bawdy-houſe are Com-incidents.* — *For ſmoke is not without fire.*

30 *wealth is better then Wit.* — *For few Poets haue had the fortune to bee choſen Aldermen.*

31 *Marriage frees a man from care.* — *For then his wife takes all vpon her.*

32 *A kennell of Hounds is the beſt Conſort.* — *For they neede no tuning from morning to night.*

33 *The Court makes better ſchollers then the Vniuerſities.* — *For when the King vouchſafes to be a* Teacher, *euery man bluſhes to bee a* non Proficient.

34 *A nimble Page is more vſefull for a Lady then a long Gentleman-vſher.* — *For a Sparrow is more actiue then a bauld Buzzard.*

35 *Tis*

35 *Tis better to* ⎫ ⎧ *For a Goose liues*
be a Coward then a ⎬ ⎨*longer then a Cocke*
Captaine. ⎭ ⎩*of the Game.*

The Mountebankes
Receipts.

*An approued Receipt against Melan-
choly Feminine.*

IF any Lady bee sicke of the Sullens,
shee knowes not where, let her take a
handfull of simples, I know not what,
and vse them I know not how, applying
them to the place grieued, I know not
which, and she shall be cured I know not
when.

Against the Scuruy.

If any Scholler bee troubled with an
Itch or breaking out, which in time may
proue scuruy; let him first forbeare
clawing

clawing and fretting meates, and then purge choller, but by any meanes vpwards.

For reſtoring Gentlemen-vſhers Legs.

If any Gentleman-vſher haue the Conſumption in his Legs, let him feede luſtilie vpon Veale, two moneths in the Spring-time, and forbeare all manner of Mutton, and hee ſhall increaſe in the Calfe.

For the Tentigo.

If any be troubled with the *Tentigo*, let him trauell to *Iapan* ; or becauſe the Forreſt of *Turnbolia* is of the ſame Altitude and Eleuation of the Pole, and at hand, let him hunt there for his recreation, and it ſhall be done in an inſtant.

For a Felon.

If any bee troubled with a *Felon* on his finger, whereby he hath loſt the lawfull vſe of his hand ; let him but once
vſe

vſe the exerciſe of ſwinging, and ſtretch
himſelfe vpon the ſoueraigne Tree of
Tyburnia, and it will preſently kill the
Felon.

For a *Tympanie.*

If a Virgin be ſo ſicke of *Cupid,* that
the diſeaſe is growne to a *Tympanie,* let
her with all ſpeede poſſible remoue her
ſelfe, changing Aire for forty weekes at
leaſt, keeping a ſpare diet as ſhe trauels,
alwayes after vſing lawfull exerciſes, till
ſhe be married, & then ſhe is paſt danger.

For *Barrenneſſe.*

If any Lady be married, yet childleſſe,
let her firſt deſire to be a mother, and eat
to her breakefaſt a new laid Egge in a
ſpoonefull of Goats-milke, with a ſcru-
ple of Amber-greece, and at ſupper feed
on a *Henne,* troden but by one *Cocke* ;
and aboue al things let her auoyd hurry-
ing in *Coaches,* eſpecially on the ſtones ;
and aſſuming a finer mold, then Nature
meant

meant her, and no doubt ſhee ſhall fru-
ctifie.

For the falling ſickeneſſe.

If any woman bee troubled with the
Falling-ſickneſſe, let her firſt forbeare
Phyſicke, eſpecially Suppoſitories and
Gliſters : neither let her trauell Weſt-
ward-Ho, becauſe ſhee muſt auoyd the
Ile of *Man.* And for that it is an euill
Spirit entred into her, let her for a
Charme, haue alwaies her legs acroſſe,
when ſhee is not walking, and this will
helpe her.

For a Rupture.

If any Merchant bee troubled with a
Rupture in the bowels of his Eſtate, ſo
that hee cannot goe abroad, let him de-
coct Gold from a Pound to a Noble;
taking the broth thereof from ſixe
moneths to ſixe moneths, and he ſhall be
as able a man as euer he was.

The

The Mountebankes Song.

IS any deafe ? Is any blinde ?
Is any bound, or loose behind ?
Is any foule, that would be faire?
Would any Lady change hor haire ?
Do's any dreame ? do's any walke ?
Or in his sleepe affrighted talke ?
   I come to cure what ere you feele,
   within, without, from head to heele.

Be Drummes or Rattles in thy head ?
Are not thy braines well tempered ?
Do's Eolus thy stomacke gnaw ?
Or breede there vermine in thy maw ?
Doest thou desire and canst not please ?
Loe here the best Cantharides.
   I come to cure what ere you feele,
   Within, without, from bead to heele.

Euen all diseases that arise
From ill disposed crudities ;

                         [From

Songs.

From too much study, too much paine,
From lazinesse, and from a straine ;
From any humour doing harme,
Be it dry, or moist, or cold, or warme.
  Then come to me, what ere, &c.

Of lazie Gout, I cure the rich,
I rid the begger of the Itch,
I fleame auoyd both thicke and thin.
I dislocated ioynts put in,
I can old age to youth restore,
And doe a thousand wonders more.
  Then come to me, &c.

The Second Song.

                                    (chin,
M<small>*Aides of the Chamber or of the Kit-*</small>
If you be troubled with an itchin,
Come giue me but a kisse or two,
And here is that shall soone cure you.
  Nor Galen *nor* Hippocrates,
  Did euer doe such cures as these.
                                Crackt

Songs.

rackt maides that cannot hold your water,
Or vſe to breake winde in your laughter;
Or be you vext with Kibes, with Cornes,
Ile cure : or Cuckolds of their hornes.
    Nor Galon nor, &c.

If luſty Sis, Maide of the Dayrie,
Chance to be blew-nipt by the Fayrie;
For making butter with her taile,
Ile giue her that did neuer faile.
    Nor Galen nor, &c.

Or if ſome miſchance betide her,
Or that the Night-mare ouer-ride her,
Or if ſhe tell all in a Dreame,
Ile helpe her for a meſſe of Creame.
    Nor Galen nor, &c.

The third Song.

HEer's water to quench mayden fires,
Heer's ſpirits for old occupiers,
                Heer's

Songs.

Heer's powder to preserue youth long,
Heer's oyle to make weake sinewes strong,
   What is't you lacke? what would you buy,
   what is it that you neede ?
   Come to me (Gallants) tast and trie,
   Heer's that will doe, will doe the deed.

This powder doth preserue from fate,
This cureth the Maleficiate ;
Lost maidenheads, this doth restore,
And makes them Virgins as before.
   what is't you lacke? &c.

Heer's cure for bone-ach, feuer lurdens,
Vnlawfull or vntimely Burdens.
Diseases of all Sex, all Ages,
This medicine cureth or asswages.
   What is's you lacke? &c.

I haue receipts to cure the Gout,
To keepe Poxe in, or put them out,
To coole hot bloods, cold bloods to warme,
Shall do you (if no good) no harme.
   what is't you lacke? &c.

FINIS.

THE SECOND IMPRESSION

PAGES A2-A3ᵛ

THE PRINTER TO
the Reader.

THY ignorance may challenge libertie
enough , not to relish the deepe Arte
of Poetry : becaufe opinion makes
thee obftinate ; and rude tradition
hath taught thee nothing but an abufe
of knowledge.   For when thou rea-
deſt a quaffing fellowe: barbarifme , a worthy-written
ſtile in Tragedies , and a collufiue flourifh onely fronted
with the name of excellent ; thou ouer-lookſt them all with
the vfuall contempt or afperfion of friuolous , and fan-
taſticke labours , putting no difference betwixt the horfe
pictured on a figne-poſt, and the curious limbd Pegaſus :
But the age giues one comfort in extremitie , that as there
is a Lizard which affailes; fo is there one, which wonders
at the maieſtie of man : fure I am if any ſhall neglect,
nay not commend the worth of this fo generally approued
Poem ; he may (if it proceeds from nice critifcifme) bee
well excluded as a churlifh retainer to the Mufes ; (if

A 2   311   *from*

from a direct plaine dealing) he must be degraded for in-
sufficiencie. For had such a volume been extant among
the ancient Romanes , though they wanted our easie con-
seruations of wit, by printing ; yet would they rather ,and
more easily , haue committed the sense hereof to brasse,
and cedar leaues, then let such an Author, haue lost his due
eternitie. If to converse with a creature so amiable,heere
described , be thought more then difficult, let then the contemplation of it be admirable , which hath expressed the
soule in so compact a forme of body. The surplusage, that
now exceeds the last edition, was (that I may bee honestly
impartiall) in some things only to be challenged by the first
author , but others now added, (little inferior to the resi-
due) being in nature answerable, and first transcrib'd by
Gentlemen of the same qualitie, I haue vpon good induce-
ments, made publike with warrantie of their and my owne
credit. Not doubting therefore to be doubly discharged,
both by the verdict of conscience and the well-
deserued thankes of all iudicious Readers, I
bid you euery one farewell,
May 16. 1614

THe only curse or blessing that betides
  To men,(made doubtful)by their beauteous brides,
Could neuer (being apparent) satisfie
The full enioyer,with satietie
Of confidence,to call them good,or bad,
So much ; as this good worke (which chiefly had
A faire creation,to create anew
The soule of some, and to confirme some few)
Hath rescued shamelesse iudgment from the suit
Of meere opinion,and speakes absolute.
This widdow booke then, wife to rauish'd skill,
Married and made by the most maiden quill
Of one,not lost to her,though she to him,
Hath leaue to liue thus single ; richly trim,
Yet neuer to be challeng'd, being so chaste
In puritie, and not to be imbrac't
Without the reuerence of hir wedlocks loue ;
Which when thou seem'st vnwilling to approue,
Scorne a compleat faire woman ; and so grudge
Because thou hast no libertie to iudge.
Nor,let thy glorious confidence presume,
To make this Lady plyant,through perfume
Of powdred phrase,and robes, or complement ;
For though on pilgrimage thy learning went
In quest of such a wonder,yet thy paines
Were lost, although thy labri'ng suit obtaines:
For woman (in the abstract) hath no more
Then hath the wife, the widdow, maiden, whore,
And altogether ; therefore thou hast none,
Except thy labours purchase such a one :
Which (to haue said) they all agreed in Eue
Is all enough ; if iealous man beleeue.
          By *I. S. Lincolniensis* Gentleman.

TO make a Wife of wit, or meere Philosophie,
And deck her vp with flowers of sweetest poesie,
Is no hard taske, but such a one of flesh to find
Would weary all the wits and bodies of mankind :
Since worse must serue the turne, then men must bee con-
To take such as they find, not such as they invent.   (tent
T . B.

THE SIXTH IMPRESSION,

PAGES M5^v-M6 AND M8^{r-v}

An excellent Actor.

VVHatfoeuer is commendable in the
graue Orator, is moft exquifitly
perfect in him; for by a full and fignificant action of body, he charmes our attention : fit in a full Theater, and you will
thinke you fee fo many lines drawne from
the circumference of fo many eares, whiles
the *Actor* is the *Center.* He doth not ftriue
to make nature monftrous, fhe is often feen
in the fame Scæne with him, but neither on
Stilts nor Crutches and for his voice tis not
not lower then the prompter, nor lowder
then

then the Foile and Target. By his action he
fortifies morall precepts with example; for
what we see him personate, we thinke truely done before vs : a man of a deepe thought
might apprehend, the Ghosts of our ancient *Heroes* walk't againe, and take him (at
seuerall times) for many of them, Hee is
much affected to painting, and tis a question whether that make him an excellent
Plaier, or his playing an exquisite painter.
Hee addes grace to the Poets labours : for
what in the Poet is but ditty, in him is
both ditty and musicke. He entertaines vs
in the best leasure of our life. that is betweene meales, the most vnfit time, either
for study or bodily exercise : the flight of
Hawkes, and chase of wilde beastes, either
of them are delights noble: but some think
this sport of men the worthier, despight all
calumny. All men haue beene of his occupation: and indeed, what hee doth fainedly
that doe others essentially : this day one
plaies a Monarch, the next a priuate person.
Heere one Acts a Tyrant, on the morrow an
Exile : A parasite this man to night, too
morow a Precisian, and so of diuers others.
I obserue, of all men liuing, a worthy Actor
in one kind is the strongest motiue of affection that can be: for when he dies, we cannot

not be perſwaded any man can doe his parts
like him. Therefore the imitating Characte-
riſt was extreame idle in calling them
Rogues. His Muſe it ſeemes, with all his
loud inuocation, could not be wak't to light
him a ſnuffe to read the Statute: for I would
let his malicious ignorance vnderſtand, that
Rogues are not to be imploide as maine ornaments to his Maieſties Reuels ; but the
itch of beſtriding the Preſſe, or getting vp
on this wodden Pacolet, hath defil'd more
innocent paper, thē euer did Laxatiue Phyſicke: yet is their inuention ſuch tyred
ſtuffe, that like Kentiſh Poſt-horſe they can
not go beyond their ordinary ſtage, ſhould
you flea them. But to concludè, I valew a
worthy Actor by the corruption of ſome
few of the quality, as I would doe gold in
the oare ; I ſhould not minde the droſſe,
but the purity of the metall.

A *Purueiour* of *Tobacco*,

Call him a Broker of Tobacco, he scornes the title, hee had rather be tearmed a cogging Merchant. Sir *Iohn Falstaffe* robb'd with a bottle of Sacke; so doth hee take mens purses, with a wicked roule of Tobacco, at his girdle. Hee takes no long time to vndoe any man hee hath to deale with, he doth it in halfe a yeare, aswell as twenty; and then brags he has nipt them by the members. Hee causes his wife to sit in his Ware-house, to no other purpose, then (as a Countrey *Poticary* hangs vp an *Aligarta* in his shop) that while his Customers are gaping at her, hee may cosen them of their waight. Hee does not loue God, because God loues plaine dealing; and tis a question, whether he loues the King, because the King loues no Tobacco. Many trades hath he filcht through; but this making of Fire-workes, brings most commodity: For hee sels his Tobacco with this condition, that they that buy it, shall bee vndone by it. Such fellowes that haue tane so many by the nose, should hang vp for their signe *Diues* smoaking in hell, and the
word

word vnder it : Euery man for himselfe, and the Diuell for them all.

FINIS.